A Remarkable Curiosity

A REMARKABLE CURIOSITY

CURIOSITY

Dispatches from a New York City Journalist's
1873 Railroad Trip across the American West

Amos Jay Cummings

EDITED AND COMPILED BY Jerald T. Milanich

UNIVERSITY PRESS OF COLORADO

Published by the University Press of Colorado
5589 Arapahoe Avenue, Suite 206C
Boulder, Colorado 80303

 The University Press of Colorado is a proud member of the Association of American University Presses.

The University Press of Colorado is a cooperative publishing enterprise supported, in part, by Adams State College, Colorado State University, Fort Lewis College, Mesa State College, Metropolitan State College of Denver, University of Colorado, University of Northern Colorado, and Western State College of Colorado.

The paper used in this publication meets the minimum requirements of the American National Standard for Information Sciences—Permanence of Paper for Printed Library Materials. ANSI Z39.48-1992

Library of Congress Cataloging-in-Publication Data

Cummings, Amos J. (Amos Jay), 1841–1902.
  A remarkable curiosity : dispatches from a New York City journalist's 1873 railroad trip across the American West / [compiled by] Jerald T. Milanich.
    p. cm.
  ISBN 978-0-87081-926-1 (alk. paper)
  1. West (U.S.)—Description and travel. 2. Frontier and pioneer life—West (U.S.) 3. West (U.S.)—Social life and customs—19th century. 4. Natural history—West (U.S.) 5. West (U.S.)—History—1860–1890. 6. West (U.S.)—Biography. 7. Journalists—New York (State)—New York—Biography. 8. Cummings, Amos J. (Amos Jay), 1841–1902—Travel—West (U.S.) 9. Cummings, Amos J. (Amos Jay), 1841–1902—Correspondence. 10. Railroad travel—West (U.S.)—History—19th century. I. Milanich, Jerald T. II. Title.
  F594.C945 2008
  917.804'2—dc22

                                                                2008025223

Design by Daniel Pratt

17 16 15 14 13 12 11 10 09 08   10 9 8 7 6 5 4 3 2 1

For Giacomo and Luca

Contents

Acknowledgments

A LARGE NUMBER OF INDIVIDUALS, institutions, and Internet information services provided me with aid, advice, and information. Notable are Andria Kuzeff, who transcribed poorly printed copies made from microfilm; Pat Payne, who worked on illustrations; Jan Coyne, my cartographer; Richard Blodgett and Deborah Snoonian, both of whom live in Amos Cummings's old New York neighborhood; Robert Singerman, James Cusick, and Joseph L. Aufmuth, University of Florida George A. Smathers Libraries; Dale D. Roach and John C. "Jack" Vrjak, Chicago Veterans of Foreign Wars; Anne Getts and David M. Hays, University of Colorado at Boulder Libraries; Susie Stepanek, Pikes Peak Library District (Colorado); Jean E. Meeh Gosebrink, St. Louis Public Library; Todd Bostwick, Pueblo Grande Museum; Jefferson County Public Library, Colorado; Kansas City Missouri Public Library; Philip J. Panum, Denver Public Library; Oberlin College archives; Jovanka R. Ristic, American Geographical Society Library, University of Wisconsin, Milwaukee; Nancy Schaefer, University of Florida Health Science Center Librarian; Bobst Library, Microforms Centre and Tamiment Library, both at New York University; Chicago Public Library; New York Public Library, especially the Irma and Paul Milstein Division of United States History, Local History and Genealogy, and the Microforms Division; the library of the New York Historical Society; Miami University Archives; and Alan A. Siegel, author and president of the Clinton Cemetery Association, Irvington, New Jersey.

I also am grateful to Darrin Pratt, director of the University Press of Colorado; his staff; and the anonymous reviewers he enlisted.

A Remarkable Curiosity

Amos Jay Cummings and
His Journey across America

W ATCHING OLD MOVIES AND RERUNS OF *F-Troop* and *Gunsmoke* on late-night television has taught several generations of viewers that it was gunslingers and gold prospectors, as well as cavalry and cowboys, who tamed the West, that huge chunk of land from the Great Plains to San Francisco Bay. To that mix of people New York City journalist Amos Jay Cummings, relying on his own firsthand observations, added bankers, business people, lawyers, and train engineers, along with Mormons and even a Canadian or two.

In 1873, less than a decade after the end of the Civil War, and fresh from a several-month-long journalistic exploration of the Florida frontier, Amos Cummings turned his attention to another portion of the expanding United States: the West. Accompanied by his spouse, Frances, Cummings ferried across the Hudson River to Jersey City's Exchange Place train station, boarded a Pennsylvania Railroad train, and headed toward the setting sun, traveling across New Jersey, Pennsylvania, and Ohio, then along another railway to East St. Louis on the banks of the Mississippi River. After crossing the Mississippi on a ferry—no bridge existed at the time—Cummings found himself in St. Louis, the gateway to the West. It was nearly seventy years after Meriwether Lewis and William Clark had set out on their own journey of western exploration.

Cummings's plan was to travel across the breadth of the American West by rail while writing articles about who and what he saw for publication in the *New York Sun* newspaper. In late May, as he traveled toward Denver over the monotonous Kansas plains west of Kansas City, Cummings began to put pen to paper, posting his stories to New York, where they appeared in the *Sun* and, in a few instances, in its sister publication, the *New York Semi-Weekly Sun*. He continued to write as he traveled west across Colorado and Utah, both then territories of the United States, and Nevada (which had achieved statehood on Halloween in 1864). It is a selection of those newspaper articles that are reprinted in this volume.

The articles Cummings wrote on his 1873 western adventure, and those he had written from Florida during the first several months of that same year, established Cummings as a bona fide human interest reporter, one of the first. Those stories, along with others written by Cummings from Florida in 1893 and his later coverage of governmental and business scandals, European affairs, and a host of other topics, built Cummings's reputation as a top-notch journalist and a superb storyteller. By the time he was first elected to the U.S. House of Representatives in 1886 to represent New York City's Sixth Congressional District, Cummings was viewed as one of America's premier newsmen. An article in the March 10, 1888, *New York Daily Graphic* news-paper, for example, included Cummings among sixteen "dis-tinguished newspaper correspondents of America . . . who have done so much for the progress of the times." Cummings used his standing as a well-known and successful newsman to launch his political career.

Cummings's death in 1902 produced an outpouring of acco-lades commemorating both his journalistic accomplishments and his status as a public personality and politician. Time erases many lives and memories, however. Today, a century after he was awarded a state funeral in our nation's Capitol building, Cummings and his journalistic oeuvre have all but disappeared from our collective consciousness. Yet some of his articles, includ-ing those reprinted here, are classics. He was a keen observer of America and its people at a time when the frontier was still moving west across the Great Plains and south into peninsular Florida.

Cummings loved to talk with the people he met on his jour-neys. On his 1873 excursion to the West he wrote about topics ranging from card sharps who preyed on tourists to the hard-ships suffered by settlers who had been enticed to move to the then-desolate plains of Kansas from the East, Midwest, and Canada. He also painted a verbal picture of the West's natural wonders, including the petrified forests of the Rocky Mountains and the Great Salt Lake. Still another facet of western life that drew his attention was the gold and silver mines of the West, especially Colorado, and the financial and other ventures, some not so legal, that resulted in fortunes made and lost. After read-ing Cummings, I now understand that mining for gold was a great deal more involved than simply picking up nuggets from a streambed or extracting gold dust from the walls of a mine, a misapprehension fueled in part by watching the 1969 classic movie *Paint Your Wagon* at least twice. Through Cummings we also learn about the ins and outs of raising and marketing sheep, and we hear tall tales, including one involving a burro tail and another that describes an early relative of the jackalope.

In his monthlong stopover in Salt Lake City, Cummings found an emerging story suited to his talents as a "man bites dog" reporter: one of Brigham Young's wives had filed for divorce against the leader of the Church of Latter-day Saints. Cummings's interviews with Eliza Young and her husband provide insight into Mormon society at a time when many in the East suspiciously viewed Utah's Mormons as members of an offbeat sect. Cummings also used his weeks in Salt Lake City to explore the region and to learn and write about Brigham Young's attempts to place Mormon colonies elsewhere in the West.

DISCOVERING AMOS JAY CUMMINGS

Who was Amos J. Cummings and how did he come to write these extraordinary articles? My initial encounter with Cummings took place in 2001, ninety-nine years after his death. "Encounter" may be too ambitious a word, because I had no idea whom I had met. Even had I known that the copy of a March 20, 1873, *New York Weekly Sun* newspaper article sent to me by a University of Florida librarian was written by Amos Jay Cummings, the name would have meant nothing.

That article, titled "Florida's Indian Mounds," with the subheading "The Mysterious Monuments of an Extinct Race," was datelined "May 20, De Soto Groves, Florida." It did not include the name of the author. Eventually, I learned De Soto Groves was a small orange-growing settlement on the Atlantic coast of Florida, not far from the launchpads of today's John F. Kennedy Space Center. The librarian, who knew of my research in Florida archaeology, thought the article might tweak my interest. He was correct.

Among other things, the 2,500-word article described the unknown author's visit to Turtle Mound, an archaeological site in modern Volusia County, Florida, just below New Smyrna Beach. That mound—actually a huge shell heap, perhaps the largest in Florida, if not the entire Atlantic coast of the United States—lies within the Canaveral National Seashore and can be visited by the public. From the sea, the mound's shape resembles a giant turtle, hence the name. In addition to Turtle Mound, the *New York Weekly Sun* article mentioned several other archaeological sites in east-central Florida.

I set out to find the identity of the author, a several-week journey with many bibliographic twists and turns, not to mention false leads. A fortuitous perusal of an 1875 book titled *Guide to Florida* led me to a second description of Turtle Mound and adjacent east-central Florida that included very similar phrases to those contained in the piece in the 1873 *Weekly Sun* article. The author of that particular section of *Guide to Florida* was "Ziska," an obvious pseudonym. It was evident that Ziska and the author of the 1873 newspaper article were one and the same. If I could discover who Ziska was, I would have the identity of my unknown *Weekly Sun* journalist and the author of "Florida's Indian Mounds."

My search for Ziska took me on some wild literary adventures through electronic databases, all chronicled in an article titled "The Historian's Craft," published in a 2003 issue of the *Florida Historical Quarterly*. Ultimately, however, I found Ziska not in a computer but in John Edward Haynes's slender volume *Pseudonyms of Authors: Including Anonyms and Initialisms*, published in 1882. On page 103, Haynes informed his readers that Ziska was a pseudonym used by New York journalist Amos Jay Cummings. I had my author.

A check of several biographical dictionaries from the late nineteenth century and later years provided a quick overview of Cummings's life, though, as it turned out, some of the important details were in error.[1] I learned that Amos Cummings had been not only a journalist but also a hero of the Civil War, receiving the Congressional Medal of Honor. He also was an elected official serving multiple terms in the United States House of Representatives. Most importantly for my search, he had indeed visited Florida on several occasions, and he wrote under the pseudonym "Ziska."

A few more bits of biographical information emerged when I consulted various sources about Congressional Medal of Honor awardees and former members of Congress.[2] Searching an online Web site documenting the final resting places of Congressional Medal of Honor war heroes, I learned that Cummings was buried in Irvington, New Jersey. That led me to another Web page containing an actual photograph of his tombstone.

My real breakthrough came when I checked the online catalogue of the New York Public Library. Listed there under Cummings's name were four scrapbooks.[3] A subsequent visit to that library and the old handwritten catalogue in the elegant Rose Reading Room revealed eleven more scrapbooks belonging to Amos Cummings.[4]

The fifteen scrapbooks had been compiled by Cummings and later, I believe, by his congressional staff over a thirty-year period, from the early 1870s until just after his death in 1902. The last scrapbook contains obituaries and information about Cummings's funerals (he had several).

It is likely the scrapbooks were retained after Cummings's death by his widow. Later, according to notes in the New York Public Library catalogue, they found their way to the Bargain Book Shop in Manhattan, where they were rescued in 1927 by a library employee and added to the library's collections.

The scrapbooks contain articles written by Cummings for the *New York Sun*, the *Weekly Sun*, and the *Semi-Weekly Sun*, as well as the *Washington Post*, along with other articles clipped from various newspapers and magazines and dealing with topics Cummings must have found interesting. The scrapbooks also hold hundreds of articles from various U.S. newspapers in which Representative Cummings was mentioned. Most likely his staff subscribed to a clipping service that monitored newspapers for information about the congressman. Within one of the scrapbooks I found a clipping of the 1873 article on Turtle Mound that I had first seen in 2001 and that had originally stimulated my search for its then-unknown author.

AMOS JAY CUMMINGS

Over the last several years I have read Cummings's fifteen scrapbooks and examined microfilmed copies of the *New York Sun* and its sibling newspapers housed in the New York Public Library in midtown Manhattan and New York University's Bobst Library in Greenwich Village. Although the articles pasted in Cummings's scrapbooks almost never include information on where they were published or even the year they appeared, I was able to find copies of every one of the articles reprinted here on one or another reel of microfilm of the *New York Sun*. Those versions of the articles allowed me to pinpoint the dates of publication. From the scrapbooks I also garnered more biographical information about Cummings.

One thing I soon learned was that Cummings and his biographers did not always provide correct or truthful information. For instance, nearly all the biographical details about him published during his life and in conjunction with his death list his birth year as 1841. In reality, it was 1838. At some point he lopped three years off his age! It is likely that he did this out of vanity; I do not believe it was simply a mistake.

Cummings was born May 15, 1838, in Conklin, New York, a small town in Broome County southeast of Binghamton. As noted above, however, most of the biographical information published about him (including several of his obituaries in the *New York Times*, his official U.S. House of Representatives biography,

7

AMOS J CUMMINGS
1838–1902

SERGEANT MAJOR
CO E 26th REGT NJ VOLS
AWARDED A MEDAL OF HONOR FROM CONGRESS
FOR DISTINGUISHED GALLANTRY
AT THE BATTLE OF SALEM HEIGHTS MAY 4 1863

EDITORIALLY CONNECTED WITH THE N.Y. TRIBUNE
AND THE N.Y. SUN FROM 1864 TO 1887

ELECTED TO THE 50th CONGRESS 1886
AND SERVED UNTIL THE 57th CONGRESS
MAY 2 1902

HIS WIFE
FRANCES CAROLINE
1833–1916
ONLY DAUGHTER OF
SEARS AND PHEBE ROBERTS

THE TEXT ENGRAVED ON THE MONUMENT ABOVE AMOS AND CAROLINE CUMMINGS'S GRAVES IN CLINTON CEMETERY, IRVINGTON, NEW JERSEY. ALAN A. SIEGEL, PRESIDENT OF THE CLINTON CEMETERY ASSOCIATION, HELPED CLARIFY THE TEXT.

and his Congressional Medal of Honor citation) give 1841 as the year he was born (a few give 1842 and only a very few, 1838). The correct year, 1838, is inscribed on the small stone on his grave in Clinton Cemetery in Irvington, New Jersey, and it is on the larger monument raised next to his grave and that of his wife, Frances Caroline née Roberts, a resident of Irvington, New Jersey, whom he married March 6, 1869 (and who died January 28, 1916, in South Norwalk, Connecticut). Frances knew Amos's true age and had the correct year carved on the small marker; later that date was put on the larger monument.

Curiously, although the correct birth date is given on the small stone—May 15, 1838—the exact day of death is in error. It is given as May 10, 1902, rather than May 2, 1902.

Cummings's correct age and birth date are found in the 1890 federal census. His and Frances's census data were collected in June of that year in New York City. At the time, Cummings truthfully listed his birth date as May 15, 1838, and his age as sixty-two years (his occupation was "Congressman"). He also listed his correct age in the 1870 census (Amos and Frances are not listed in the 1880 census; perhaps they were out of New York City at the time). Stretching the truth for a biography apparently was one thing; lying to the federal census takers was another.

In a story told to Fred Mather, fishing editor of *Forest and Stream* magazine, who recounted the story in his 1901 book *My Angling Friends*, Cummings mentions moving to Honesdale, Pennsylvania, presumably from Conklin, New York, where he had been born, when he was seven years old. Honesdale is in Wayne County in northeast Pennsylvania in the lake region of the Pocono Mountains. Two years later Amos was still living in Honesdale. An April 16, 1896, issue of the magazine *20th Century Cookery* features a story written by Cummings in which he talks about eating keg oysters when he was nine years old and living in Honesdale (the article is titled "The Dishes of Childhood"; keg oysters were oysters preserved in liquid in wooden kegs, which, according to Cummings, gave them a "peculiar, delicate flavor"). In the same story, he mentions a brother.

In his book *Out of Our Past: A History of Irvington, New Jersey* (124–128), Alan A. Siegel provides information about Amos Cummings and his family's years in Irvington, New Jersey (in Clinton Township), where the family moved in the winter of 1852–1853. Amos was fifteen at the time. In Irvington, his father, Moses Cummings (his mother was Julia Ann Cummings, née Jones), worked as a dentist and jeweler and served as a lay minister. In 1855, Moses took over the editorship, including printing, of the *Christian Palladium*, a twice-monthly publication of the Christian Publishing Association. Later the paper merged with another to become the *Christian Messenger and Palladium*. Moses also published at least one religious book.

As a teenager, Amos learned the art of typesetting in his father's composing room on the first floor of the Cummingses' Irvington home. Later he would claim he first served as an apprentice typesetter when he was only twelve, which probably was not true. The elder Cummings, a staunch abolitionist who also preached against "atheism, evolution (and) ignorance" (*Out of Our Past*, 125), died in New York City in 1867. He was buried in Clinton Cemetery in Irvington. Julia Cummings, Amos's mother, continued to live in Irvington after the death of her husband, subdividing and selling their relatively large landholdings for income. In the 1870 federal census, her occupation is listed as "boarding"; she probably also was renting out rooms in the old family house.

The 1860 federal census for Essex County, New Jersey, records the Cummings family's presence in Irvington in Clinton Township. In that year, Moses, a native of New Hampshire born in 1812, was forty-seven. Spouse Julia, a native of New York, was fifty years old. Within their household lived Charles W. Cummings, nineteen, Amos's brother, the one mentioned in the 1896 article about keg-oyster eating. Charles, whose birth state appears to be Pennsylvania (the written census record is smudged; probably he was born in Honesdale), worked as a printer apprentice, as did four other young men living with Moses and Julia: Charles Hadden, twenty-one; John Jaroleman, seventeen; Frederick Loyd, seventeen; and John Schreibner, fifteen. Bridget Henry, nineteen and a native of Ireland, worked for the Cummings family as a live-in domestic.

Where was Amos at the time the 1860 federal census was taken when he would have been twenty-two years old? According to stories he told that are quoted in various *New York Times*

AMOS CUMMINGS'S BOYHOOD HOME IN IRVINGTON, NEW JERSEY. (FROM "MAP OF IRVINGTON & VICINITY, CLINTON TOWNSHIP, ESSEX CO., N. JERSEY. SURVEYED & PUBLISHED BY THOS. HUGHES, 1858. LITH. OF FRIEND & AUB. 332 WALNUT ST. PHILADA."; THE IMAGE, PROVIDED BY ALAN A. SIEGEL, IS REPRODUCED IN SIEGEL, *OUT OF OUR PAST*, 121; A COPY OF THE MAP IS IN THE AMERICAN GEOGRAPHICAL SOCIETY LIBRARY AT THE UNIVERSITY OF WISCONSIN, MILWAUKEE, CATALOGUE # 860-D/IRVINGTON/D-1858)

and *Washington Post* articles, obituaries, and memorials written after his death, he left home at age fifteen and began traveling around the country, working for various newspapers as a "tramp printer." Presumably, like his brother, he learned how to set type from his father. One newspaper source embellished the story, stating that Amos "ran away" from home to take up the life of an itinerant typesetter.

These stories, however, are at least partially made-up. We know for certain that Amos had only just moved to Irvington when he was fifteen years old. He would have been about seventeen when his father took over the *Christian Palladium*, thus giving Amos the opportunity to learn typesetting. Perhaps he did travel while in his late teens (in a *Chicago Daily Tribune* story published July 8, 1888, he states he was first in Chicago in 1857; at the time, he would have been eighteen or nineteen), but by the recording of that 1860 census, he was back living in Clinton Township, having married Maria Van Harten (in *Out of Our Past*, 128, Alan Siegel says Amos's spouse was Ida Van Houten; Maria may have been her nickname or middle name). Amos, whose occupation in the census is given as printer, was living with twenty-one-year-old Maria in the household of her parents, Horace, a dairy farmer, and Mary. Several other Van Harten families lived nearby.

Ida (or Maria) died in childbirth. I found a note in death records from New Jersey mentioning a child, Percy Byron Cummings, born to "Marie Cummings," on the Fourth of July 1860. The child died on the same date, his birthday, in 1861. That may have been the child of Amos and his deceased wife.

Amos Cummings always thought of Irvington as his boyhood home. As noted above, Frances Cummings, Amos's second spouse, was a native of that town and Irvington is where Amos chose to enlist in the army after the outbreak of the Civil War. It also is the town where he and Frances are buried. Alan Siegel (in *Out of Our Past*, 128) notes that after he was elected to Congress, Amos maintained an apartment in Irvington at 1068 Clinton Avenue.

Just prior to 1860—several of the *New York Times* and *Washington Post* newspaper obituaries say 1857—Amos supposedly interrupted his career as itinerant typographer to join one of the several expeditions organized and led by William Walker, who wanted to overthrow political regimes in the Central American country of Nicaragua. A few biographical sketches, such as that in the *New York Times* published on May 3, 1902, the day after Cummings's death in Baltimore, have Cummings traveling to Nicaragua with Walker on Walker's second expedition in 1857. In Nicaragua, Cummings and his fellow adventurers, according to the article, were taken captive aboard the sloop of war *St. Marys*, a U.S. Navy vessel, but were later allowed to return to the United States through the intervention of John Forsyth, U.S. Minister to Mexico. Another version of the story in a second obituary adds the detail that Cummings joined the expedition in Mobile, Alabama, in 1857. Interestingly, I found a clipping from the *New York Daily Graphic* in one of Cummings's scrapbooks recounting the capture of Walker's men by Commodore Charles Davis, the captain of the *St. Marys*.

Still other sources, including his U.S. Congressional biography, have him with William Walker on Walker's "last invasion of Nicaragua in October 1858" (which actually was not the last), whereas another has him on Walker's 1860 expedition (which became Walker's last expedition when he was executed by Honduran authorities).

I am suspicious of all these stories, none of which fits all the facts. For instance, it was Walker's first expedition (which sailed from San Francisco) when his men were taken aboard the *St. Marys* and transported to Panama City. Later they were returned to the United States. Cummings could not have been on that expedition because he was not in San Francisco at that time. Walker's second expedition did leave from Mobile, Alabama, in November 1857, but the sloop *St. Marys* was not involved. A third expedition also sailed from Mobile (in December 1858), but Walker's schooner *Susan* wrecked off the coast of British Honduras and the men were returned to the United States.

In September 1859, Walker arranged for two steamships to leave from New York City as part of another coup attempt. The first, the *Philadelphia*, loaded with arms, docked in New

Orleans, where it was seized by authorities. The second, the *St. Louis*, loaded with volunteers, was never allowed to cast anchor in New York City's harbor.

Walker's last voyage sailed out of Mobile in August 1860. He faced a firing squad several weeks later on September 12. Cummings certainly was not on that 1860 voyage, since he was working for the *New York Tribune* (and commuting to New York City from a farm in Irvington, New Jersey?). Knowing Cummings's penchant for telling a good story, and lacking further documentation, it seems safest to declare his participation in Walker's schemes as uncertain. Perhaps he was on the steamship that left New York City in 1859.

After his involvement with Walker, whatever that involvement was, Cummings was hired by the *New York Tribune*, whose editor-in-chief was the famed newsman Horace Greeley. Union records show he joined the New York Typographical Union, Local 6, on February 4, 1860. He remained a paid-up union member until his death.

Later that same February in 1860, Cummings rubbed elbows with Abraham Lincoln, then a candidate for the presidency. Lincoln was supported by Greeley and the *Tribune*. According to Robert S. Harper's book *Lincoln and the Press*, Lincoln presented a speech at the Cooper Union near the Bowery in Manhattan. Seeking a scoop, Greeley, who had sat on the stage with Lincoln, received a copy of the candidate's speech as soon as Lincoln finished and rushed off to have it set in type for publication in the *Tribune*. Later, Lincoln went to the *Tribune* offices to read and correct the typeset copy. He arrived just as Cummings, serving as proofreader, had been handed the galleys. Lincoln is said to have sat down next to Cummings, donned his glasses, and proofed the speech himself. He made corrections and stayed around to read those proofs as well. After he left, according to Cummings, the original draft of the speech was tossed into the trash.

After the outbreak of the Civil War, Cummings, who was still with the *New York Tribune,* enlisted in the U.S. Army. One account written at the time of his death says he tried twice to enlist in New York City but was rejected for some "trifling physical incapacity." I suspect this story was made-up. Cummings most likely chose to enlist in Irvington.

The circumstances of his enlistment were these: President Abraham Lincoln, in accordance with an Act of Congress passed July 1861, had issued a draft on August 4, 1862, to the State of New Jersey for 10,478 men, each to serve for nine months in the U.S. Army. The draft went into effect September 1, 1862, and within three weeks, the quota was filled. The new soldiers were allotted to army units, and officers assigned.

Many men, Cummings among them, had chosen to volunteer rather than wait to be drafted. Military records show Cummings enlisted on September 1 and was assigned the rank of sergeant in Company E in the Twenty-sixth New Jersey Infantry Regiment (volunteers). He was one of seven noncommissioned officers of that rank. Amos's brother, Charles, enlisted at the same time and served in the same regiment.

On September 26, the Twenty-sixth Regiment left New Jersey for Washington, DC, where the men encamped on Capitol Hill as part of the Second Army. Less than a week later the regiment was relocated in Hagerstown, Maryland, where it became part of the Sixth Army Corps.

Cummings and his regiment saw action at Fredericksburg, Virginia, in December 1862, and during the Chancellorsville campaign in May/June 1863. He was promoted to sergeant major in March 1863. During the war, Cummings sent letters back to New Jersey that were published in Newark newspapers. Some are humorous; others describe bloody, horrific scenes. All are worth reading. Historian Alan Siegel draws on a number of quotes from Cummings's letters in his two books *Beneath the Starry Flag: New Jersey's Civil War Experience* and *For the Glory*

of the Union: Myth, Reality, and the Media in Civil War, New Jersey,
both of which provide important details about New Jersey soldiers in the Civil War.

After the war, probably in the early 1870s, Cummings
researched newspapers to find contemporary accounts reporting on the various military engagements in which his regiment
had been involved, pasting them in one of his scrapbooks and
adding his own annotations in the margins. Included in his
scrapbooks are other newspaper articles about the Civil War,
the assassination of President Abraham Lincoln, and the arrest
of John Wilkes Booth.

It was at the battle of Salem Church on May 4, 1863, during the Chancellorsville campaign that Amos Cummings performed the gallantry that earned him the Congressional Medal
of Honor. In their book *Deeds of Valor: How America's Heroes
Won the Medal of Honor* (1903, 1:166–168), Walther F. Beyer and
Oscar F. Keydel offer a general description of the battle, which
is followed by a more colorful account written by Cummings
himself:

> The Twenty-sixth New Jersey Infantry, of which Amos
> J. Cummings was sergeant-major, was part of General
> Sedgwick's Corps, which was heavily engaged in the ever
> memorable struggles between Federal and Confederate
> forces around Chancellorsville. The culmination of the
> engagements and maneuverings came with the battle of
> Salem Church on May 4, 1863. Generals Early, Anderson
> and McLaws had left Lee's Army at Chancellorsville to
> drive General Sedgwick's troops into the river. The con-
> flict, which followed, was most obstinate, and lasted all
> day. Though largely outnumbered, the Northerners bravely
> repulsed each assault until darkness fell, when they were
> forced to yield to the superior strength of the enemy, and
> retreated, in good order, across the Rappahannock. Up to
> midnight the armies wrestled for supremacy. Both sides
> displayed bravery and daring, and many were the deeds

of heroism performed by friend and foe. The Union soldiers especially were conspicuous for their gallantry. Some
incidents occurred which give one a clear conception of the
fierceness of the fighting and the heroism of the fighters. In
this connection Sergeant-Major Cummings, who earned his
medal on that memorable day, furnishes an inspiring narra-
tive in the following:

"At sundown on this fourth of May, the Twenty-sixth
New Jersey, Second Brigade, Second Division, lay in line of
battle in a depression along a ditch dug by a farmer to drain
his land. We were supported by the regular battery occupying a slight elevation in our rear. Our position was about
three-fourths of a mile north of Salem Church.

"The Confederates massed and came down on us five
lines deep. As they advanced I could hear the officer in
charge of the battery behind us giving his commands. He
was gauging his fuses by the advance of the enemy.

"'Second and a half' he shouted.

"'Blim! Blim!' responded his guns.

"'A second and a quarter!' he cried.

"'Blim! Blim! Blim' was the reply.

"'A full second!' he roared.

"'Blim! Blim! Blim!' answered the guns.

"'Three-quarters of a second!' came next.

"'Blim! Blim! Blim!'

"The shrieking of the shells as they swept over our
heads was appalling. Suddenly, right in front, there was
a flash all along the line. The Confederates were within
thirty yards of us and had commenced firing. The rebel yell
was still heard, but the column had lost its impetus. As the
yell died away our lieutenant-colonel shouted: 'ten-tion!'

"The order was heard by every man of the regiment. In
a second everybody was on his feet. The colonel continued:
'Right about face!'

"The regiment obeyed the orders as if on parade.

"Then came, probably, the most singular command
ever heard on a battle-field.

"'Regiment, left half wheel!'

"The left wing of the regiment on our right had swung back, doing so to take advantage of the natural depression of the field and thus had left a gap between its left and our right.

"Our colonel saw the opening and realized that by left half wheeling he could again cement his line. Hence his singular command. But, when our regiment tried to obey the order, beginning the movement steadily and in perfect form, the result was disastrous. Suddenly there was a waver, then a break and then a rush for the river.

"A few brave men remained, but only a moment, when they began to swear and to coolly walk after their fugitive comrades, trying by shouts and curses to rally them. A lieutenant of the battery confronted the demoralized men. He stood straight as an arrow with drawn sword. All of his guns had disappeared but one. It stood unmanned, subject to capture. His amazement knew no bounds. Our men had been acting like veterans and were now running over him like frightened deer. His oaths were terrific. He called them all the names in the vocabulary of indignation. There was a score of our regiment, however, who did not lose their heads.

"'Let us save the gun!' I shouted, at the same time seizing it by a wheel. The enemy were making for the gap, but four of my comrades were with me around the gun. On came the Southerners and our little group was increased by the coming of a few more of our men.

"The piece began to move backward in answer to our efforts, but, suddenly there was a change of scene.

"The enemy had passed through the gap and were upon us. They were holding our gun by the muzzle and then muskets were clubbed, bayonets were used. If the combatants had been personal enemies for years, the cursing and reviling could not have been more bitter. On both sides the wounded fell, uttering oaths and imprecations, but without groans.

"Enough of our men had rallied to the cannon to keep it moving until a Vermont regiment in the woods on our left, a regiment which had stood firm through all, was able to bring an enfilading fire to bear, when the Confederates were quickly dispersed.

"The gun was saved, the metal won."

The Medal of Honor citation that Cummings received on March 28, 1894, succinctly describes Cummings's heroic actions: "Rendered great assistance in the heat of the action rescuing a part of the field batteries from an extremely dangerous and exposed position."

Cummings and a number of other men who had enlisted when he had were mustered out of the army on June 27, 1863. Of the seven original sergeants from the Twenty-sixth Regiment, it appears only four came home.

Cummings was awarded the Medal of Honor three decades after the battle of Salem Church, several years after he was first elected to Congress. Did he receive the medal in part because he was a congressman? I looked at the records of thirty-five soldiers from New Jersey who received the Medal of Honor for gallantry in the Civil War. At least twelve of the thirty-five, more than a third, received their medals after the war, many about the same time as Cummings, and at least one as late as 1906. Cummings was a bona fide war hero.

His fellow Medal of Honor winners must have thought so, too. According to a short article in the June 10, 1897, *New York Times*, the Medal of Honor Legion at their meeting in Scranton, Pennsylvania, elected Amos Cummings as commander (their highest office) for the coming year. Cummings also was an active and respected member of the Grand Army of the Republic, an organization of Civil War veterans. Years after his death, Post 1612 of the Veterans of Foreign Wars, located in Chicago, named itself the Amos J. Cummings Post. That honor was due both to Cummings's status as a heroic war veteran and his long membership in the typographical union. Post 1612, according to an April 27, 1950, article in the *Chicago Daily Tribune*, was known as "the printers' post," having been founded by veterans of World War I and World War II who also were members of the International Typographical Union, Local 16, based in Chicago.

In several of the newspaper obituaries written about Cummings in the *New York Times* and *Washington Post*, there are mentions of an unspecified health problem that led him to take extended journeys out of New York City, such as the one to the American West in 1873. One memorial in the *Times* says it was an illness that caused him to leave the U.S. Army during the Civil War, but that is not true. He was mustered out at the end of his tour of duty. Another account says he had "a physical breakdown which left him permanently impaired." The exact nature and cause of any physical problems he had remain a mystery.

After he was discharged from the army in mid-1863, not long after the Battle of Salem Heights, Cummings returned to New York City, where he was rehired at the *New York Tribune* and its sister publication, the *Weekly Tribune*. At some point, he was working as night editor for the paper. That may have been his job when, according to several biographical sketches, including one obituary in the *New York Times*, he helped to ward off rioting military draft protestors who were intent on raiding the *Tribune* offices in retaliation for the stance Horace Greeley had taken regarding the draft.

During a printer's strike, Cummings briefly lost his newspaper job and went to work for the *Law Transcript*, published in New York City. By 1866, however, he was back at the *Tribune*, holding several different editorships over the next few years. By 1867, he had moved into Manhattan and was living at 95 Second Avenue.

On January 1, 1869, Cummings left the *Tribune* for the *New York Sun*, where Charles Anderson Dana made him managing editor. According to Frank M. O'Brien's 1928 *The Story of the Sun* (p. 241), Cummings told Dana, "I am leaving the *Tribune* because they say I swear too much." Alan Siegel (in *Out of Our Past*, 125–126) supplies the details:

> Cummings resigned from the *Tribune* in the fall of 1868 after the managing editor, whose habit of issuing numbered orders raised the hackles of the entire staff, dispatched two of his pronouncements to Cummings in one night:
>
> Order No. 756—There is too much profanity in this office.
>
> Order No. 757—Hereafter the political reporter must have his copy in at 10:30 P.M.

Cummings turned to his desk and wrote his reply:

> Order No. 1234567—Everybody knows damn well that I get most of the political news out of the *Albany Journal*, and everybody knows God damn well that the *Journal* doesn't get here until eleven o'clock at night, and anybody who knows anything knows God damn well that asking me to get my stuff up at half past ten is like asking a man to sit on the window-sill and dance on the roof at the same time.

The details of Cummings's move, associated with the switch of several newspeople within and between the *Tribune* and the *Sun* staffs, are announced in two clippings pasted in one of Amos's scrapbooks, both with the date January 1, 1869, penciled in beside them (one clipping from each of the two papers, most likely). The first, headlined "Journalistic Changes," reads:

> Mr. England, for many years city editor of the *Tribune*, and at present managing editor of the *Sun*, of the 1st day of January relieves Mr. Byington of the business charge. Mr. Cummings succeeds Mr. England, and Dr. Wood takes the place of Mr. Cummings.

And the second:

> In the *Tribune* office, Dr. Wood, the well-known night edi-
> tor, leaves on the 1st prox. to take a similar position on the
> *Sun*. Mr. Cummings, the *Tribune* sketcher and city editor,
> has left that "Happy Family," and will assume the manage-
> ment of the *Sun* on the first of January.

At some point after Amos left the *Tribune* for the *Sun*, probably after he married Frances (in 1869), he was living in Manhattan at 114 Varick. It was at the *Sun* that Cummings made his reputation as a journalist, writer, and public figure.

AMOS JAY CUMMINGS, JOURNALIST

In the winter of 1873, four years after moving to the *New York Sun*, Cummings took leave of New York and headed south. After a stop in Savannah, Georgia, he reached northeast Florida, and then traveled down the peninsula, probably on a steamship on the St. Johns River, to the Indian River and Cape Canaveral region of east-central Florida. He spent the months of March and April 1873 in the area, writing a series of stories that were mailed back to New York and published in the *Sun* and its related publications. Cummings also traveled north to Lake City and Jacksonville, Florida, to write about Reconstruction-period racial strife and governmental corruption in Columbia County, Florida.

His articles, all unsigned, were a hit with his New York audi-ence. The stories describe a frontier land of extraordinary natu-ral bounty that was being settled by a cross section of people who were not always gentle in their attempts to wrest a living from the land. Cummings pulled no punches in reporting what he saw and heard, whether it was a man trading his daughter for another man's wife and twenty cows or a farmer feeding thou-sands of sea turtle eggs to his mule.

Cummings returned to New York from Florida and almost immediately set out on the western odyssey that is the focus of this book (the route of which is explored in more detail below). It was on that western journey that Cummings began to sign his *Sun* stories with the pseudonym Ziska.

In December 1873, following the western trip, Cummings was once again back in New York. In only a matter of days he packed for a return to Florida. His journey south was a leisurely one that took him to Columbia, South Carolina, and then Augusta and Savannah, Georgia. By March 1874, he was back in the Indian River area on the Atlantic coast of central Florida. On the way back north in May and June 1874, Cummings spent time in Charleston and Florence, South Carolina. During that trip, he sent stories back to the *Sun* from Georgia and South Carolina, as well as Florida. The 1874 articles all appear over his pseudonym Ziska. Selections from the 1873 and 1874 Florida visits (and a later one in 1893) are published in *Frolicking Bears, Wet Vultures, & Other Oddities: A New York City Journalist in Nineteenth-Century Florida*, a book I compiled in 2005.

The 1873 and 1874 journeys to Florida apparently were not Cummings's first, and certainly were not his last. In a letter written to the editor of the *Sun* signed Ziska (who, of course, was Cummings; I found several instances where Cummings wrote letters to the editor—himself—just so he could make a point in the editor's published answer), Cummings mentions spending five winters in Florida, each averaging four months. The letter, from its placement in one of Cummings's scrapbooks, probably was written in the late 1870s. One of his biographical sketches also says he spent five winters in Florida, including in 1875 and 1876. There is a piece of stationary from the Hotel Ponce de Leon in St. Augustine, Florida, dated Valentine's Day 1888 in another of his scrapbooks, suggesting he again was in that state in the 1880s. It is certain he returned in 1893.

Throughout the 1870s and 1880s, Cummings, sometimes writing as Ziska, wrote numerous other articles for the *Sun*, at least some of them penned while on still more trips around the United States. In the late 1870s and early 1880s, he wrote a series of stories, some with interviews, about Thomas Alva Edison and his discoveries, including the electric lightbulb. The stories, based in part on visits Cummings made to Edison's Menlo Park laboratory, have headlines like "The Genie of Menlo Park," "Four Hours with Edison," and "Edison's Electric Light." Cummings clearly saw the changes that the lightbulb was going to bring.

Late summer 1880, which was hurricane season in Florida, found Cummings in New York City when one of the tropical storms sank the steamship *City of Vera Cruz* in the Atlantic Ocean off Cummings's old east-central Florida stomping grounds, the area that today is New Smyrna Beach and Daytona Beach. Bound from Havana to New York with both passengers and cargo aboard, the hurricane literally broke the *Vera Cruz* in half. Even while the ship's owners in New York City were denying anything was amiss, local residents in Florida were finding cargo, bags of mail, timbers from the ship, and bodies along the Florida coast from St. Augustine to Cape Canaveral. At first it was feared all seventy-eight aboard were lost, but that turned out not to be the case (twenty-two people were washed ashore and lived).

The fate of the ship and its passengers and crew gripped the attention of the nation. From September 4 through September 15, 1880, the *Sun* carried articles about the disaster, most, I suspect, written by Cummings. For at least one of the articles, Cummings used information wired him by one of the men he had befriended on his earlier trips to east-central Florida.

On September 10, 1880, the *Sun*'s editorial staff had no new information on the wreck, so Cummings, writing as Ziska, sat down and drafted a marvelous account of what a Florida hurricane was like ("A Florida Typhoon: A Graphic Description of a Hurricane near Mosquito Inlet"; Mosquito Inlet, just north of New Smyrna Beach, Florida, today is known as Ponce de Leon

Inlet). Cummings must have been through at least one hurricane while in Florida.

At times frustrated with the slow pace of information coming out of east-central Florida where most of the survivors were being found, one of the *Sun's* editors, most certainly Amos Cummings, wrote: "Had those survivors of the *Vera Cruz* whose names were so long unknown reached Smyrna in Asia Minor instead of [New] Smyrna in Florida, we should several days since have learned a great deal more about them and their ship."

A decade after the Menlo Park interviews and nearly a decade after the *City of Vera Cruz* coverage, the *Sun* carried a series of seven stories by Cummings under the rubric "Fortunes in the South." The articles, datelined from June 6 to August 1, 1889, were based on a swing through the post–Civil War South made by Cummings to take the pulse of the region. All are signed "Amos J. Cummings."

Later that same year Cummings headed west to the new state of South Dakota. Among other things, he was interested in the tin mining boom in the Black Hills, hence the name "Tin Letters" that is written in a short table of contents in the scrapbook in which clippings of six *Sun* articles were pasted. Three are datelined Rapid City, one each from Grizzly Gulch and Hill City, and another one from Deadwood ("A Cold Day in Deadwood"). The latter was written thirteen years after 1876, the date of the town of Deadwood as portrayed in the HBO television series of the same name.

During the late 1870s and 1880s, Cummings also was known for covering several notable murder trials. In 1877 he wrote a lengthy article on the Loomis family gang, a multigeneration band of outlaws who terrorized a wide swath of central New York State in the mid-1800s. Cummings also attended the national political party conventions in 1880, 1884, and 1888, covering them for the *Sun*.

Cummings, probably from the *New York Sun*, ca. 1884. The drawing, labeled "Amos J. Cummings, The Worker," was published with the following text: "Among the working journalists of New York few stand more deservedly higher than Amos J. Cummings, of the *Sun*. He knows everybody of note, and in turn is known by thousands he has never met. Amos enjoys life and a large salary, and as he has a roving commission, writes when he feels like it, lives like a prince and writes like an expert. . . . Amos is a good-looking and good-natured man, and is a friend to young journalists." (Print Collection, Miriam and Ira D. Wallace Division of Art, Prints and Photographs, the New York Public Library, Astor, Lenox, and Tilden Foundations)

The *Tribune* and the *Sun* were not the only papers for which Cummings worked. At some point before mid-1875, Cummings had been involved with the *New York Evening Express*, itself associated with the *Weekly Express* and the *Semi-Weekly Express*, whose editor-in-chief was Erastus Brooks. All three of the papers ceased publication around 1881. Also, for a time in the late 1880s, he was managing editor for the *New York Evening Sun* newspaper, one of whose writers was social reformer Jacob Riis. The *Evening Sun* was said to be the first afternoon sporting newspaper.

Just as Cummings wrote for more than one newspaper, so did he write under more than one pseudonym. Uncle Rufus Hatch[5] is listed as the author of articles Cummings penned for the *Sun* during travels in England and to Paris during the period 1879–1882.

Cummings clearly saw some humor in his dual personae. In a *New York Times* article of October 29, 1881, it was reported that the *City of Rome*, billed as the largest steamship in the world, was sailing for Liverpool that day. She had arrived in New York on October 24 on her maiden voyage from England. Highlighted among a list of 200 people booked in cabin class (as opposed to steerage) on the return voyage to England were six dignitaries, including "Ernest S. Inman [owner of the steamship line to which the *City of Rome* belonged], Rufus Hatch, [and] Amos Cummings." The other three upper-class passengers were a former U.S. Consul to Liverpool, a bishop, and a general who later would become president of Panama. Amos must have loved the joke, which was picked up by other newspapers, such as the *Brooklyn Daily Eagle*.

In addition to articles on Europe, Uncle Rufus Hatch wrote articles about Wall Street and the financial dealings of people like Jay Gould. Cummings also published "Sayings of Uncle Rufus" (1880), a small collection of humorous sayings with political overtones (I have not been able to locate a copy).

Although writing under pseudonyms may seem peculiar today, pen names were popular at the time that Cummings was writing as Ziska and Uncle Rufus Hatch. Two well-known contemporary authors whose works Cummings no doubt read were Charles Dodgson and Samuel Clemens, whose pseudonyms were, respectively, Lewis Carroll and Mark Twain. (Cummings met Clemens in Manhattan, where they both belonged to the same social club.)

As noted above, Cummings's newspaper articles brought him journalistic acclaim. John Hicks, in his book recounting his own adventures as a printer (*Adventures of a Tramp Printer, 1880–1890*), met Cummings in New York City about 1889 and describes him as "a newspaper genius" (p. 270), whereas Frank O'Brien (in *The Story of the Sun*, 241) calls Cummings "the best all-round news man of his day."

Cummings's popularity led to his being elected president of the New York Press Club in 1885–1886 (he later served on its board of trustees as well). His popularity was the topic of an editorial from the *Brooklyn Daily Eagle* dated April 26, 1885:

> All practical newspapermen will admit, I think, that Mr.
> Amos J. Cummings is the most popular journalist in the
> United States. . . . When that easy going and tranquil man
> strolls up Broadway with one hand in his pocket, a very
> large cigar in the corner of his mouth and genial smile
> backing up the cigar, he seems to know every other man
> on the street, and if three or four newspaper men gather
> to chat in New York, New Orleans, Manitoba, or Mexico,
> Mr. Cummings is sure to be mentioned before they leave in
> some characteristic anecdote or story. . . . [Cummings] is
> one of the most unassuming but influential men on the New
> York press.

Cummings also gained acclaim as a sports reporter. The *National Police Gazette* (issue of March 28, 1885) offered this flattering literary portrait:

> Amos J. Cummings, the well-known journalist and founder
> of the *Sun*'s reputation, is, among other things, an admirable
> sporting reporter. His first sporting reports were written in
> 1867, when he reported the Saratoga ⌈horse⌉ races for the
> New York *Tribune*. . . . Mr. Cummings has reported many
> prize fights and cock fights for the *Sun* . . . he is skillful in
> making sporting reports as in reports of . . . other events to
> which he is more frequently assigned.

In the gaslight era of the 1880s and 1890s, social gatherings organized around elaborate meals were very popular. With no radio, television, or movies, one's dining companions provided the entertainment. Amos, no shrinking violet, must have loved such occasions, including Press Club meetings, events usually reported in the *Sun* and other newspapers and in periodicals. Two of Cummings's scrapbooks in the New York Public Library (as well as *Field and Stream: A Journal of Outdoor Life* . . .) contain articles recounting the culinary adventures of the New York "Ichthyophagous Club" (Fish-Eating Club) and celebrating the eating of a variety of fish, shellfish, and crustaceans. Cummings was behind some of the articles and is mentioned in all of them.

That Amos loved a good time is also evident from his membership in the Pleiades Club, formed in 1896 by a number of New York residents who met in Greenwich Village in an Italian restaurant (Maria del Prato) on MacDougal Street. Members, both male and female, got together weekly during the winter months for dinner and entertainment. The club formally incorporated in January 1902, taking "Pleiades Club" as their name. It was at that club that Cummings met Samuel Clemens. Amos also belonged to the Hoboken Turtle Club (founded in the 1790s and known for legendary shore dinners and excursions by boat) and the Typothetæ, an association of master printers who dined each year on the occasion of Benjamin Franklin's birthday.

More evidence that Amos enjoyed social events is reflected in an anecdote in the *Brooklyn Daily Eagle* (June 12, 1901). After

THIS DRAWING OF CUMMINGS APPEARED IN THE *NEW YORK SUN*, CA. 1885, ACCOMPANIED BY A THREE-PARAGRAPH STORY (ALMOST CERTAINLY WRITTEN BY CUMMINGS) THAT READS IN PART:

A few of the jolly old friends of Amos J. Cummings, the brilliant journalist and president of the New York Press Club, last evening gathered in George Hopcroft's parlors at No. 57 Franklin street. The occasion was intended to be a surprise to Mr. Cummings, and it was a complete one in every detail. He was presented with a gold watch, chain and locket which cost $350. Jolly speeches were delivered and a magnificent banquet was enjoyed. Mr. Cummings was the proudest man in New York. . . . The poet Geoghegan was the moving spirit in the whole matter, and to his untiring energy the charming success of the affair was entirely due. The poet sang himself to sleep in his own little cot at 4:30 this morning, while Mr. Cummings was guarded on the way home by four of Inspector Byrnes's most lynx-eyed detectives.

A MEMBER OF THE NEW YORK PRESS CLUB, WILLIAM GEOGHEGAN RAN THE SALOON CALLED POET'S CORNER LOCATED AT GRAND AND JACKSON STREETS IN LOWER MANHATTAN; HE ALSO WROTE FOR THE *EVENING SUN* NEWSPAPER. THOMAS BYRNES WAS THE WELL-KNOWN CHIEF OF THE NEW YORK POLICE DEPARTMENT'S DETECTIVE BUREAU, WHILE HOPCROFT WAS THE ASSISTANT TO THE NEW YORK CHIEF OF POLICE AND A FISHING BUDDY OF CUMMINGS. (PRINT COLLECTION, MIRIAM AND IRA D. WALLACE DIVISION OF ART, PRINTS AND PHOTOGRAPHS, THE NEW YORK PUBLIC LIBRARY, ASTOR, LENOX, AND TILDEN FOUNDATIONS) one particularly notable dinner that included New York governor Roswell P. Flowers, the governor is said to have told Cummings, "You'll see two carriages waiting at the door to take you home, Amos. Take the first one; the other isn't there."

Like dining, fishing expeditions were another acceptable male social activity. Wherever he went, Cummings dropped a line in the water. He told Fred Mather (in Mather's book *My Angling Friends*, 187–197) that he had "set type and fished in every State in the Union." He went on to claim he had fished from "almost every dock in New York and New Jersey" south to Lake Worth in Florida and west to San Lorenzo Creek in California. He also recalled fishing in Bunnell's Pond near Honesdale, Pennsylvania, when he was a boy.

Not only were there extravagant meals, social clubs, and fishing expeditions to keep Amos entertained, there also were travel junkets in concert with fellow newspapermen. One, recorded in the *Winfield* (Kansas) *Courier* on New Year's Eve 1885, describes a "Jamboree," an excursion by rail from Chicago to New Orleans. Along with Amos Cummings, the newsmen included male editors from the *Philadelphia Times*, *Philadelphia News*, *New York Tribune*, *Boston Herald*, *St. Paul Globe*, *St. Paul Dispatch*, and *Minneapolis Tribune*. The newsmen departed Chicago at 8:30 at night on Saturday, December 26, 1885, arriving in New Orleans in time to celebrate Press Day the following Monday at the New Orleans Exposition. The editors were accompanied by wives and "other female relatives." In New Orleans, the journalists met "their brethren from Mexico and Central and South America."

On the trip south it was not intended that the members of the party should suffer. According to the newspaper article, their journey on the Illinois Central Railroad was "in a special train of the handsomest excursion cars ever built in the world. They include drawing rooms, parlors, state rooms, sleeping berths, pantries and kitchens complete, and are supplied with all the essentials of luxurious travel." Upon arrival in New Orleans the press corps was "received in state by the Mayor, municipal authorities, and Exposition management."

In reality, the New Orleans Exposition had already closed and the journey actually was to its stepchild, the American Exposition. The latter turned out to be less than a financial success, although the press corps must have enjoyed their opulent visit.

For much of Amos's career, he and Frances resided in New York City in Greenwich Village at 32 Charlton Street, east of Varick Street and west of Sixth Avenue (now also named Avenue of the Americas; today Charlton runs only three blocks, from Sixth Avenue to Greenwich Street; in the nineteenth century, it went east all the way to the Hudson River). According to an entry in Trow's New York City directory, they were living at that address by 1879. In one of Cummings's scrapbooks, there are two small (undated) clippings, each reporting on their purchase of that and other adjacent Charlton Street properties. The Cummingses owned not only their own residence at 32 Charlton Street but also the three adjacent row houses at 26, 28, and 30 Charlton Street. They lived in number 32 and rented out at least portions, if not all, of the other three.

Amos Cummings maintained a personal home library that he used for research and for his own enjoyment. In used book dealer catalogues, I have run across three books that belonged to him. Two of them (*Personal Recollections of Distinguished Generals*, published in 1866, and *History of the United State Secret Service*, 1867) have "Amos J. Cummings, Tribune Office" written in them along with the dates July 30, 1866, and January 20, 1868, respectively. A third book (*Manual of Bayonet Exercise: Prepared for the Use of the Army of the United States*, 1862) has the inscription "Col. A. J. Morrison, 26th Reg't New Jersey Vols., 'Camp Meder' Frederick, Md., Oct 9, 1962" written on the flyleaf. Morrison commanded Cummings's Civil War regiment. On the front free endpaper is the inscription "presented to

THE CUMMINGSES' HOME AT 32 CHARLTON STREET IN NEW YORK CITY. A SLIVER OF 34 CHARLTON STREET CAN BE SEEN ON THE FAR RIGHT; 32 CHARLTON IS THE ADJACENT BUILDING TO THE LEFT. (MILSTEIN DIVISION OF UNITED STATES HISTORY, LOCAL HISTORY & GENEALOGY, THE NEW YORK PUBLIC LIBRARY, ASTOR, LENOX AND TILDEN FOUNDATIONS)

Sergt-Major Amos Jay Cummings." Morrison must have given the book to Amos.

A bookplate pasted inside the front cover of the same book is stamped "ACCESSION NO 9147 SHELF NUMBER NO 293" (with the numbers added in different ink). Under that information is another stamp in the same ink color as the words "accession no" and "shelf no," which reads "CUMMINGS LIBRARY." Was there a Cummings Library? To find out I initially turned to the *New York Times*, where, in a December 8, 1902, article, Mrs. Cummings is quoted as saying it was her intent to "give a library" to the Union Printers Home in Colorado Springs, Colorado. The home, opened in 1902, was to be a retirement home for union members in need of special care. In a later article in the *Washington Post* (August 9, 1903), a plan for a memorial library to be funded by the union is mentioned, and in the same story it is noted that "Mrs. Cummings, the widow, has a big collection of books of her deceased husband, which she is willing to contribute."

To find out the rest of the story I turned to the *Typological Journal*, a monthly periodical of the International Typographical Union. In addition to the publication of numerous articles and reports about the union and the Union Printers Home, once each year the journal carried a supplement detailing the actions taken at the union's annual convention.

The 1902 union convention in Cincinnati, held just weeks after Amos Cummings's death, voted to appoint a committee to come up with an idea for the "erection of a monument . . . in memory of the Hon. Amos J. Cummings." In February 1903 the committee announced plans for a boulder with a suitably inscribed marble or bronze plaque. The monument was to be placed on the grounds of the Union Printers Home.

The location was chosen in part because Amos Cummings had served from 1890 to 1892 as one of thirteen members of the Home's original board of trustees that had helped to finalize plans for building the home in Colorado Springs and had approved construction of the facility. The Home had been dedicated on May 12, 1892, as the Child-Drexel Home for Union Printers (the name was unofficially changed to Union Printers Home in 1899 and legally changed three years later).

After his death, Amos Cummings's role as a former Home trustee, along with his long support of the union, led to numerous memorial resolutions from union locals, including in Denver, Houston, Kansas City, Knoxville, New York City, Washington, and Binghamton, New York. Many of those union members thought a boulder was not enough of a monument, and in June 1903 the Denver local called for the Amos Cummings Memorial Hall to be built as an addition to the Printers Home. The new wing would include an assembly room, library, and reading room. Later that year at the union's annual convention in Washington, the decision was made to see if enough money could be raised for such a project. Frances Cummings pledged donation of Amos's personal library (765 books), and the gift was accepted by the Home's board of trustees.

From 1903 into 1908, fund-raising efforts continued, supported by letters from Mrs. Cummings to the trustees and fund-raising committee. As Amos's memory among union members faded, donations grew fewer. Finally, in something of a compromise, the plans for a Cummings memorial were meshed with the need for more space at the Home for retirees and union members who needed medical care. An addition to the Home was funded and constructed. Dedicated in February 1910, the addition, a wing off the northeast corner of the building, included a library dedicated to Amos J. Cummings (the February 17, 1910, issue of the *Colorado Springs Gazette* carried a full history of the Union Printers Home and the efforts to raise funds for the new library dedicated to Cummings). At the time, the library's holdings included 10,000 volumes and numerous newspapers. As late as 1966, the library still existed, although even by the 1930s, few if anyone remembered Amos Cummings. *A Pictorial Presentation of the Union Printers Home*, put out by the International Typographical Union in 1935, even failed to mention that the library had been named for Cummings.

In the 1980s the International Typographical Union, victim of the computer technological revolution that had negated the need for typesetting, merged with the Communication Workers of America. The Union Printers Home is now an independent facility.

What ultimately happened to Amos Cummings's 765 books sent to Colorado Springs? I don't know. I suspect many were "deaccessioned" after the Home became a privately owned facility and found their way to the used book market.

Fortunately, Amos Cummings's fifteen scrapbooks were not among the boxes of books donated to the Union Printers Home by Frances. She apparently retained those in New York. A decade later when she moved to South Norwalk, Connecticut, to a nursing home (in 1911 or 1912), Frances, in declining health, likely left the scrapbooks in the house at 32 Charlton Street, which she still owned.

A brief obituary in the *New York Times* (January 29, 1916) notes Frances's death "yesterday" in South Norwalk, where "she had lived . . . for four years." On August 3 of the same year, the *Times* carried an article headlined "Estate of A. J. Cummings's Widow," which details the fate of the Cummingses' Charlton Street properties after Frances's death:

> The New York Estate of Mrs. Frances C. Cummings, who died Jan 28 last and was the widow of Amos J. Cummings, was appraised yesterday at $48,000 and consisted entirely of real estate she owned [at] 26, 28, 30, and 32 Charlton Street, appraised at $12,000 each. She held personal property outside New York State valued at $19,758. These assets included five shares of stock in the Sun Printing and Publishing Company, par value $1,000 each, the value of which was stated by the executors to be $710 a share, based on a recent sale of the stock at auction. She was a resident of Norwalk, Conn. The residuary legatees were Margaret A. Bronson and Mable F. Fitch, cousins of the decedent. Amos

J. Cummings was managing editor of *The Sun* and later a Congressman.

The story in the *Sun* the same day (under "Wills and Appraisals") includes much the same information but adds: "[T]here were 23 beneficiaries, all friends of decedent."

In 1927, the same year Amos Cummings's scrapbooks were found in the Bargain Book Shop, the four Charlton Street properties were sold for $260,000 and then razed so a new six-story brick apartment building could be built. That building is still there today. Perhaps the scrapbooks were still at 32 Charlton Street in 1927 and were taken to the Bargain Book Shop at that time, later finding their way to the New York Public Library.

The block of Charlton Street where Amos and Frances Cummings once lived today is within the Charlton-King-Vandam Historic District, designated in 1966 by the New York City Landmarks Preservation Commission. Richard Blodgett, in his study *The Story of Charlton Street*, calls Charlton Street "one of the great historic streets in New York City," noting "the north side of Charlton today contains the longest unbroken row of Federal and early Greek Revival homes extant in New York City." The Cummingses' properties on the opposite side of the street once faced that row of townhouses.

Those townhouses today are high-priced, well-kept, and desirable properties. The neighborhood, however, was not as fashionable when Amos and Frances lived there. That observation is substantiated by Blodgett, who, in *The Story of Charlton Street*, notes that Charlton Street west of Varick, a block from the Cummingses' house, had become home to Irish immigrants, with many of the men working on the docks while the women took in washing. In an 1874 article in the *New York Times* (quoted in *The Story of Charlton Street*, 11), the gutters of Charlton Street are said to flow with wastewater, "sending forth an offensive odor on a warm day."

In the 1870s, trolley rails were laid down Charlton Street, making it an even "less desirable place to live because of the noise and dirt of the cars and horses" (*The Story of Charlton Street*, 12). Charlton Street in the late nineteenth century was not an upper- or even upper-middle-class New York neighborhood.

Eulogies after his death noted that Amos was not a rich man, which was true, especially when compared with the businessmen, investors, and gentleman farmers who served with him in the House of Representatives. Even so, Amos and Frances Cummings maintained a seemingly well-financed middle-class lifestyle, one that included numerous extended journeys abroad and around the United States. Part of their income came from Amos's success as a journalist. An article in *Current Literature* (titled "General Gossip of Authors and Writers," March 1889, 194) notes that Amos's salary was $15,000, no small amount at the time. There were other sources of income as well. The *Washington Post* (November 4, 1886) noted that Cummings "made a lot of money in the first boom of Edison's electric-light stock, when it rose in a month from $80 a share to $3,000." According to the article he also derived annual income of $4,000 from "syndicate letters." Amos was not above deriving income from a patronage job, either. The *Chicago Daily Tribune* of November 22, 1894, carried a short article ("Amos Cummings Is Given a Good Job") noting that New York mayor Thomas F. Gilroy had appointed Congressman Cummings as New York Subway Commissioner with an annual stipend of $5,000. But what a Tammany mayor gave, an anti-Tammany mayor took away. In a June 28, 1895, *Washington Post* article, it was announced that new mayor William L. Strong had removed Amos from office.

Still other income came from renting out floors and rooms in the townhouses the Cummingses owned on Charlton Street. That is borne out by the 1890 federal census. Although the particular census pages that document the residents of Charlton Street are extremely messy, hard to read, and often mixed in with data from Van Dam and MacDougal streets, it is clear that Amos and Frances lived in an ethnically diverse neighborhood that included immigrants from Italy, Ireland, England, and Germany. The building next to the Cummingses (34 Charlton, later the site of the Charlton Street Memorial Church) housed a family of Italian immigrants, whereas the Cummingses' houses at 30 and 26 Charlton Street, or at least portions of them, were rented out to immigrant families from England and Ireland. (I could not discern the census data for 28 Charlton.) To generate income, the Cummingses even took in two adult boarders at their 32 Charlton residence: Mortimer Sandworth(?) and James Avery. The Cummings household in 1890 also included a forty-year-old servant, Louise Lewis, and her three children (daughters aged eight and seventeen, and son, five). By remaining in their neighborhood, shrewdly investing in property and collecting rent money, Amos and Frances Cummings could afford to feed their penchant for travel.

AMOS JAY CUMMINGS, POLITICIAN

In 1886, Cummings, already a successful journalist, decided to enter the U.S. political arena, something he had been writing about for years (he was initiated into the Tammany Society in late December 1885). His first campaign for the United States House of Representatives was successful. Supported by the Tammany Hall political machine, he ran as a Democrat for the Sixth New York District, then around Wall Street in what today is the financial district in Lower Manhattan. Cummings subsequently served in the Fiftieth Congress from March 1887 to March 1889.

When election time for the Fifty-first Congress neared in 1888, either Cummings or the Tammany Hall leadership (or both) decided he should not defend his old House seat. But when Samuel S. Cox, the incumbent in the seat for District Nine in New York City died on September 10, 1889, Cummings ran in an election to fill the vacancy and won the seat, holding it through the remainder of the Fifty-first Congress and through the Fifty-second (December 1889–1893). Next he ran for the seat from the Eleventh District, which he also won, although he resigned the seat on November 21, 1894, a ploy that allowed the Tammany machine to fill the vacancy with one of its own while Cummings ran for another vacancy in the upcoming Fifty-fourth Congress. He won that vacant Tenth District seat, holding it until his death in 1902 during the Fifty-seventh Congress (terms of 1895–1897, 1897–1899, 1899–1901, and 1901–1902). While in Congress, he served on the Committee on Naval Affairs, chairing it for several terms, and on the Committee on Library, chairing it for a term.

Cummings's scrapbooks are filled with numerous clippings about his congressional activities, including mentions of him in various U.S. newspapers and copies of speeches he gave, especially ones published in the *Congressional Record*. He had a reputation as an orator and was in demand in both Washington and New York City. By 1891, he was frequently described as one of the "prominent leaders" of the New York Democratic Club, giving speeches at the clubhouse on Fifth Avenue near Fiftieth Street in Manhattan in support of Tammany Hall and other Democratic candidates and causes.

He also was often cited in the newspapers as a major Tammany Hall politico, although he sometimes was at odds with some of the Tammany Hall leadership. Disagreements in 1897 may have cost him the opportunity to run for the office of New York City mayor (he was mentioned as a possible candidate for that office as early as 1888; see *Life*, March 1, 1888, 2). Cummings also served on the House Democratic Caucus Committee representing New York until a coalition of Long Island congressmen managed to oust him by getting their own candidate elected. Even so, Cummings remained a major Democratic figure both in New York City and in the House of Representatives.

One of his congressional speeches ("On the Naval Appro-
priations Bill"), delivered in the House of Representatives
in April 1900 during Cummings's second term as congressman, is reprinted in volume 6 of *Famous American Statesmen &
Orators, Past and Present* (compiled by Alexander K. McClure
and Byron Andrews). Another, a pro-union oration delivered on
Memorial Day 1894 on the occasion of the unveiling of a statue
of Horace Greeley in Manhattan's Greeley Square (just south of
Macy's department store at the intersection of Sixth Avenue and
Broadway), is reprinted in a 1912 history of his union (Stevens,
New York Typographical Union Number 6). Others of his printed
speeches are preserved in the Library of Congress and other
libraries.

My favorite Cummings speech is one I ran across in one
of his scrapbooks in the New York Public Library. It was given
October 14, 1888, when he presented the pennant to the New
York "National Base Ball League" champions. The team, coached
by James M. Murtie, was preparing for the interleague playoff
known as the World Championship against the St. Louis Browns
of the American League. The New York team, founded five
years earlier in 1883 when they were known as the Gothams,
had been renamed the Giants in 1885. New York won the 1888
series and the team won the next year as well, defeating the
Boston Beaneaters.

Throughout the decade and a half Cummings served in the
House of Representatives, he remained a staunch labor and union
supporter. At one time he was the only member of a labor union
in Congress. In June 1894, when President Grover Cleveland
signed into law the bill making Labor Day a national holiday,
the pen he used was turned over to Cummings, who sent it
to Samuel Gompers, president of the American Federation of
Labor. Cummings had been a sponsor of the bill in the House.

Cummings was as popular a politician as a newsman, and
as fervent a Democrat as a union man. In the times in which

he lived, those roles often overlapped. One example is the sixty-four-page pamphlet called "The *Sun's* Greeley Campaign Songster," published and distributed by the *New York Sun* in 1872 and authored by Amos. The pamphlet contained lyrics—most written by Cummings and often set to popular tunes of the day—that poked fun at "Useless" Grant, the Republican candidate for president of the United States, and supported Horace Greeley, the Democratic candidate (often referred to in song as "the farmer from Chappaqua"). Although the *Sun* had no love for Greeley or his rival newspaper, the *New York Tribune*, the *Sun's* editorial staff and publisher always backed the Democratic Party. Amos also wrote *The Political Handbook: Political Information for Present Use and Future Reference*, which was published in 1896.

Cummings was chosen as New York's Eighth Congressional District delegate to the Democratic National Convention, held in Chicago in 1896. Conference proceedings record that he was introduced as a "member of the famous Tammany Society of New York." At least one of his Democratic supporters suggested in September of that year that Cummings should be the party's candidate for governor of New York. Four years later in 1900 he was being considered as a possible vice president for presidential candidate William Jennings Bryan. Instead, Adlai E. Stevenson, grandfather of Adlai Stevenson, the Democratic nominee defeated twice by Dwight D. Eisenhower, was named as Bryan's running mate. Stevenson had already served as vice president for Grover Cleveland from 1893 to 1897. In the 1900 election, Bryan and Stevenson lost to William McKinley and Theodore Roosevelt.

Throughout the period he served in the House of Representatives, Cummings continued to travel and to write. The "Fortunes in the South" and "Tin Letters" series of articles both were written in 1889. The trips he took to gather the information for the stories were done after the adjournment of the Fiftieth Congress. As noted above, in 1893 he was back in

Florida, enjoying his status as a visiting congressman. I found a short clipping from the *Charlotte Observer* in one scrapbook indicating that he was in Charlotte, South Carolina, in May 1899 on still another southern visit.

Beginning in December 1897 and continuing until the time of his death in 1902, Cummings wrote political commentary for the Sunday *Washington Post.* Those articles, some of which were reprinted in other newspapers, further cemented his reputation as a politician/journalist.

In early March 1898, Cummings, three members of the United States Senate, and another member of the House traveled to Cuba on a "personal visit" to report back on conditions there. They traveled aboard a yacht owned by the famed Florida developer Henry Flagler as guests of William Randolph Hearst, owner of the *New York Tribune* and a noted proponent of war with Spain over Cuba. The report subsequently filed by the five politicians received wide coverage in the press, especially by pro-war newspapers. The *Chicago Daily Tribune,* for example, headlined an article quoting the report at length: "Tell of Cuba's Woe; Death on Every Shore; Spain's Cruelty Fills Half a Million Graves." Such examples of yellow journalism, and other numerous examples being published about the same time, were in part instrumental in pushing through a joint resolution of Congress passed in April 1898, authorizing President McKinley to use force to protect Cuban "patriots" from Spain. The short-lived Spanish-American War was on.

Not all of his trips out of New York and Washington were successful for Cummings. A September 23, 1899, clipping from an unknown newspaper says he had suffered a broken leg. A second clipping (September 26, 1899) adds more information: Cummings was injured in a bicycle wreck while in the mountains of Pennsylvania a month earlier. Perhaps he was back to Honesdale in the Pocono Mountains, where he had lived as a youngster. A third clipping (January 4, 1900) says he was confined to bed with a severe cold. I suspect it was not a cold at all, but the broken leg.

In another scrapbook I found a handwritten note signed "Amos J. Cummings" that reads: "Broke my leg December 27, 1900. Letters discontinued." According to a December 30 note in the *Brooklyn Daily Eagle* newspaper, he broke his leg in New Haven and had been transported by train back to his home in New York, accompanied by his physician, Dr. Girdner (most likely John H. Girdner, who was active in Democratic politics in New York). That would have been more than a year after the first broken leg. Did the leg not heal properly? I do not know. The last few years of his life could not have been too pleasant for Amos Cummings.

CUMMINGS'S DEATH

In 1902 while serving in the Fifty-seventh Congress in Washington, Cummings became ill with a kidney infection. The news was first printed in the *Washington Post* on April 1 in a short article that noted Cummings maintained a residence in Washington at 46 B Street, an address near the U.S. Capitol (North and South B streets are now Constitution and Independence avenues). Throughout most of the remainder of the month, the *New York Times* and the *Post*, as well as other papers, printed relatively upbeat updates. On April 11, Cummings was moved to the Christ Church Home and Infirmary in Baltimore, where he underwent surgery four days later. Updates continued in the newspapers every several days.

The news turned bad on April 29, when Cummings, according to newspaper accounts, was diagnosed with double pneumonia. By May 1, the *Times* admitted the "worst is feared." At 10:15 in the night of May 2, 1902, just prior to his sixty-fourth birthday and while still at the Church Home and Infirmary, Cummings died. His wife, Frances, and a cousin, Charles H. Cummings, were with him.

Just before his death, Cummings wrote his last words on a piece of letterhead from the U.S. House of Representatives' Committee on Library for the Fifty-sixth Congress: "[F]or this is a great world and God moves in a mysterious way." That leaf of stationery with Cummings's shaky, barely legible penciled writing on it is preserved on the final page of the fifteenth scrapbook in the New York Public Library.

I obtained a copy of Cummings's certificate of death from the Maryland State Archives. On it, his age is given as sixty-one years, eleven months, and eighteen days, meaning the birth year given to the official who filled out the form was 1840, not 1838, his true birth year. On the same certificate it is recorded that Cummings's "Last Sickness" was several months in duration and that the "Cause of Death" was "First, (Primary)": "Enlarged Prostate," and the "Second, (Immediate)" cause was "Pneumonia, Pyelitis." According to medical dictionaries and databases I consulted, pyelitis is an infection of the kidneys commonly caused by bacteria from an untreated urinary tract infection, such as a bladder infection caused by an enlarged prostate cutting off the normal flow of urine. The infection could also have spread to the lungs.

Amos Cummings's death was national news. Over the next several days, both the *New York Times* and the *Washington Post* carried multiple stories recounting his life and his career as a journalist and a politician. On May 3, his desk in the House was draped in black and covered with "purple orchids and Spring flowers." A series of resolutions were read on the House floor and a funeral committee was appointed (later made a joint committee of the House and Senate). Flags were lowered to half-staff.

On May 4, Cummings's body was placed aboard the 9:34 A.M. train in Baltimore and taken to Washington, traveling over the Pennsylvania Railroad. Capitol policemen served as pallbearers, and the body was accompanied to the Baltimore train station by war veterans and representatives of the Typographical

Union and Letter-carriers Association. Several hundred people gathered to see the train off. A contingent of Baltimore journalists accompanied the casket to Washington, as did members of the congressional funeral committee, who earlier that morning had traveled to Baltimore.

That same day a state funeral was held at 3:00 P.M. in the Hall of Representatives. Cummings was said to be only the third member of the U.S. House to be so honored "in recent times." Two thousand people, according to the *Washington Post*, paid their respects.

Cummings's body lay in state until that evening, when it was again placed aboard a train, this time bound for New York City. Originally, Frances Cummings had planned a New York funeral to be held at their home at 32 Charlton Avenue, but it soon became clear that the space was not large enough, and it was announced that the funeral, scheduled for 11:00 A.M., Tuesday, May 6, would be held at Merritt Chapel at Eighth Avenue and Nineteenth Street in Manhattan.

Cummings's New York funeral was attended by throngs of people, including dignitaries from Congress and labor unions. Among the floral displays was a "full-rigged ship," a symbol of Cummings's membership on the House Naval Affairs Committee. The crowd was so large only a limited number of people were allowed into the chapel at a time.

Following the two-hour service, the casket was taken to the West Thirty-third Street pier, put aboard a ferry, and transported across the Hudson River to New Jersey. A large funeral procession, including a band, marched with the casket to the ferry through the New York streets. From the New Jersey pier the funeral procession traveled to Clinton Cemetery in Irvington, New Jersey, where Cummings was interred in the Roberts family plot. A color guard from Cummings's old Civil War New Jersey regiment was in attendance, along with more union officials.

Over the next several days more memorials were held. The Columbia Typographical Union No. 101 held theirs on the afternoon of May 11, 1902, at Chase's Theater, an opera house in Washington, DC. An orchestra played "Tannhäuser" and "Beyond the Pearly Gates." Samuel Gompers, president of the Federation of Labor, was the speaker. The *New York Times* estimated the audience at 2,000 people. A second memorial service under union auspices was held June 22, 1902, at Carnegie Hall in New York City. Sponsored by Typographical Union Local 6, Cummings's old union, the service featured music by an orchestra, soloists, and speeches by union presidents, congressmen, journalists, ministers, and vicars.

Two out-of-the-ordinary events transpired as a result of Cummings's death. The first was a memorial service held by the House of Representatives on Sunday, June 29, 1902, at 11:00 in the morning. Cummings was again eulogized, this time to the accompaniment of the Marine Band sent by the Secretary of the Navy. What was odd is that it was the first regular session of the House held on a Sunday since 1811. Mrs. Cummings and some of her friends were in the gallery for the service.

The second event, which had occurred a month and a half earlier on May 15, might better be described as brazen rather than extraordinary. Certainly, Amos Cummings would have seen some humor in it. According to the *Washington Post:*

> There appeared at the door of the House of Representatives yesterday a neatly dressed woman arrayed in black and armed with all the habiliments of grief. Armed with a moistened handkerchief and sniffling and sobbing, she sought interviews with several Congressmen.
>
> She claims to be the only sister of the late Amos J. Cummings, and asked for relief. She pleaded amid her sobs for assistance and claimed her dead brother had left her unprovided for and starvation was rapidly approaching.
>
> A number of the members to whom she applied were aware that Mr. Cummings never had any sister. The police

of the Capitol have been notified of the sister in black and
will be on hand when the next scene is enacted.

The voluminous literary legacy of Amos Jay Cummings
exists in his fifteen scrapbooks in the New York Public Library
and on reels of microfilm housed in that and other libraries.
There also are small numbers of published speeches and correspondence—even a menu—in a number of repositories, including the Library of Congress, University of California–Berkeley,
Georgetown University, University of Nevada, New Jersey
Historical Society, Radcliffe College, and Syracuse University.
Other materials no doubt exist elsewhere. We still have much to
learn from Amos Cummings.

THE WORLD AND THE WEST IN 1873

When Amos Cummings crossed the Mississippi River in 1873,
he was entering a part of the United States that was a geographical mosaic of states and territories. Missouri had been the first
western state in 1821; California, with its newly found wealth,
was awarded statehood in 1850. Kansas (1861) and Nevada (1864)
also were states, but Colorado was still a territory, as were Utah,
Arizona, New Mexico, and Wyoming.

Perhaps the biggest event uniting the West with the East
took place in May 1869, when the golden railroad spike was
driven near Promontory, Utah, about a half mile west of Ogden,
connecting the rail line coming from the west with that from
the east. Cummings passed over that very stretch of track on his
1873 journey.

To say that the West was sparsely settled when thirty-five-
year-old Amos Cummings made his trek across it is an under-
statement. In the 1870 federal census, 1,721,399 people were
recorded in Amos Cummings's hometown of New York City,
and the total U.S. population was pegged at 38,558,371. By comparison, the total population of the territories of Colorado and

Utah and the state of Nevada together numbered only a paltry 169,141 people.

There was no electricity to run appliances in 1873. The phonograph and electric lightbulb were not patented until later in the decade. Gas, oil, and wax fueled lights. There were no automobiles, and trains ran on steam.

In 1873, Remington and Sons first began to mass-produce the manual typewriter. Amos Cummings, who apparently dictated his stories for much of his professional life, later learned to compose on a typewriter.

The telegraph was around in 1873 and was a major means of cross-country communication. Telegraph lines strung on poles generally followed the railroads across the West. It was also in 1873 that Alexander Graham Bell moved to Boston from Canada; three years later he patented the telephone.

Charles Darwin's *Descent of Man* appeared in print in 1873 (fourteen years after *The Origin of Species* was first published), and Ulysses S. Grant was president. In some parts of the southern United States, federal troops left over from the Civil War were still stationed. It was the period of Reconstruction following that strife. In England it was the Victorian Age, and the Industrial Revolution was well under way.

The year before Cummings crossed the Great Plains, Jacob Davis, a tailor in Reno, Nevada, asked Levi Strauss to help him apply for a patent on Davis's invention: riveted overalls. In 1873 the patent was obtained and the two men went into business together as Levi Strauss & Company, and Levi jeans were born. I doubt that Cummings ever wore a pair. In 1873 the one-cent postcard and the first mail-order catalogue appeared.

The year after Cummings crossed the Kansas plains, Joseph Glidden obtained a patent for barbed wire. Three years later Lt. Col. George Armstrong Custer and 647 men of the Seventh Cavalry lost the Battle of Little Bighorn. Eight years later in 1881 in the Territory of New Mexico, Sheriff Pat Garrett plugged Billy

A WAGON TRAIN CROSSING THE GREAT PLAINS. (YOUNG, *WIFE NUMBER 19*, FACING 120)

the Kid. In 1882, Jesse James went to his final rest in the state of Missouri at the hands of his new partners, Bob and Charlie Ford.

In 1873 much of the Wild West was still wild and rugged. When Amos Jay Cummings crossed the Mississippi River in the spring, he was embarking on a great adventure, one that we can join, thanks to the articles he left behind.

CUMMINGS'S 1873 TRIP WEST

Travel by train was not new when Cummings set out on his journey, but traveling by train across the North American continent from Atlantic to Pacific was. Only four years earlier the Union Pacific and Central Pacific railroads had been united with the driving of the golden spike in Utah, making coast-to-coast rail travel possible. By 1869, there was a spiderweb of rails laid between towns east of the Mississippi River, with a much less dense web expanding over the West.

In 1869, had one the inclination, the rail trip from East Coast to West could be made in ten days; had one the fortitude,

a seven-day crossing was possible—what a contrast from traveling across the West by prairie schooner, the preferred method
from 1843 to 1869, when the journey took four to six months.
It is estimated that several hundred thousand people made the
2,000-mile wagon journey from St. Louis across the Great
Plains and over the Rocky Mountains during that earlier quarter century. The trip by covered wagon was hard and dangerous;
one out of every ten travelers died along the route.

No wonder travel by train became the preferred mode of
transportation across the West. Trains were infinitely quicker
and more comfortable than wagons, walking, or horseback. After
1869, one could reserve a berth in a Pullman car pulled behind
a steam-powered locomotive. Generally, although not always,
trains had dining cars attached, adding to the ease of travel.
Otherwise, there were stops in stations where meals could be
purchased, usually at a hotel.

For those wishing to pay a lesser fare there was the option
of sitting upright for the entire journey as the train bumped
its way from New York or Philadelphia to Sacramento and San
Francisco. Even that less comfortable option was certainly better than what had existed before the rails were laid.

Having sampled the southern frontier in Florida in 1873,
Amos Cummings was eager for another course, and ready to
take advantage of the new rail system on a journey that would
take him through the relatively new states and older territories west of the Mississippi River and deposit him in California.
Along the way he planned to see the sights, visit with people,
and report back to his readers in New York City, hundreds of
miles and many lifestyles away.

Cummings was well aware of the stories of new mineral
wealth emanating out of the West, something to be investi-
gated and written about. The California gold rush, which had
began a quarter century earlier in 1849, had run its course
and a new generation of miners and entrepreneurs were in

the throes of tapping silver and gold mines in Colorado and Nevada.

Amos's great journey began in mid-May when he and Frances left their townhouse on Charlton Street. It may have taken more than one horse-drawn carriage to transport them and their luggage to the pier at the foot of Desbrosses Street on the Hudson River, several blocks south of their townhouse and two blocks south of the modern Manhattan entrance to the Holland Tunnel. At the time, there were no tunnels or bridges connecting Manhattan with New Jersey.

From Manhattan a ferry carried the Cummingses across the mile-wide Hudson River to Jersey City's Red Star Line pier, where porters moved their luggage the short distance from the landing to Exchange Place Terminal. Both the pier and terminal belonged to the Pennsy, the Pennsylvania Railroad. Exchange Place, long torn down, was a huge train shed quite like Victoria Station in London. The name of that Jersey City train terminal still lives on today as the Exchange Place PATH (Port Authority Trans-Hudson) commuter train station in Jersey City.

An advertisement for the Pennsylvania Railroad in the May 14, 1873, *New York Sun* records:

> Trains leave New York from foot of Desbrosses and
> Cortlandt sts. As follows:
> Express for Harrisburgh, the West, and South with
> Pullman palace cars attached, 9:50 A.M., 5, 7, and 8:30 P.M.
> Sunday 5, 7, and 8:30 P.M.

I would bet that Amos and Frances followed the advice offered by guidebooks of the time and took the morning train, allowing them to see Pennsylvania by daylight. They retained their same berths in the same Pennsylvania Railroad Pullman car for the two-day journey to St. Louis. That was possible because in the several years prior to 1873, the Pennsy had bought up, leased, or signed agreements with numerous formerly independent railway companies in the East, consolidating Pennsy's grip on the burgeoning rail-travel industry and providing passengers with nearly seamless rail service from New York and New Jersey to Chicago and St. Louis. Cost of a berth for the trip from New York to St. Louis was $6; meals ranged from $0.50 to $1.00.

Henry T. Williams's guidebook to travel in the western United States (*The Pacific Tourist: Williams' Illustrated Trans-Continental Guide of Travel from the Atlantic to the Pacific Ocean*, which went through multiple editions in the 1870s) offered prospective travelers a hint of what to expect on their journey, while trying to convince them train travel in the West was even better than in the East:

> The sleeping-cars from New York to Chicago, proceeding at their rushing rate of forty or more miles per hour, give travelers no idea of the true comfort of Pullman life. Indeed the first thousand miles of the journey to Chicago or St. Louis has more tedium and wearisomeness, and dust and inconveniences than all the rest of the journey. . . .
> [In the West the] slow rate of speed, which averages but sixteen to twenty miles per hour, day and night, produces a peculiarly smooth, gentle and easy motion, most soothing and agreeable.

From Jersey City the Pennsylvania Railroad's rails took Amos and Frances to West Philadelphia, a trip of ninety-nine miles. Then it was along the Main Line to Harrisburg (another 105 miles). Along that leg of the trip, civilization was still only a glance out the window, as the train steamed past one small town after another. After Harrisburg, Altoona was next, then Pittsburgh; the latter was 440 miles and eleven hours or so from Jersey City.

West of Pittsburgh the rails led across the northern portion of the panhandle of West Virginia and then into Ohio. Near Bradford, Ohio, just west of Columbus, the tracks forked,

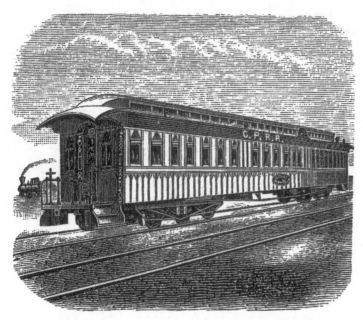

One of the Central Pacific Railroad's palace cars touted for their luxury. Similar cars carried passengers on the Pennsylvania Railroad. (Williams, *Pacific Tourist*, 161)

with the right rails leading to Chicago and the left continuing west past Cincinnati and then southeasterly to East St. Louis in southeast Illinois, across the Mississippi River from St. Louis, Missouri.

Two lines of evidence make it clear that Amos and Frances took the route past Cincinnati and on to St. Louis and not the more northerly one through Chicago. In a signed article extolling the virtues of Chicago that Amos wrote for the *Chicago Daily Tribune* (dated July 8, 1888, and headlined "Good Pie and Good Beer"), he wrote that his first visit to Chicago was in 1857 and his second in 1878. He was not in Chicago (a city he says to have preferred to St. Louis and Hoboken, New Jersey) in 1873. And had the Cummingses gone through Chicago on their 1873 rail journey, they most likely would have taken the railroad leading

to Omaha, Nebraska, which then went on to Utah. They would not have needed to pass through St. Louis and Kansas City, nor would they have traveled across the Kansas plains, an experience that Cummings wrote about.

There was no bridge spanning the Mississippi River from East St. Louis to St. Louis. The first bridge, built by James Eades, opened the next year. To cross the Mississippi River, train cars (with passengers aboard) were loaded on one of the train ferries operated by the Wiggins's Ferry Company and transferred from eastern rails to western rails. It must have been an incredible experience. The date the Cummings couple crossed the Mississippi was probably May 21, 1873.

In St. Louis, on the west side of the Mississippi River, and having left the Pennsylvania Railroad, Amos and Frances found themselves in the "Gateway to the West." They stayed in St. Louis for several days (until around May 24), seeing the sights and resting up from the nonstop journey from Jersey City.

From St. Louis it was on to Kansas City, where the Cummingses may not have stayed at all, simply stopping there briefly to change trains before heading out across the Kansas plains on the Kansas Pacific Railroad, which took them to the foothills of the Rocky Mountains and Denver. Along the rail route, the train puffed through Fort Riley, Junction City, Ellsworth, Hays City, and Kit Carson before reaching Denver about May 26. In one article, Amos says the journey from St. Louis to Denver had taken two days and two nights of travel.

Denver served as the base of operations for the Cummingses for visits to Boulder City, Manitou, Pueblo, Colorado Springs, and Greeley, as well as other locales (from June into early July). Within Colorado they traveled by railways, some on small-gauge tracks, and by horse and buggy and stagecoach. According to one of Amos's articles, the couple spent a month in Colorado Territory.

From Denver the Cummingses went northward on the Denver Pacific Railroad to intersect the famed Union Pacific Railroad at Cheyenne in Wyoming Territory. Along the way the train passed through Greeley, Colorado, north of Denver, a small town of interest to Amos, who had once worked for

Horace Greeley. Amos and Frances probably stopped there, perhaps for only a night, before proceeding on to Cheyenne, where
they might also have spent time. It was probably mid-July. Back
aboard the Union Pacific, they continued their westward journey until they reached Ogden, Utah, where they took the newly
built southern spur line (the Utah Central Railroad) to Salt Lake
City, arriving in late July. By rail it was 36.5 miles from Ogden
to Salt Lake City. The *Salt Lake Tribune* on July 24 noted the
presence of the Cummingses in the city.

Like Denver, Salt Lake City served as a base for more explorations of the West. Amos and Frances stayed in Utah for more
than a month, traveling to see different sights and towns. A
short note in the personals section of the *Salt Lake Daily Herald*
on September 2, 1873, records: "Mr. A. J. Cummings of the New
York *Sun* and Mrs. Cummings, left yesterday for the west after
a pleasant stay of some six weeks." On the same day a longer
farewell was published in the *Salt Lake Tribune.*

From Salt Lake City, Amos and Frances Cummings took
the Utah Central back to Ogden and boarded the Central Pacific
Railroad headed west. The Union Pacific and Central Pacific
railroads met at Ogden. On the way west out of Ogden the
Cummingses traveled through Promontory, Utah, then through
the Nevada towns of Toano, Elko, and Reno before reaching
Truckee, California. The Cummingses stayed in Truckee and the
general area, including western Nevada, for a week or so. One
place they visited (by stage from either Truckee or Reno) was
Carson City, Nevada, where Amos's arrival was chronicled in a
short article in the *Nevada Tribune* on Wednesday, September
10, 1873. Headlined "A Welcome Visitor," it reads:

> The *Tribune* office was yesterday honored by a visit from
> Mr. Amos J. Cummings, managing editor of the *New York
> Sun.* Mr. C. is a lively genial gentleman, and meeting as he
> did Senator Israel Crawford, a fellow townsman of the State
> of Pennsylvania, his visit to our *sanctum* was especially

AMOS CUMMINGS'S RAILROAD JOURNEY ACROSS THE UNITED STATES.

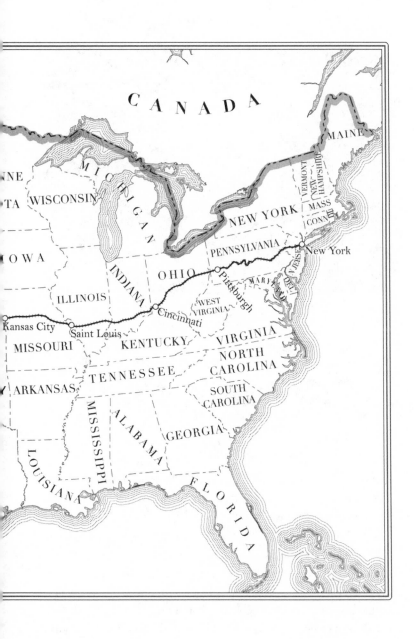

LAKE TAHOE IN THE 1870S. (WILLIAMS, *PACIFIC TOURIST*, 215)

pleasing. Mr. Cummings went to the lake last evening where he will remain a week or so in order to write up the scenery and doings of this out-of-the-way sage-brush State. We hope to renew the acquaintance of this very pleasing gentleman before he leaves for New York.

Amos and Frances spent several days in the general Lake Tahoe area, perhaps going by stage from Carson City to Lake Tahoe, and then proceeding again by stage to Truckee, arriving there about the end of the second week of September. I am not certain of their exact itinerary after leaving Salt Lake City, although it is certain the Cummingses spent about two weeks in western Nevada, Lake Tahoe, and Truckee.

Truckee, where the Truckee section of the railroad met the Sacramento division, featured a large roundhouse where locomotives were switched. One locomotive pulled the train westward to Truckee from Ogden, while another was needed to pull the train from Truckee to Sacramento over the Sierra Nevada Mountains.

From Truckee it was 259 miles, a day's journey, to San Francisco. Along the route, Amos and Frances and other travelers continued on the Central Pacific Railroad to Sacramento, passing first through Summit (elevation 7,017 feet) and Cisco as the train climbed up and over the Sierra Nevada Mountains, and then through Colfax and Newcastle. From Sacramento it was about sixty miles on the Western Pacific Railroad to Oakland, across the bay from San Francisco. In Oakland, train passengers and their baggage were transferred to ferries for the 3.4-mile voyage across the bay to the ferry-house at the foot of Market Street in San Francisco.

The arrival of Amos Cummings in the City by the Bay elicited this short note headlined "A Distinguished Journalist in Town" in the *San Francisco Chronicle:*

> Amos J. Cummings, managing editor for the New York
> *Sun,* arrived in this city last night, and is sojourning at the
> Cosmopolitan Hotel. His trip to the Pacific Coast is one of
> pleasure and observation. A series of brilliant letters from
> his pen have recently appeared in the *Sun,* descriptive of life
> in Colorado, Utah and Nevada. Mr. Cummings is accompa-
> nied by his wife, and is on his way to Yosemite.

Handwritten in pencil on the clipping, which is pasted in one of Cummings's scrapbooks, is the name of the newspaper and the date "September 1873." The Cummingses' arrival in San Francisco was on September 17; the article was in the *Chronicle* the following day (as was a list of guests checking into the Cosmopolitan Hotel on September 17, including Amos and spouse). The article, in the "Local Melange" section of the newspaper, was certainly written by Cummings himself.

Over the next six weeks, Amos and Frances traveled around California, but he did not do any writing. Perhaps he declared himself on vacation, his work in the West done. Fortunately for us, that work is preserved in the pages of his scrapbooks and on microfilm in the New York Public Library. I hope you enjoy reading the following articles by Amos Jay Cummings as much as I relished finding and annotating them. More than a century after his death Amos Cummings is still a lot of fun.

ORGANIZING, TRANSCRIBING, AND ANNOTATING AMOS CUMMINGS'S ARTICLES

There are innumerable combinations and permutations that I could have employed in organizing and grouping these nineteen articles. In the end I decided to group them topically—at least as I perceived them—rather than solely in geographical or chronological order. For each group of articles I have provided some brief introductory comments to help orient readers and to provide, as appropriate, a bit more information.

While assembling a previous book on Amos Cummings and his visits to Florida I discovered that although computer scanning technology is sometimes a wonderful thing, it is not at all efficient for prints made from microfilms of old newspapers. Consequently, all the articles were transcribed by hand on a word processor. Often prints from two different microfilm copies of the same article needed to be consulted because the microfilm had deteriorated.

Amos Cummings either wrote out these articles by hand or dictated them to someone (perhaps his wife); then the handwritten versions were sent by mail back to New York City to editors at the *New York Sun*. Those editors must have deciphered the handwriting, had the articles put in print and proofed, and then published them in the *Sun* and sometimes the *Sun*'s sister publications. (Interestingly, the reprints in the sister publications were published without resetting the type; the same typos appear in the different versions of those articles published in more than one newspaper.)

In 1873, when all but one of these nineteen articles appeared in the *Sun* (one was published the following year), that newspaper was four pages in length with seven columns of text (or ads) on each page. Cost was $0.02 per copy and subscription rates were $0.50 per month and $6.00 per year. The editors claimed circulation was 120,000.

In general, each of Cummings's longer articles was laid out in print in the same fashion as the *Sun*'s other long articles (those that were more than one column in length). Each has a headline of 14-point font, all in capital letters. A linear dingbat (a symbol or sometimes just a line) separates the headline from a subhead. The subhead, in 8-point font and italicized capital letters, was set off by another linear dingbat from a readout. Readouts, intended to further draw reader interest to the article by providing more information about its content, often were made up of section headings from within the article. Thus, for the first article that follows, the headline is "OVER THE KANSAS PLAINS," and the subhead reads, "*THE LEVEL PARADISE SOUTH OF THE MISSOURI RIVER.*" Both are followed by the readout "*The Mysterious Footprint—Editorial Mincemeat— Beware of Monte Players—Information for Overworked New York Clerks—The Bone Pickers of the Prairie.*"

Each Cummings article has a dateline, whether a town or place-name, which is followed by month and day. For example, the dateline for the first article is "DENVER, Col., May 30," indicating the article was written from Denver on May 30, 1873 (a Friday). Most of the longer articles also have "Correspondence of The Sun" between the run-out and the dateline to let readers know the article was written by a *Sun* journalist. Shorter articles in the *Sun*, including several reprinted in this volume, were not given a large-font headline but received the other introductory treatments.

I did almost nothing to edit Cummings's own prose. Where there was an obvious typo or mistake—e.g., "thee" instead of "the" or "east" instead of "west"—I corrected it. I left archaic and quaint spellings or inconsistencies as they were, for example, "moosied" instead of "moseyed," "per cent" and "percent," "cañon" versus "canyon," or "cut worm" and "cutworm." Where appropriate, commas were added or deleted and capitalization corrected.

Where I thought an annotation to explain a term or identify a person was warranted, I put in a note. There were times, however, when I could not find any additional information, especially when trying to identify individuals mentioned in the articles. Even though I was not always successful in finding information about the people Cummings wrote about, I had a great time trying to cover at least some of the same ground he did in 1873.

NOTES

1. Nineteenth-century sources included *The National Cyclopedia of American Biography* (New York: James T. White & Co., 1891) and *Appleton's Cyclopedia of American Biography*, 6 vols., ed. James Grant Wilson and John Fiske (New York: D. Appleton & Co., 1888–1889); also see *Dictionary of American Biography*, vols. 1–20 (New York: Charles Scribner's Sons, 1928–1936).

2. *Medal of Honor Recipients, 1863–1994*, 2 vols., comp. George Lang, Raymond L. Collins, and Gerard F. White (New York: Facts on File, 1995); *Biographical Directory of the American Congress, 1774–1927* (Washington, DC: U.S. Government Printing Office, 1928).

3. Catalogued as "Cummings, A. J. Scrapbook of newspaper clippings," call number "*CZ+."

4. "Scrapbooks of newspaper articles, pamphlets, etc., [1927]," call number "AN+."

5. In using "Uncle Rufus Hatch" as a pseudonym, Cummings likely was tweaking Alfrederick S. Hatch, one of the principals of the banking and brokerage firm of Fisk and Hatch. Hatch, whom Cummings often referred to in print as "the good Mr. Hatch," served as president of the New York Stock Exchange in 1883 and 1884 but was forced to resign over dealings that came to light at the time of the financial panic of May 1884.

The Flat Earth Society

WHEN AMOS CUMMINGS LEFT ST. LOUIS, he next traveled to Kansas City, Missouri. He probably was there on Sunday, May 25, 1873, perhaps only for a few hours while changing trains. There is little information about the city in his article "Over the Kansas Plains."

Kansas City had been a relatively small city until 1869, when a railroad bridge was built across the Missouri River, tying the town to outside markets and awakening the populace to a new future. By 1873 Kansas City already was developing a meatpacking industry that eventually would be second only

THE KANSAS CITY BRIDGE IN 1869. (FRONTISPIECE IN CHANUTE AND MORISON, *THE KANSAS CITY BRIDGE*)

to Chicago's. In 1870, Kansas City's population was just over 32,000. Four years later Cummings gave the figure as 40,000.

Leaving Kansas City aboard the Kansas Pacific Railroad, the Cummingses traversed the Great Plains on their way to Denver. Throughout his trip, Cummings's journalistic modus operandi was to gather information by observing and talking with people, including, if he could find them, local newspaper editors. Although there were none of the latter on the train, Amos still found plenty to see and write about, both inside the railroad cars and out.

Like many other visitors before and since, Cummings found the plains to be "treeless," "nearly level," and "monotonous." To help pass the time he set out to count buffaloes and American Indians out the train window, but he saw neither. Instead he observed antelopes, prairie dogs, birds, and telegraph poles that had been hit by lightning. In his writings he wanted to give his readers back in New York an idea of what life was like for people on the Kansas plains and provide them with a firsthand account of the realities of travel by train through the West.

Opting for the less traveled railroad route from St. Louis west to Ogden, Utah, which took him across Kansas and through Denver—as opposed to the Union Pacific Railroad route that ran across Nebraska through Omaha to Ogden—Amos had made a conscious decision to see what other travelers often did not. In his visits to St. Louis, Kansas City, and Denver he was seeking adventures (and articles?) beyond the descriptions offered in most popular guides to the West. Indeed, *The Pacific Tourist*, which appeared in multiple editions during the 1870s and mapped and described the rail journey from Omaha across the West to California, does not even list Kansas in its index!

The 1877 edition of *The Pacific Tourist* does tell us that it was 636 miles along the Kansas Pacific Railroad from Kansas City to Denver, the latter a growing city of 16,000 people that was becoming important as a rail center. Amos would have welcomed the information provided in the same book that trout fishing was excellent in the mountains of Colorado.

Both of Amos's articles in this section are datelined May 30, one from Denver and the other from Gypsum Creek Valley, Kansas. The latter is east of Salina and west of Abilene, both towns on the route of the Kansas Pacific Railroad. The two articles almost certainly were mailed back to New York City from Denver. The first, "Over the Kansas Plains," was published in the *New York Sun* on June 6, 1873, and in the *Semi-Weekly Sun* on June 13, 1873. "The Earthy Paradise," written tongue in cheek with Cummings assuming the guise of a settler on the Kansas plains drawn there by promises that it was heaven on earth, appeared in the *Sun* on June 5.

The stories that Cummings wrote while on his transcontinental journey provide modern readers with an extraordinary firsthand chronicle of a large portion of the West at a time when most of it was still a frontier. The articles allow us to hop aboard the Kansas Pacific Railroad car that was transporting Amos Cummings from Kansas City to Denver and share his view of the Great Plains and the people settling that vast region as they were in the spring of 1873.

OVER THE KANSAS PLAINS.

THE LEVEL PARADISE SOUTH OF THE MISSOURI RIVER.

*The Mysterious Footprint—Editorial Mincemeat—
Beware of Monte Players—Information for Overworked New
York Clerks—The Bone Pickers of the Prairie.*

Correspondence of The Sun.

DENVER, Col., May 30.—It takes two nights and two days
to reach this city from St. Louis. I stopped a day in Kansas City.
As I alighted at the depot I saw a score of citizens in flannel
shirts and buckskin trousers measuring a footprint in the mud.
There appeared to be considerable excitement about it. The foot
track was measured a half dozen times, but it was finally settled that it was thirteen inches in length. There was a rumor
that the impression was from the foot of Susan B. Anthony.[1]
The citizens believed it to be true, but they were mistaken. The
footprint turned out to be the work of the accomplished cattle

market reporter of the *New York Times.*[2] This lady has attracted much attention in Kansas and Colorado. While the stock breeders laugh at her personal appearance, they acknowledge that she thoroughly understands stock raising and breeding, and many horsemen say that they are indebted to her for valuable hints. It is said that she has purchased or is about to purchase several thousand acres of land either in Kansas or the Territory,[3] and go into business on her own account.

A QUEER NEWSPAPER.

Kansas City contains nearly 40,000 inhabitants. It looks as though it had been pitched into a heap of sandy bluffs, through which great gaps or streets are cut, and on which white residences stand like bird houses on garden poles. It contains a massive brick court house, surmounted by a sham clock, a half dozen second-class hotels, and a theatre. Its journals are usually newsy and bright, the *Kansas City Times*[4] appearing to take the lead. While walking at the intersection of Seventh and Main streets, I saw the following sign:

OFFICE OF KANSAS CITY MINCE MEAT.

As it was Sunday the office was closed, and I did not see the editor, but I understand that the *Mince Meat* has a fair circulation.[5]

ON THE PLAINS.

The trip by railroad over the plains is monotonous. It is generally understood that passengers have not a thing to do during the journey but to gaze at immense buffalo herds and shoot antelopes. Although it was in the buffalo season, I saw none of the animals. I counted twenty-one antelopes, but they were at a great distance. We passed about fifty prairie dogs, one prairie hen, any quantity of snipe and turtle doves, four black ducks, and a weasel—and that was all. Not an Indian. The plains spread north and south as far as the eye could reach, but a tree was a rarity. At one time we ran 150 miles without seeing a leaf or a branch. There was neither wood nor water—not a stick as big as a man's thumb. A line of telegraph poles followed the railroad track. Beyond Fort Riley[6] I counted nine successive poles shattered by lightning in a thunder storm that occurred during the night. The only natural curiosity seen was Table Rock.[7] It stands alone on a rolling prairie, and weighs several tons. It is balanced so evenly upon a natural stone post that one fancies he could shove it over without much effort.

A REMARKABLE CURIOSITY.

As interesting a curiosity as I saw during the trip was the following placard in the smoking car:

BEWARE

OF

CONFIDENCE MEN

AND

THREE-CARD MONTE PLAYERS.

This car was filled with second-class passengers. Occasionally a Pullman's car traveler dropped in to take a smoke. He was delighted. The hard-fisted emigrants invariably took him for a confidence man. If he wore diamond studs or gold sleeve buttons he was set down for a three-card monte player, and treated to a seat all by himself.[8]

INFORMATION FOR OVERWORKED CLERKS.

Within four hundred miles west of Kansas City the land is nearly level, and very rich. The soil is a black loam, and resembles the soil of the Illinois prairies. Water is said to be plenty, and enormous crops of grain can be produced. Large cattle ranches are found within twenty miles of the railroad, but not one-seventieth of the land is cultivated. It looks as though it had been seeded down for grass. All that a farmer has to do is to stick a ploughshare into it and turn the sod. It ploughs as easily as an Ohio corn field. The only trouble appears to be that there is no wood for fences, but I saw hundreds of acres under cultivation without a foot of fence. In some cases men had just taken up their land, and were living in wall tents until they could erect houses. Some had dug holes in the ground and boarded them over. Such residences are called "dugouts." Toward the territorial line these houses outnumbered the others two to one. The earth, however, is filled with a soft limestone, which can be sawed into blocks as it is dug from the ground, and which hardens from exposure to the weather. Many of the railroad stations are built of this stone. It is clean and white, but it will not take a polish.

HOW TO PRE-EMPT LAND.[9]

For ten miles on either side of the road the alternate sections are owned by the Kansas Pacific Company. The other sections are open for preemption. The railroad company sells its land for from $2 to $6 an acre, with five years credit, one-fifth cash, and no other payment, except interest, within two years. A discount of ten percent for cash within sixty days is allowed. As the company is anxious to fill the country with settlers, they offer extra inducements in the way of tickets. Government land can be pre-empted for $1.25 per acre. Payment cannot be made, however, until the party has actually resided on the land for six months, and made the necessary improvement and cultivation. This proof can be furnished by one witness.

WOMEN ALLOWED TO PRE-EMPT.

It is not generally known that an unmarried woman over twenty-one years of age, and not the head of a family, can pre-empt her 160 acres the same as a man. I have not seen or heard of any woman who has done this, though I have seen several women who ought to do it. Officers, soldiers, and sailors who have served in the army or navy for ninety days, have the privilege of entering 160 acres of land within railroad limits at $2.50 per acre. Civilians are restricted to 80 acres. These are called "double minimum lands." Many thousand acres have been taken up by colonies. Between Junction City and Ellsworth, ranging from 138 to 223 miles from Kansas City, there are a number of large and prosperous colonies. There is an English colony in Clay County, a Scotch colony near Solomon City, two Swedish colonies in Saline and McPherson counties, and an Ohio colony in Saline County.

ENGLISHMEN TURNING AMERICANS.

A wealthy Englishman named George Grant[10] has purchased about twenty square miles of land near Hays City, 200 miles west of Kansas City. The company has built him a commodious house of soft limestone, and Grant began operations on Saturday last with about a dozen colonists. He intends raising blooded stock. Your correspondent passed through it on Monday.[11] The land is well watered. A hot sun was shining on the broad, leafless plain, and a flock of blooded sheep just imported was quietly grazing a quarter of a mile away. Two corrals had been built, and a note had been sent to the railroad agent at Ellis[12] for lumber to make a third one. Grant himself was walking about this purchase, with a sun umbrella over his head. His face was very red, and the passengers laughed a little at his large nose, but he looked like a man who had a well-settled plan, and who was determined to carry it out. The ladies of the party were sent to Ellis, there to remain until the colonists have made arrangements for their accommodation. Mr. Grant calls his settlement Victoria. The whole colony went before Senator Edwards[13] in Ellis yesterday, and declared their intention to become American citizens. They are daily expecting a consignment of short-horned cattle from England.

YOUNG ELLIOTT, THE TREE-SEED MAN.

Ellis is the finest station on the road between Ellsworth and Denver. It contains a beautiful hotel and three or four houses, and is the breathing place between Kansas City and Denver. State Senator Edwards lives here. He has planted trees about his residence, and he says they are thriving finely. Mr. R. S. Elliot,[14] the Industrial Agent of the railroad company, has been planting tree seeds between Ellis and Wallace, 118 miles further east. He believes that they will prove a success, but the Senator declares that Elliot will be an old man before his trees shade the plains. Elliot is remarkably handsome and has a wonderful intellectual development. He seemed to be about 25 years old, and is regarded as one of the rising young men of Kansas.

THE THREE DRAWBACKS.

So much for the land in Kansas. Any healthy retail clerk with $500 capital can become independent through its cultivation. The cattle looked fat and tempting. They were grazing on the prairies by thousands. There may be a drawback in the shape of sickness. It seemed to me that fever and ague and prairie fevers would feed upon the settlers, though I heard no complaints. The snow storms of winter must be severe as there are miles upon miles of high racks along the railroad to prevent the snow from drifting into the cuts. These racks are always on the north side, about a hundred feet from the track. They are nearly six feet high and resemble huge sawbucks with slats nailed across the arms of the buck. They prove of great service, even where the road is cut not more than a foot below the surface. Only two weeks ago Sunday the plains were visited by a snow storm so severe that the locomotives were frozen up and the cars stopped running. One man in Ellsworth lost 400 head of cattle. The third drawback is an occasional visit from grasshoppers. At intervals of years these insects spread over the prairies by myriads, destroying every green thing.

The grass grows less green as we approach the Rocky Mountains. There is less moisture in the soil, and it looks sterile. For more than 200 miles east of Denver the land is valueless without irrigation and this can be obtained only through artesian wells. There are few settlements along the railroad in the Territory. All the houses between Ellsworth and Denver, over 400 miles, could be dropped into Washington square,[15] with room to spare.

THE BUFFALO BONE HUNTERS.

I saw no buffaloes, but plenty of buffalo bones. These bones are gathered up from the prairies, and delivered at the railroad station for $5 a ton. Every second station between Ellis and Kit Carson[16] had its monument of buffalo bones. Some of them contained many tons, being from forty to fifty feet long, and from ten to twelve feet high. The bones are used in separating ores.[17]

Curing buffalo hides and bones. Note the stacks of bones in the background. This scene is thought to be from near Wichita, Kansas. (*Harper's Weekly* 18 (April 4, 1874):307; original engraving by Paul Frenzeny and Jules Tavernier)

Acres of buffalo hides were spread about various stations, and in certain sections the ground was strewn with animals that had been slaughtered for their skins. The raw hides bring $1.50 apiece. I saw an old hunter who said he had just come in from the buffalo country, 800 miles to the south. He declared that for hundreds of miles the buffalo paths were like rows of corn, about three feet apart and a foot deep. He was a very gentlemanly hunter, but nobody asked him to drink, and he departed somewhat discouraged. He wore buckskin breeches, with an old barn-door flap ornamented with beautiful Indian bead work.

SOD-WALLED GARDENS.

Toward Denver the shanties were surrounded by walls made out of prairie sods. I noticed the garden, containing half an acre of ground, encircled by a sod fence with a good-sized ditch outside. The sods were piled up about two feet high, which served to keep the cattle out. The race course in Denver is shut in by a high mud wall, similar to the sod walls. Some of the passengers were so innocent as to assert that these walls were thrown up for protection against the Indians. No savages appeared upon the route, but gravestones of white limestone occasionally marked spots where they had massacred parties of whites. I am told that Indians rarely appear upon the line of the road. They seem to have given up the thing for good, and to have withdrawn to the north and the south.

A PLEASING INCIDENT.

Pleasing incidents, however, relieve the monotony of the long ride. While the passengers were eating supper at Ellis a few days ago a trapper and a conductor indulged in a little intellectual conversation. The conductor endeavored to persuade the trapper into an endorsement of his peculiar views by drawing a revolver upon him, whereupon the trapper whipped out a brace of six shooters, and began snapping them promiscuously about the room. Sixty people, men and women, made a rush for the door. It is averred that a colored palace car porter jumped ten feet high, and landed on his stomach across a windowsill. The conductor whizzed out of the door like a comet, and a gentleman weighing 295 pounds managed to stow himself away under a small dining table. He said that he had dropped his watch key, and was looking for it. After all were safe on the cars it was discovered that the trapper's pistols were not capped, and that fifteen of the railroad men and passengers ran out of the dining room with loaded revolvers in their pockets.

A SECOND PLEASING INCIDENT.

A few days ago two hunters got on a spree in Wallace. One of them was a notorious character known as Mud-Eater. Under the influence of whiskey his bump of self-esteem began to swell, and he had a desire to let the people know who he was. "I'm a coyote! I'm a wolf!" he shouted. One of his comrades said, "Well, I've knowed you a good many years, an' I've heered you howl; but I never knowed you to hurt anybody." Mud-Eater's destructiveness arose. He drew a navy pistol, and shot the speaker dead. After procuring another drink he moosied[18] off over the plains. A party followed him and returned a day after with his clothes, declaring that they had lynched him. As they were nearly all intimate friends of Mud-Eater, their story is doubted.

Another version of the affair is that one of the crowd shouted, "I'm a wolf!" Mud-Eater replied, "I'm a wolf eater!" and put a bullet through him, making a hole big enough for a rabbit to jump through. He then disappeared, but returned within a half an hour. Lifting the dead body, he tore the shirt away from the breast, and pointing to the hole in the heart, chuckled out, "Popped just whar I aimed, by —!" He then mounted his horse and left the settlement unmolested. The man's body laid around Wallace for days before it was buried.

A THIRD PLEASING INCIDENT.

We arrived in Wallace[19] on Monday after dark. The little town, consisting of an eating house and four or five mud shanties, was in a spasm of excitement. There is a military post near by,[20] under command of a Capt. Irwin.[21] The captain is alleged to have grossly insulted the wife of Mr. George Barry,[22] a well-known master mechanic. When the latter gentleman heard of it, he shouldered his rifle and began to look for the captain. The officer, however, was too shrewd for him. He ordered out a guard of soldiers, and is determined to have a general fusillade in case Mr. Barry makes his appearance. This is the story told the passengers. Mr. Barry's provocation may be lesser, or even greater than reported, and the captain may be as innocent as a whip-poorwill, but it is certain that both are on the war path, and that Wallace is boiling over with excitement.

INVALIDS ON THE ROAD TO PARADISE.

These delightful incidents are duly appreciated by the passengers. To further entertain them the railroad officials kindly point out the trees along the road where men have been hanged. The trees are so scarce that an invalid is overjoyed to see one, and he absolutely thrills with satisfaction when he is told that half a dozen desperadoes have been strung up to its branches without a judge or jury. It is particularly pleasant to have such a tree pointed out and hear such a story about dark. It produces so refreshing a sleep and such charming dreams that the poor consumptive experiences a sensation of being much nearer heaven than he was on the previous day.

NOTES

1. The famous suffragist was five feet five inches in height, tall for her generation. I believe that here Cummings is tweaking the people of Kansas. In 1867 an amendment to the Kansas constitution that would have allowed women to vote had been defeated. The vote had drawn

national attention and the *New York Tribune* and its editor, Horace Greeley, rivals of Cummings's own paper, had opposed the amendment. Earlier in 1873, Ms. Anthony had stood trial for illegally voting in New York.

2. The *New York Times* journalist was certainly Middie Morgan, described by contemporaries as "the most respected live-stock reporter in New York" and "the best judge of horned cattle in this country" (Stanton, Anthony, and Gage, *History of Woman Suffrage*, 403). Ms. Morgan, who also covered footraces and cattle shows, is generally said to be the first woman sports reporter in the United States.

3. He is referring to Colorado, which was still a territory in 1873.

4. In 1990 the venerable *Kansas City Times* merged with the *Kansas City Star*, formerly the evening paper. Today the *Star* is a Knight Ridder paper.

5. Cummings is poking fun both at Kansas City and his newspaper colleagues. There was no *Mince Meat* newspaper. The Sunday Cummings was in Kansas City almost certainly was May 25.

6. Established in 1852 as Camp Center because it was near the geographical center of the United States, the fort was renamed the next year to honor Maj. Gen. Bennett C. Riley (1790–1853), who is credited with commanding the first military escort along the Santa Fe Trail, which led from Franklin, Missouri, to Santa Fe, New Mexico. Fort Riley was intended to help protect people and trade traveling the Santa Fe Trail. In 1867, George Armstrong Custer was stationed there and Wild Bill Hickok was an army scout. Fort Riley continues to be an important U.S. Army facility today.

7. The western (as well as the eastern) United States has a number of table rocks. The one Cummings is referring to was on Table Rock Creek in eastern Lincoln County, Kansas, north of the railroad: Kansas's Table Rock. According to author Frank Blackmar (in *Kansas*, 795), the rock "consisted of two columns of stone surmounted by a cap. Originally the stone was about 5 feet high and overlooked the surrounding country. The late B. F. Mudge of Manhattan brought the curiosity to the attention of the public in an article on the geology of Kansas, which was published in the report of the state board of agriculture for 1877–78, in which a photograph of the rock was reproduced. It is said that the rock was inscribed with the names of the members of one of Fremont's parties which camped here during one of his expeditions.

The rock was partially, if not wholly, destroyed a few years since by parties who failed to appreciate its value."

8. Three-card monte was (and is) a classic con game rather than a legitimate card game. The dealer takes three cards, one of which is a queen, mixes them, lays them facedown, and the player bets on which one is the queen. Because the dealer manipulates the cards, players always end up losing.

9. Preemption is the right to buy land.

10. George Grant was actually a native Scotsman who had made a fortune in the cloth business. His colony, Victoria, was southeast of Hays City in Ellis County, Kansas.

11. Probably Monday, May 26, 1873.

12. Ellis was the next small town on the rail line west after Hays City. The railroad had established a water station at that location in 1867; the town received a post office in 1870. In the 2000 federal census the town's population was 1,873.

13. John H. Edwards, from Ellis, was a ticket agent for the railroad before being elected state senator. Edwards County, Kansas, is named for him.

14. Cummings also spells the name "Eliott." R. S. Elliot would go on to write scientific papers on the industrial resources of Kansas and Colorado, among other things.

15. Washington Square Park is at the foot of Fifth Avenue in New York City's Greenwich Village. It is less than ten acres in size.

16. Kit Carson, in eastern Colorado (today in Cheyenne County), was a flourishing railroad town and a major shipping point for cattle when Cummings visited in 1873.

17. To extract silver and gold from ore, lead was added in the smelting process. The resulting alloy was then transferred to a cupellation furnace that contained bone ash. Heating the alloy in the furnace caused the lead to take up oxygen. The resulting lead oxide was absorbed by the bone ash, leaving behind the valuable metals.

18. Moseyed.

19. Wallace originally was a station on the stagecoach line that once crossed the plains. In mid-1867 it had been raided by Cheyenne Indians.

20. Fort Wallace, originally established as Camp Pond Creek in western Kansas in 1865 and renamed in 1866, was about two miles

southeast of Wallace. From 1865 to 1878 it is said to have been one of the most active military outposts in terms of encounters with Plains Indians. The fort was abandoned in 1882.

21. Captain Irwin may have been Bernard John Dowling Irwin, an Irishman, who was stationed at Fort Riley, where he served as post surgeon at various times from 1867 to 1873. In that latter year he left to become chief medical officer of the U.S. Military Academy. Irwin was awarded the Congressional Medal of Honor in 1894 (the same year as Amos Cummings) for bravery at Apache Pass, Arizona, in 1861. Forts Riley, Harker, and Wallace, among others, were on the east-west trail along which the railroad that carried Amos Cummings west in 1873 had been built only several years earlier.

22. George Barry, master mechanic, may have been James Barry, who in 1870 was at Fort Harker (between Fort Riley and Fort Wallace), where he served as a foreman for the company building the railroad across Kansas. A native of Ireland, he was forty-three years old in 1870 (according to the federal census). His wife, Mary, born in New York, was thirty-six that year. Fort Harker was closed in 1872. James Barry might well have moved west to Fort Wallace from Fort Harker, especially because railroad construction had moved west past Fort Harker (in 1867). All of this, however, is speculation.

THE EARTHLY PARADISE.

A MAN WHO HAS HAD ENOUGH OF WESTERN KANSAS.

Farming on the Old Buffalo Range in Kansas—A Racy Letter from a Saline County Angel—The Extraordinary Winds That Blow Wheat Fields and Herds of Cattle into the Next County.

Correspondence of The Sun.

GYPSUM CREEK VALLEY, Kan., May 30—Perhaps the readers of THE SUN may feel an interest in learning the experience of a settler in Kansas, who has made a home some 200 miles west of Kansas City. They probably knew what the Kansas Pacific Railroad men represent this country to be, and may also have a faint recollection of the earthly heaven the imaginative land agents talk about. The heaven described to me was situated in Saline County, Kansas, and as I had the desire to go to the abode of good men after my death, and thought that a residence in an earthly paradise would tend to prepare me, I came here.

In short I am a Saline County angel, and am living in a valley, Gypsum[1] by name, with a lot of the meanest angels ever heard of.

In regard to the crops that are sure out here my information may be depended on. We get a crop of northers in the winter that are as sure as death. And that is the only sure crop in the country. Corn is generally sure; but the lack of rain is the curse of that crop. I suppose, one year with another, that thirty bushels to the acre is an average crop. Now and then a field that was planted at just the right time, and on which the rain falls at exactly the right time, will make over 100 bushels to the acre. But this is very rare.

Winter wheat is a very uncertain crop. It winter kills badly, and then we have a trouble with this crop in the spring that would appear to Eastern farmers to be impossible. This trouble is wind—wind so strong and continuous as to blow the wheat plants out of the ground. That is something that I would not have believed if I had not seen it. I know of fields this spring that have not a dozen wheat plants on as many acres; and this wheat was blown out after it had stood the arctic winter of Kansas. I lost five acres of winter wheat by having it blown out, and about thirty-five by having it frozen out. Spring wheat, oats, and barley do well enough. In 1872 spring wheat made about ten bushels to the acre, but the wind often uncovers the spring grain before it gets set, and the result is a half crop.

TOBACCO AND COTTON.

To judge about the practicality of raising tobacco and cotton, one should be here in the summer when the wind blows, and see the haying suspended for a week at a time on account of the wind; see a set of haymakers lying around, "reckoning that this 'ere wind won't be so smart to-morrow"; and then he would realize that the broad leaves of the tobacco plant would be blown into shreds. I do not believe that sound, whole tobacco leaves enough to make a cigar wrapper could be grown on one thousand acres of Kansas land. As to cotton; well, well; let me see. Did you ever see a cotton field when it was white? I can imagine a Kansas farmer looking in dismay at the cotton being blown out of his field into the next county. Cotton and tobacco would grow here, but the crop would not be worth much to harvest. Hemp I know nothing of from experience; but I am told by men who raised hemp in Kentucky, that you could not rot it here in five years. At least they refuse to grow the crop, though they have tried it on a small scale. The climate is too dry.

Prices are low for all a farmer grows and has to sell, and high for all he buys. Reason: It is known that the people of the United States built a few charity railroads. The Union Pacific Railroad, Central Pacific Railroad, and Kansas Pacific Railroad are the three great charity railways of the nation. Built by the bounty of a generous people, and given to those who "put money where it does most good," a man in the simplicity of an honest heart might think that these roads would be run for the benefit of the people, or at least run at living rates. But such is not the fact. The Kansas Pacific Railroad's freight tariff should be posted up in every town in the Eastern States, so as to induce those who may think of emigrating to Kansas to alter their plans and invest their little all in fitting up a few rooms in the county poorhouse, and there live in ease and comfort among their friends. The effect of this outrageous tariff is that corn, oats, and barley are worthless. It takes a bushel to send a bushel from Saline to St. Louis—that is, the railroad tolls the farmer one-half of the result of his industry. Wheat brings a fair living price because we never have a full crop, and generally have to import flour. I am using Colorado flour in my house.

THE PLEASURES OF WINTER.

Of Kansas winters the least said the better. Cattle have to be well fed for five months, and it requires the greatest care to get them through without loss. I can winter cattle in New York on less hay and corn than the same cattle would require in Saline County, Kansas. We are cursed with the winter storm I have mentioned called a "norther." It is a storm that freezes cattle to death, freezes men to death, freezes the ground to the depth of two feet, and forms ice on the ponds fifteen inches in thickness where the wind cannot keep the water in motion. This wind blows sheds down and fences over, and if the cattle get out of the corral it will blow them on the run forty miles in a single night.

Oh, it is a pleasant, mirth-provoking sight on a January evening to see your band of cattle starting south on a fast trot. How happy you feel, and how much you love the country as you hasten to saddle a horse, get your blankets and money—the latter to pay the damages the cattle will surely do—and start after the long-horned brutes. A night's ride in a norther, fifty vain endeavors to get the cattle turned against the wind, and then daylight. You find you are on the banks of the Arkansas River, and have lost some twenty or thirty animals. You are cold, frost bitten, hungry, and want to sit down and die. That is Kansas winter.

Of course we have voted bonds to those humbugs of ours, called "railroads." Saline County, a poor poverty-stricken frontier county, must needs vote $500,000 to railroads [*sic*]. How we are to pay the interest on the bonds is not yet settled, but I suppose the railroads will be satisfied if we give them all our property, and our notes endorsed by parties who live in other counties where there are no railroads, for the remainder of the debt. This we are all prepared to do, as we believe in developing the natural resources of the country.

THE ONLY HOPE THAT REMAINS

to us is to entice strangers to leave the East and come here. Then we borrow their money, sell them things at two prices, stick them with land when we can, and plunder them generally. So, if you know of any unsophisticated young farmers who have a farm or money, send them here, and let us have a chance to peel them. Don't encourage any poor people to come here, as they cannot be plundered, but very unjustly and to the injury of us old settlers, assist in robbing those who have something. Keep all those poor devils in the East. My nightly prayer is "Oh Lord, send me a stranger with money, an unsophisticated stranger, and give me a chance to go through him."

We have fevers of course. So if you have a lazy enemy whom you would like to punish, send him to Saline County, and I'll warrant he will have the fever and ague; and when he gets it I'll watch him and write you a full account of his performances. The ague will enliven any man; it will stir him up and make a bustling person out of him. Bilious fever[2] and the rattlesnakes will surely kill your enemy if the ague does not shake his liver out.

If you will come out, and bring along a pair of pistols, you and I will go down into my cellar, and sitting on a couple of barrels I have for that purpose, we will see who can kill the most rattlesnakes in one hour. I have not got a first-rate rattlesnake cellar, but still one can have an hour's lively sport in it.

NOTES

1. Gypsum Creek is east of the intersection of Interstates 70 and 135 in central Kansas, about 185 miles west of Kansas City. The creek and its tributaries extend north from McPherson County into Saline County.

2. An archaic medical term used for a fever accompanied by intestinal disorders.

Crops of Grain, Stumps of Stone, and a Town without Rumbirds

RAVELING FARTHER WEST ON THE KANSAS PACIFIC RAILROAD, Amos Cummings left the Kansas plains, climbed the foothills of the Rocky Mountains, and reached Denver. He and Frances stayed a month in the region, exploring Colorado. Traveling aboard the rails of the Denver and Rio Grande Railway Company, they went southward to Colorado Springs, seventy-six miles from Denver, then on to Pueblo, at that time the end of the rail line. From Colorado Springs, Cummings hired a coach to take them to Manitou, about six miles from the famed springs where the town of Manitou Springs later was founded.

Henry T. Williams's 1877 guidebook, *The Pacific Tourist* (pp. 75–77), provides this information about the region:

> The uniform railroad fare in the Territory [of Colorado] averages ten cents per mile. Stage routes run all through the mountains, fare from ten to twenty cents per mile. The uniform rate of board is four dollars per day, and almost every-where can be found excellent living; the nicest of beef steak, bread and biscuits. In many of the mountain resorts plenty of good fishing can be found, and delicate trout are common viands of the hotel tables. . . .
>
> The Denver and Rio Grande Railroad will carry the traveler southward from Denver, along the base of the Rocky Mountains, to some of the most noted pleasure resorts of the territory. . . . Seventy-six miles south of Denver, on this line, are clustered three little places of resort, practically one in interest, Colorado Springs, Colorado City, and Manitou Springs. The former is the railroad station, a lively town, which in five years has risen from the prairie. . . . The location of this resort, with its wonderful collection of objects of natural interest and scenery, have earned for it the title of "Saratoga of the Far West." . . .
>
> We know of no country better worth the title of the *"Switzerland of America"* than Colorado, with its beautiful mountain parks, valleys, and springs. Go and see them all.

That is exactly what Amos Cummings did.

The first two articles presented in this section were written while Amos was staying at the Manitou House, a tourist hotel built the year before. Manitou, in the Rocky Mountains, was four miles west of Colorado Springs. In the 1870 census only 987 people lived in the entire county of El Paso, where Manitou and Colorado Springs are located. Colorado City, founded more than a decade earlier than Colorado Springs, also is in that county. In 1871 when General William Palmer, a Civil War veteran (for the Union) and teetotaler, began building the Denver and Rio

COLORADO SPRINGS SEVERAL YEARS AFTER CUMMINGS WAS THERE. (FOSSETT, *COLORADO*, 38)

Grande Railway, he found Colorado City too rough and ready (and wet) for his tastes, so he decided to establish his own town. Thus, Colorado Springs was born. It stayed dry until after Prohibition in 1933.

The railroad brought just what General Palmer wanted: tourists. Today, Manitou Springs remains a major tourist destination. Its local population in the 2000 census was just under 5,000, and El Paso County had more than 500,000.

I originally thought that Moses Ouellette, the Canadian whom Amos interviewed for his article "A Canadian in Colorado," was not a real person but a composite made up of several different farmers interviewed for the piece. But that turns out not to be true. Moses "Ouillet" is listed in the 1870 Jefferson County, Colorado, census as living in an agricultural area near Golden, Colorado. Golden is several miles west of Denver, just as described in Cummings's article. Golden already was a growing town in 1870 with a population of 2,390. Early on, it was the territorial capital of Colorado, and in 1873, Adolph Coors opened a brewery there. Moses Ouellette died in 1899 and his will was

THE SMALL TOWN OF MANITOU. (FOSSETT, *COLORADO*, 114)

probated in Jefferson County. As we will see below, Amos never went to Golden. He interviewed Mr. Ouellette in Manitou.

Cummings traveled west from Manitou through Ute Pass to the Florissant Valley on the flanks of Pikes Peak about thirty-five miles west of Colorado Springs. The valley was not yet known by that appellation. It would later acquire its name from the very small settlement of Florissant, founded by Judge James Costello, who figures prominently in the second article in this section, "The Petrified Stumps." Costello (Cummings calls him "Castello") was born in Florissant, Missouri. He moved to Fairplay, Colorado, in the mid-1860s, a victim of gold fever. In 1867 he was appointed a United States Commissioner, which gave him certain judicial powers (and, hence, the title "judge"), and later he represented Park County in the Colorado Territorial Convention.

When gold became scarce, Costello and other Fairplay residents moved on. In 1870 the judge resettled in a beautiful, park-like valley where the Oil Creek and Ute trails met, an area well-known to early fur trappers. Calling his new settlement "Florissant" after his old home in Missouri and, perhaps, in response to the wildflowers for which the valley still is known, Costello eventually built a hotel, trading post, general store, and post office.

The petrified stumps that Cummings wrote about continue to interest visitors to the area. Most are the petrified remains of giant sequoia trees and are the largest petrified stumps known. Today, many are protected in the Florissant Fossil Beds National Monument. The monument also is renowned for extraordinary fossil deposits, all dating from the Eocene epoch, 34 to 35 million years ago. After reading Amos Cummings's article, I was heartened to learn that some of the petrified stumps survived the exploding attentions of the early settlers in the region. Cummings also mentions Pikes Peak. Although he certainly would have enjoyed the vista from the top, Cummings, like Zebulon Pike for whom the 14,115-foot mountain is named, never made it to the summit.

In trying to learn more about some of the people mentioned in "The Petrified Stumps," I stumbled upon the online Colorado Historic Newspaper Collection. It is a magnificent resource and it taught me a thing or two about Amos Jay Cummings. First, with one exception (the third article in this section) the datelines on the articles for the *Sun* accurately reflect each place he was when he wrote that article; the dates also are correct. Second,

Amos was content to relax at a hotel such as the Manitou House and interview people in order to gather information for articles. I would not be at all surprised to learn he had his best conversations in hotel bars or on verandas with a drink in hand. The third thing I learned was that Amos put a host of inside jokes in his articles, giving people imaginary or honorific titles and upping their stations in life.

How do I know these things? The Colorado Historic Newspaper Collection led me to both the *Colorado Springs Gazette* (published in Colorado Springs) and the *Colorado Chieftain* (often called the *Colorado Daily Chieftain*, published in Pueblo; its modern-day descendant is the *Pueblo Chieftain*). Amos's presence in specific towns and the existence of people mentioned in his articles are corroborated by news accounts in various historic Colorado newspapers I found in the newspaper collection. For instance, in the June 21, 1873, issue of the *Gazette*, I found a list of "Hotel Arrivals" for the Manitou House. There among the people who had stayed at that hotel "during the week" was "A. J. Cummings and his wife, New York." As I printed out the article, the name of another guest caught my eye: "M. Ouellette, Denver," the very farmer Amos interviewed for "A Canadian in Colorado." A second look revealed a third name: H. Damhoyt from St. Louis. That certainly is Hermann Danhorst, also mentioned in the article. Amos never went to Moses Ouellette's farm; he took advantage of the farmer's coming to him.

Further searches in that same newspaper led me to the identification of another person mentioned in "The Petrified Stumps," the "Hon. Mr. Swisler." That person, certainly a typographical error for Swisher, is Marshal D. Swisher, co-owner of the Swisher and Homes Livery Company. The company maintained a stable in Manitou, and Swisher and associates regularly drove tourists out to the Manitou House from the train station in Colorado Springs, a lucrative undertaking. The year before Amos's visit, Swisher and company had purchased a new Concord brand stagecoach, a transaction highlighted in the *Gazette.* The stagecoach was manufactured in Concord, New Hampshire, and shipped west on the railroad. Cummings must have enjoyed Swisher, awarding him in print the title "Hon. Mr."

Further south on the Denver and Rio Grande line, Cummings, as he often did, stopped at the local newspaper. In Pueblo he visited the *Colorado Chieftain* editorial office on June 21, 1873. A short note appeared the next day in the paper: "Amos J. Cummings, associate editor of the New York *Sun,* favored the CHIEFTAIN office with a most acceptable call yesterday."

Cummings probably dropped off this longer, handwritten announcement of his visit to the area, one that was published in the *Chieftain* two days later. It is quintessential Cummings:

> Amos J. Cummings, managing editor of the New York *Sun,* now on a visit to Colorado, is interviewing the country very thoroughly, and making himself familiar, not only with the grand, novel, and beautiful scenery peculiar to the "Switzerland of America," and the objects of interest usually noticed by tourists, but with our materials inter- ests, resources, advantages, and possibilities. His graceful and able pen forms his impressions of what he sees and learns about the country into articles that do full justice to Colorado, and from their ability, and the medium through which they are given to the public, the New York *Sun,* with its one hundred and sixty thousand circulation, daily, and high reputation as a newspaper, these will do us good service. Mr. Cummings's wife accompanied him. Her just appreciation of the beautiful and sublime in our surround- ings, and her nice perception of what is really advantageous and superior in our new country, enable her to find much enjoyment during their sojournings, and make her an excel- lent judge, and, we trust, a firm friend of Colorado.

The phrase "Switzerland of America," used here by Cummings and also by Williams in *Pacific Tourist,* came from another ear- lier volume, *The Switzerland of America: A Summer Vacation in the*

Parks and Mountains of Colorado, authored by Samuel Bowles and published in 1869.[1]

Amos could have posted the letters containing the first two articles, written at the Manitou House, in the town of Colorado Springs, or he may have waited until he was back in Denver. Either way, the stories reached New York. "A Canadian in Colorado" was published in the *Sun* on July 7, 1873, and "The Petrified Stumps" appeared in the *Sun* on July 5.

On their way north out of Colorado to meet the Union Pacific Railroad at Cheyenne, Amos and his spouse went through the town of Greeley, named for Horace Greeley, who had died the previous year. Greeley had been a major force in the Democratic Party as well as the long-serving editor of the *New York Tribune*, a major competitor of the *New York Sun*. Greeley had used the newspaper to support his political and social agenda (he was strongly against slavery as well as against alcohol, tobacco, and gambling). Cummings, when starting out in journalism, had worked at the *Tribune*; I cannot imagine Greeley and Cummings ever becoming close social friends. Cummings used his trip to Greeley to tweak Greeley's memory as well as his anti-alcohol stance.

The town of Greeley had started out as the Union Colony, a utopian enterprise intended to incorporate Horace Greeley's social views. Thanks to Greeley's *New York Tribune*, the colony had received a great deal of attention in New York City. Cummings's rendition of the colony's founding is quite different from that which appeared in the *Tribune*.

Cummings's recounting of the founding and present condition of the utopian Union Colony, "The Town in the Desert," did not appear in the *Sun* until September 20, although it is datelined Cheyenne, August 8. By August 8, he already was in Salt Lake City, so exactly where he was when he wrote and posted this article is uncertain. What is certain is that it is classic Cummings.

NOTE

1. Ten years after his Colorado book, Bowles wrote about another "Switzerland in America": New Hampshire.

A CANADIAN IN COLORADO.

A Farmer's Experience at the Base of the Rocky Mountains.

*A New York City Farmer Tackles the Old Gentleman—
The Result—What Crops Can Be Raised in Colorado, and
What Can't Be Raised—The Wonderful Instinct of the Potato
Bug—The Old Farmer Saved.*

Correspondence of The Sun.

MANITOU, Col., June 17.—I had a talk today with Mr. Moses Ouellette,[1] a Canadian, who has cultivated a farm in Colorado for the last nine years. He owns 160 acres of land, about six miles west of Denver. Mr. Ouellette is a sound-headed, practical man. Believing that his information would prove interesting to farmers in the States, I interviewed him in the old brass-mounted style.[2] As I had had several years' experience in farming in New York City,[3] I felt that I was thoroughly posted, and therefore tackled the old gentleman with considerable confidence. He panned out as follows:

City Farmer—What crops turn out the best in Colorado?

Mr. Ouellette—Wheat and oats. Of course we can raise vegetables, but they thrive better on low bottom lands along the streams, wherever there is a new formation caused by the shifting of the water. We can raise good barley, but the trouble is in harvesting and threshing it. A few farmers raise it, but the mass of them prefer other grains which pay just as well.

City Farmer—Is it any more trouble to thresh barley in Colorado than in the States?

Mr. Ouellette—I never raised but one crop of barley, and the grasshoppers reaped that for me. You see the majority of the farmers here wear flannel shirts. The air is very dry, and when they use the threshing machines in the open field, exposed to the winds, as we always do, the grain breaks and the beard of the barley fills the flannel shirts and throats of the laborers, making it excessively disagreeable. They don't like it, and won't stand it.

COLORADO WHEAT.

City Farmer—What kind and quality of wheat do you raise?

Mr. Ouellette—We raise the Sonora wheat, but more of the Chilt. There is the Club mixed with it.[4] In fact the whole thing is rather mixed, as the seed wheat comes from everywhere. Some came from New Mexico, some from the States, some from Salt Lake, and it is hard to say what kind of wheat we really do raise. But it is of the best quality, far superior to either Eastern or Salt Lake wheat. California wheat may be as good. It has a great reputation, but as I have never seen any of it I can't give an opinion.

City Farmer—I have heard it said that the kernels of your Colorado wheat are plumper and better filled out than other wheat. How is it?

Mr. Ouellette—Well, I don't think that it is much plumper. I have seen Salt Lake wheat and wheat from the States with a larger and plumper kernel—equal to ours, anyway. I have never seen large quantities of it, and I only speak from what I have seen. Our wheat is flinty and brighter in color. It is so hard that the millers are compelled to dampen it before they can grind it. If this was not done, the bran would cut as fine as the flour, and the meal would be speckled and not clear. The first year's wheat puzzled the millers, but a Californian turned up who discovered what was the matter, and began to sprinkle the grain. Now all of our mills run their wheat into a conveyer where the water drops upon it until it is fit to go under the burrs. The miller must use his own judgment. If the wheat is too wet, it clogs the burrs, and he has to do his work over again.

SOAKING WHEAT IN BLUE VITRIOL.[5]

City Farmer—When you do plant your wheat?

Mr. Ouellette (laughing and accenting the words "plant" and "sow")—We plant corn and potatoes, but we usually sow our wheat in Colorado. We never raise winter wheat. It don't do well. The winds bother us. I sow wheat from the first of March to the latter part of May. You see, early wheat will stool better.

City Farmer—What do you mean by stool?

Mr. Ouellette—What we call stooling is the branching out of the wheat. You see, the most of the snows we get fall in March and April. For example, a spear of wheat comes up, and the snow beats it down. Then two or three spears take its place, and the snow beats them down. The more snow up to a certain point, the greater the increase in wheat. This is what we call stooling. But as to the sowing, I have always found that late sown wheat has longer heads than that put in the ground earlier in the season, but it don't stand so thick on the ground. It ripens almost as early as the other. I have sown wheat in March and in April, and harvested all of it within a week. We have to soak our seed wheat either in brine or sulphate of copper[6] before we sow it. We generally soak it for six hours and then lime it—that is, sprinkle it with slacked lime.

City Farmer—What do you do this for?

Mr. Ouellette—To prevent smut.[7] If we didn't do this, and should continue to sow the same wheat for three or four years in succession, the grain would become smutty.

THE FINEST WHEAT IN THE WORLD.

City Farmer—How many bushels of wheat do you raise to the acre?

Mr. Ouellette—Well, I can't exactly say. I have never myself raised over twenty-five bushels to the acre. I have been told that some farmers have raised thirty and even forty bushels, but I think that twenty-five would be a strong average. Probably it would run nearer twenty.

City Farmer—What do you get for your wheat?

Mr. Ouellette—It is now lower than I have ever seen it before. It is sold by the pound and not by the bushel. It is down to two and a half cents per pound. It sold last fall a little higher. In 1864 and 1865 it sold for from fifteen to eighteen cents per pound, but that was in war times, when men had more money than brains. The highest price I ever received was fourteen cents. I think that was in 1866. You see the crop of 1865 was all eaten up by grasshoppers, and there was very little seed in the country.

City Farmer—Is any of your wheat shipped East?

Mr. Ouellette—There was some sent to St. Louis some time ago, but the millers didn't understand how to grind it. I have heard that a few car loads were sent to Kansas City, where it was mixed with Kansas wheat before it was ground. We send East considerable flour. It goes as far as Boston. It is more advantageous to send flour than grain. The bran and shorts[8] are worth more here than they are East. The flour is of the finest quality, and makes the whitest and best bread in the world.

City Farmer—I can certify to the truth of that assertion. But what do you think causes this?

Mr. Ouellette—I think there are two reasons—irrigation and climate. Wheat always heads in a dry season. As soon as it begins to head in this country we turn the water upon it, and the kernels seem to fill up better and plumper than they do in the East, where farmers have to depend upon the rain. And still I think something is due to the quality of the water, for millers say that wheat irrigated by the water of Clear Creek[9] is the best raised in the Territory. Wheat north of the Divide—that is, on the Platte—is considered better than that raised south of the Divide, or along the Arkansas.[10]

OATS IN COLORADO.

City Farmer—How about oats? When do you plant them?

Mr. Ouellette (again laughing, and accenting the words "plant" and "sow")—We plant corn and potatoes, but we usually sow our oats in this country. I believe that in the States you put in your oats before you do your spring wheat. Here we never do. We always sow oats last. The reason for this is obvious. In the States the spring opens differently from here. Eastern farmers sow their oats and wheat after the heavy frosts are over. Here we can sow wheat in February if we want. Our snows fall later, and instead of injuring the wheat they benefit it. It is not so with oats. If our oats were sown at the same time with our wheat, they would be damaged by the frosts, which sometimes run pretty stiff late in April.

City Farmer—How do your oats turn out?

Mr. Ouellette—I guess they will average forty bushels to the acre, and they will average forty pounds to the bushel. In Colorado every kind of grain except corn improves in quality. I have seen common or "shoe-peg" oats, as we call them, brought from the East, that ran about thirty-two pounds to the bushel. They were sown here, and they turned out from thirty-eight to forty pounds. South of the Divide, along the Fontaine-qui-Bouille,[11] oats have been raised that reached fifty pounds to the bushel, but they were what is called the "barley oat." Sixty bushels to the acre is not uncommon in the Territory, but it will not run through the whole field. We tried Norway oats, and they were a failure; so now we sow the common white and black oat.

City Farmer—What do your oats bring?

Mr. Ouellette—Well, just now they bring in Denver about $1.90 per hundred.[12] In the mountains they bring more. Our oats will sell for from a quarter to a half cent more per pound than Eastern oats.

City Farmer—How often do you irrigate your oats?

Mr. Ouellette—Wheat and oats we generally irrigate twice in a season. Sometimes once is sufficient. It depends upon the fall of rain. You see, the late snows start the grain, and it is seldom necessary to turn the water on more than twice.

A MILLIONAIRE'S OPINION OF COLORADO BARLEY.

City Farmer—How about barley? When do you plant that?

Mr. Ouellette (accenting the words "plant" and "sow" in apparent astonishment)—We plant corn and potatoes, but we usually sow barley in this country. As I said before, we raise but little barley, but what we do raise is of superior quality. Mr. Hermann Damhorst, the great millionaire brewer of St. Louis,[13] tells me that he has never seen better barley than we produce in Colorado. He says it will be equal, if not surpass, the barley raised in Upper Canada. Barley will bring about the same price as wheat, and will average about the same as wheat to the acre. We can sow it at the same time as we do wheat.

COLORADO NOT A CORN COUNTRY.

City Farmer—Do you sow any corn?

Mr. Ouellette (accenting the two words "sow" and "plant" with charming dignity)—We sow wheat and oats, but we generally plant corn in Colorado. [After a pause]—North of the

Divide, say fifteen miles from the foot hills of the Rocky Mountains, we can't raise corn. Corn needs warm nights and dews, and those we don't have. Our nights are cool and our dews wouldn't dampen a spider's web. Further east they grow corn. It is a passable crop, very flinty and hard. South of the Divide, with good luck, the farmers raise a fair crop, say fifty bushels to the acre. But this is not corn country. In full three-quarters of the Territory the crop don't pay. In the mountain valley it is impossible to secure a crop. It is altogether too cold. You see our farms are nearly 6,000 feet above the sea level, and that is pretty high-up for corn. Corn will irrigate on a clay soil, and turn out middling, but it won't irrigate on a sandy soil, because the ground gets too wet. Corn, you see, has a kind of a tender root, and too much water will damage it.

THE GRASSHOPPER AND THE CUT WORM.

City Farmer—Are you bothered with crows here?

Mr. Ouellette—No. There are no birds in the Territory that destroy our crops. We never have any weevil, and rust[14] is unknown, because we have no fogs nor a superabundance of rain. Our greatest agricultural curse is the grasshoppers, and a kind of cut worm that makes its appearance as soon as the ears of corn form. The cutworm attacks the end of the ear and eats a hole between the rows of kernels. The grasshoppers in 1865 made a clean sweep of everything. This is the only time that they have overrun the Territory. They generally appear, say, in August and lay their eggs. On the following year these eggs hatch, and the young grasshoppers feed upon the grain and vegetables until their wings grow out. Then, if the weather is fair, they raise in the air like a cloud and sail off with the wind. They are all gone in a day, and are so numerous that they almost obscure the sun as they sail away. Their course is generally east or southeast. They attack the vegetables first, and afterward feed upon anything they can get hold of. I knew them to destroy clothing in Minnesota in 1857, but they never have been as bad as that in Colorado.

City Farmer—What price do you get for corn?

Mr. Ouellette—The prices are regulated by the Eastern markets. As I have told you, there is but little corn grown in the Territory. Corn is brought to Denver from the States. It is softer and brings a better price than Colorado corn. This is the only grain raised in the East that sells for more than grain raised here. Generally it is the other way.

POTATOES.

City Farmer—How about potatoes? When do you sow them?

Mr. Ouellette (accenting the words "sow" and "plant" in a confidential tone of voice)—We sow corn and wheat, but we generally plant potatoes in Colorado. Potatoes run from one to three hundred bushels to the acre. The best potato ground is along the streams, where the soil is dark and moist, though they turn out splendid crops in the mountains when the frost doesn't interfere. Potatoes grow nearly 10,000 feet above sea level. They will stand water, and thrive well under irrigation. We generally plant them in rows running from east to west.

City Farmer—Why don't you run the rows north and south?

Mr. Ouellette (laughing)—Because the fall of the land goes toward the east, and water runs down hill instead of up, though you Eastern fellows seem to think that we make it run up hill. We plant our potatoes in April or May. We use principally the Early Rose, the Goodrich, and the Morton Whites. There are a few Peach Blows, Bloomershanks, Prince Alberts, and Neshannocks.[15] They turn out all about the same. There is very little difference in the yield. We have to change the seed every two or three years. If we plant the same kind of potatoes four years in succession, the crop falls off, and the potatoes decrease in size.

INTELLECTUALITY OF THE
COLORADO POTATO BUG.

City Farmer—I have been in the Territory over a month, and have not had a decent potato since I left the States. They are soft and watery, and half of them are so blue after they are boiled that they appear to be mortifying. How do you account for this?

Mr. Ouellette—About the blue part, that is owing to the kind of potato. We call them the blue Neshannocks. But potatoes here have not been so good for the past two or three years as they were formerly. You see, we have been terribly pestered by the potato bug. Take a big marrowfat pea and split it in two, and you will have an idea of the size and shape of this bug. The young ones are the most disgusting bugs that I have ever seen. They are soft, and a man cannot touch one of them without a shudder. Some seasons you will find a half dozen bugs standing on their hind legs in a circle waiting for a potato vine to come up. The old bugs don't appear to do much damage, but they lay from fifteen to twenty eggs each on the underside of a leaf, and these eggs hatch in a very short time. The young ones then pitch in and strip the vines. The only way we can get the best of them is to sprinkle the vines with Paris green.[16] The moment they touch the poison they drop dead. The use of the Paris green puts the growth of the potato back by stunting the vine, and this may possibly account for the poor quality of which you complain. I think, however, that we can raise better potatoes here than you do East. I saw a potato raised here in 1882 that weighed eleven pounds and a quarter. It was a Neshannock. That year was the greatest year for potatoes that we have ever had. They were so plentiful that the farmers offered to give them away to any one who would carry them off.

City Farmer—What is the weight of your potatoes?

Mr. Ouellette—They will average sixty pounds to the bushel, the same as they do everywhere. They are worth from a cent and a half to two cents per pound.

COLORADO VEGETABLES.

City Farmer—Tell me something about vegetables.

Mr. Ouellette—Well, there is one thing curious. It is warmer south of the Divide than it is north of it; but the crops mature north quicker than they do south. We set out early cabbages in April, and late cabbage in June. I have seen cabbages planted in July, and they turned out good. We plant them the same as you do East. If it is very hot, we run a furrow along the row, and turn a small stream of water into it. This gives the plants a start, and they don't wilt. When the cabbages are grown, we bury them in damp soil instead of a dry one, as you do East. Some of our days in winter are almost as warm as summer, and if cabbages are buried in a dry place, they will rot. Our fall cabbages average twenty pounds after they are trimmed and cleaned. I have seen them in fairs weighing sixty pounds. In the fall they will bring about a dollar a hundred pounds, and in the spring from two to three cents a pound in Denver. We are rarely troubled by cutworms.

A TALK ABOUT ONIONS.

City Farmer—What about beets? When do you plant them?

Mr. Ouellette (profoundly)—We usually sow beets in this country. Carrots, beets, parsnips, radishes, tomatoes, lettuce, and such things do better under irrigation than they do East. You see, we can make them grow as long as we are of a mind to until frost comes by simply turning the water upon them. They all bring a fair price. Onions require a damp soil. Where they have this they turn out good. I think they are not so strong and rank here as they are East. I have seen onions raised here that would average a pound a piece to the bed, and I saw several that weighed over four pounds each. They were grown from Mexican seed. We raise onions from the seed in one season, but the seed must come from either Massachusetts or Mexico. Other seed turns out in scullions,[17] that is they grow just as big above the ground as they do below, and are not good for much. We raise early turnips on the plains, but those grown in the mountains are far superior. Ours are pithy, while theirs are solid, and of an excellent flavor. They grow to an enormous size, and fetch a good price. Asparagus and cauliflower do well. It requires work to keep asparagus in good condition, and consequently there is but little grown. Cauliflower is just the same as cabbage. The heads are much larger than those grown in the States. To sum up, if a farmer thoroughly understands irrigation, and has the right kind of land and experience, he can raise larger and better vegetables of all kinds here than he can in the East.

WILD HAY.

City Farmer—How about hay? When do you sow that?

Mr. Ouellette (gravely)—We never sow hay.

City Farmer (quickly)—When do you plant it?

Mr. Ouellette (with great gravity)—We never plant hay. We cut the native grass that grows on the bottoms. There is but little or no timothy sown. We have what we call the bottom hay, the second bottom, and upland hay. The latter is the finest, and brings the higher price. It grows thin, however, and a farmer has to go over a good deal of ground to scrape up a ton. Of the bottom hay we can cut from two to three tons to the acre. In the mountains they cut a light blue grass, which is considered the finest hay, and which brings the highest price. The climate is so dry that we can cut and cock our hay[18] on the same day, and it cures in the stack. Hay fetches about $15 per ton for bottom, $20 for second bottom, and $25 for upland in Denver. At Fairplay,[19] in the mountains, it will sell for $60.

FRUITS IN COLORADO.

City Farmer—What do you do in the way of fruits?

Mr. Ouellette—Strawberries turn out splendidly. Gooseberries and currants the same. Blackberries and raspberries need protection in the winter. They must be laid down and covered with dirt or straw to preserve them. Peaches, pears, apples, and quinces do not thrive. They must have something to protect them from the dry west winds.

City Farmer—How about labor?

Mr. Ouellette—There has been a great scarcity of laborers in the country, but this year we have a surplus. We can get farm hands for the season at from twenty-five to thirty dollars per month. During harvest time they get forty dollars. If they are hired by the day, they get from $2.50 to $3.

A NARROW ESCAPE FROM DEATH.

Here Mr. Ouellette began to suffer. The weather was warm. He grew faint, and it was evident that the interviewing was too much for him. He began to gasp for breath, as if he were being talked to death. As he was quite an old man, and a friendless bachelor, your correspondent took pity on him, and this saved him from an untimely end.

NOTES

1. The 1870 federal census lists the then-forty-two-year-old, unmarried Moses "Ouillette" as a native of Canada who lived in Golden City, Colorado. His occupation is "farmer," and the values of his real estate and personal estate are given as $2,000 and $1,000, respectively.

2. "Brass-mounted" means "tough."

3. Cummings is making a joke about having farmed in New York City.

4. Sonora and Club were varieties of wheat. I cannot find any mention of "Chilt," nor could heritage wheat buffs whom I consulted. It may be that what is meant is "Spelt," a common wheat variety in the West at the time of Cummings's visit. Perhaps a New York City editor, who knew nothing about wheat, misread the handwritten story submitted by Cummings.

5. Copper sulfate.

6. Soaking the wheat seeds in a saline brine or in copper sulfate (a process called "bluestoning") killed smut spores that could attack the wheat.

7. Wheat smut (sometimes called "bunt") is a parasitic fungus that attacks wheat plants.

8. Bran is the coarse outer covering of the wheat kernel removed in milling; shorts are fine pieces of bran and other fibers left behind after the grain is milled into flour.

9. Clear Creek runs across Jefferson County, the county where Mr. Ouellette's farm was located.

10. The South Platte River runs from Denver to the northeast corner of Colorado and beyond into the Great Plains; the Arkansas River is roughly parallel, running across southeastern Colorado and east into the plains. The "divide" is not the Continental Divide but the rolling grasslands between the two river valleys.

11. Fountain Creek, as it is known today, flows south from the Colorado Springs / Manitou Springs locality to Pueblo, where it joins the Arkansas River.

12. Per 100 pounds.

13. Hermann Jacob Damhorst was one of the three owners of H. Grone & Co., brewers and soda water manufacturers. The Grone brewery was on Clark Avenue in St. Louis. The other principals were John Whelan and Henry Grone. Damhorst, as noted in the introduction to this section, was a guest at the Manitou House at the same time as Amos Cummings.

14. Corn rust is another parasitic fungus.

15. These are varieties of potatoes. "Goodrich" is more commonly "Gooderich." The names are little used today.

16. Paris green, a copper- and arsenic-based compound, was used as a pigment in paint before it was found to be an effective insecticide. It is highly toxic.

17. Scullions (not scallions) were a problem of onion growers. The newsletter of a farmers' club in Illinois in 1869 carries the admonition "If you plant onion seed from scullions, you'll reap scullions."

18. Cocked hay is hay that has been cut and then arranged in small rounded piles that are subsequently moved to a barn or silo.

19. Fairplay is about sixty-five miles west-southwest of Denver in the Rocky Mountains in Park County (elevation is just under 10,000

feet). The town was founded in 1859 at the onset of the Colorado mining boom. Its population in 2000, according to the federal census, was
610. In 1870 the census listed 447 people for all of Park County. Today,
Fairplay may best be known as the model for the town of South Park,
Colorado, in the animated television series *South Park.*

THE PETRIFIED STUMPS.

Stone Trees in the Heart of the Rocky Mountains.

Judge Castello and His Wonderful Shirt—How to Find the Valleys of the Petrified Stumps—Wiping a Natural Curiosity from the Face of the East—Nature's Magnifying Glass—Rocks with Silver Linings.

Correspondence of The Sun.

MANITOU, Col., June 15.—I believe that a petrified stump, or a piece of a petrified stump, is to be found in every house or cabin within forty miles of Pike's Peak. Some citizens own several hundred pounds of these curiosities. They take great pride in exhibiting them to tourists, and they are always ready to sell them at a bargain or to give them away. These stumps come from a valley in the Rocky Mountains about thirty miles west of Pike's Peak. Last week your correspondent visited this valley. He drove through the celebrated Ute Pass, and lay over night at the residence of old Judge Castello,[1] thirty-seven miles from Colorado Springs.

A ROCKY MOUNTAIN JUDGE.

Judge Castello lives in a beautiful valley, near the foot of a pyramidal mountain. He was once the sheriff of St. Louis.[2] He is as portly as the Hon. Judge Anthony Hartman[3] of your city, but his nose is much larger and his face is more flushed, though he drinks less beer. Judge Castello keeps a house of entertainment for man and beast. His hotel is a modest unplanned one-story house, walled with illustrated papers, and comfortably furnished. His table is the best I have found in Colorado. The house contains but one bedroom, but that is always open to tourists, who are welcome for a night or two if they have an abundance of money; but no longer, as the Judge's good lady declares that she will have no New York boarders. The mansion is surrounded by a half dozen log cabins, which are the bedrooms of the teamsters who throng the road to Fairplay.[4] These wagoners sleep in their own blankets, and are given horse feed, victuals, and lodging for a fair remuneration. Tourists are charged more. I arrived at the Judge's at 3 P.M. and left at 8 o'clock the next morning. My bill was $11, but there were three in the party,[5] and it was worth something extra to gaze at the Judge and his museum. The latter consisted of nearly a thousand pounds of petrified wood, elk horns, and horns of Rocky Mountain rams. A pair of the latter weighed twenty pounds. The elk horns were of great size. A pair of them were nearly six feet high, and were branched out like the limbs of a gnarled oak. The Judge says he picked up these curiosities in the valley about his house. He don't know[6] who killed the animals, but he thinks it was the Indians.

THE PETRIFIED STUMPS.

The country is unsettled and the Judge has but few neighbors. The land, except on the edge of one or two little streams, is as dry as tinder. Trees are scarce. The principal crop appears to be prairie dogs. They turn out well, and can be raised without irrigation. The valleys are dotted with branded cattle, and wolves, bears, and occasionally mountain lions roam over them with impunity.

"The petrified stumps," said the Judge, "are over the hill there, about a mile and a half from here. Take that right-hand road that you see at the top of the hill, and you can't miss them. They are at the right hand of the road. You can tell the spot easy enough. At a distance it looks just as though somebody had been sprinkling lime around the stumps. Some travelers mistake them for kilns."

The Judge wore an old straw hat, a pair of slippers, gray pantaloons, and a collarless shirt, which, owing to the absence of suspenders, slumped heavily over the front of his breeches. As he waved my party a parting adieu he looked gloriously dignified. His form seemed bursting with legal lore.

Over the hill we went, and then down a gentle slope. A black, sluggish stream, about two feet wide, crawled through the valley. This we forded, sinking to the hubs[7] in the slimy mud. Ten rods further some gentleman had run a fence across the street, and had appropriated the road for three-quarters of a mile. We followed the line of the fence, driving carefully through fear that our horses might snap off their legs in the dog holes. A little hillock hove in sight on our right. There was a large chalky spot upon its side. We alighted, climbed the fence, and walked up the hill. A hundred prairie dogs scattered at our approach. The white spot was the remains of a petrified stump. Somebody had blasted it out, and the ground was covered with chunks of petrifaction. The hole was a good-sized one, and there was nothing but the roots left from the original stump. At the top of the hill we saw a small stump rearing its head from the ground. We made a rush for it, but it proved to be a genuine wooden affair, showing no signs of a change. On the other side of the hill we discovered a second stone stump. It had been shattered by the use of powder, and the earth was covered with its debris; but the body of the trunk remained, and the roots were not in sight.

THE GIANT OF THE STONE STUMPS.

Within a square of a half mile there were thirteen of these pet-rifactions. All but one had been ruined by curiosity seekers. That one had evidently been a tree of gigantic size. It stood at the foot of a picturesque ledge of rocks. The stump arose from the soil to the height of three feet, and it was at least ten feet in diameter. Though preserving the grain and even the color of the wood, it was a mass of solid stone. The heart of the tree bore a beautiful polish. The petrifaction was smooth and hard, and resembled the creamy whetstone that used to be so common in the East. It was more brittle, but it would sharpen a razor or a knife as quickly and as well as a whetstone. Where the sun had baked the wood dry and black before it was turned into stone the color and the almost imperceptible cracks in the grain of the wood were perfectly preserved. Some of the splinters of the stump seemed to have been rotten before petrifaction, and pre-sented a remarkable appearance. They were pure stone, but their edges were frayed like the chewed end of a rattan, and the stone was so thready and limber that in some cases it might be used as a paint brush. Most if not all the trees appeared to have been spruce or pine, though the large stump looked like the Southern cypress. The gum or rosin exuded from their trunks is petrified. It sparkled in the sun like tiny dewdrops. Occasionally, when pieces of the stone were cracked open, great flakes of petri-fied rosin were revealed. They encrusted the wood like frosted silver.

THE PETRIFIED CHIPS.

But our most singular discovery was a nest of petrified chips. Some of them were as large as a sheet of foolscap paper.[8] They seemed to have jumped red hot from the axe of a stalwart back-woodsman. Who made these chips is thus far an unanswered question. Their appearance warrants the assertion that some of the trees were cut down before they were petrified. If so, who swung the axe? The size of the chips precludes the idea of the use of a tomahawk. If the trees were chopped down by white men, who were they, and when did they visit the Territory? I have heard four theories advanced for the origin of these stone chips.

In 1805 Col. Pike[9] discovered the peak that bears his name. His party may have wandered into the mountains and leveled the trees; but if so, the trees must have been turned into stone within the last sixty-five years. Geologists laugh at this idea, but the appearances bear out the conjecture. I saw pieces of the stumps that seemed to be in a state of transition from wood to stone. But while petrified chips were plentiful, I could find no petrified bark. The surfaces of the trunks were as smooth and round as though they had been planed.

AN ANCIENT EXPEDITION.

The second theory is more interesting. It is known that after the conquest of Mexico an army of six hundred Spaniards, under a Col. Coronado,[10] swept up the valley of the Rio Grande and through Colorado in search of gold. Major Bigbe[11] of the *Pueblo Chieftain,* who has overhauled old Spanish documents, tells me that he thinks the party penetrated as far north as the Yellowstone region. However this may be, there is a possibility that Coronado's army may have visited the valley of the petri-fied stumps and laid low a few of the trees. This would allow nearly 250 years[12] for the petrifaction of the stumps and chips. If corpses petrify within ten or twenty years, as has frequently been the case in various parts of the United States, the stumps might easily have turned into stone since Coronado swept over the country, or even since the time that Pike was wandering around the head of the Arkansas.

Allowing either of these theories to be correct, neither Coronado nor Pike could have destroyed more than one or two of the trees, for the Hon. Mr. Swisler[13] of Manitou informs me that six years ago the most of the stumps were from ten to twelve feet high. Selfish curiosity seekers have blown them to pieces and lugged off the rarest specimens, thus destroying what in time might have turned out one of the most attractive spots in the Territory.

THE MYSTERIOUS RACE.

The stone chips are the subject of a third theory. They may have been made by either the mysterious race who built the wonderful aqueducts of the great Arizona desert,[14] or by the mound-builders of the West.[15]

Geologists say that the trees were turned into stone during the icy period of the earth's formation. They declare that the valley has at some time been filled with water strongly impregnated with the mineral substances of the mountains, and that this impregnation caused the petrifaction. This is a learned theory, but it doesn't account for the chips. Nor does it account for the petrified palm trees that were discovered at the foot of South Park[16] a few years ago. These trees, however, laid upon the surface of the ground, and might have floated where they were found. There is not a palm tree within hundreds of miles of the Territory.

SOIL AND CLIMATE OF THE PETRIFIED VALLEY.

The soil of the petrified valley is composed of grains of quartz and red sandstone from the size of a pinhead to that of a large white marble. Grass grows in dry tufts, dotting the red earth like the squares of a checker-board. Prairie dogs have preempted the land, and have a clear title to it. They appeared to be deeply interested in my researches, for they yelped continually, but scampered in all directions when I endeavored to form their acquaintance.

The air of the petrified valley is wonderfully soft, dry, and clear. Every breath expands the lungs and invigorates the system. The atmosphere is so clear that a visitor can hardly rid himself of the notion that he is looking through an immense magnifying glass. The snowy summit of Pike's Peak must be forty miles away. It does not appear to be over six. Rocks and trees a mile distant seem to be but a few rods off. But there were no trees, and the sun beat hot upon us. I could not have been warmer on the corner of Nassau and Fulton streets[17] during a hot day in July. Dead animals, however, never decay in the petrified valley. Their hides shrivel up and their remains gradually waste away without a scent until nothing but bleached bones are left. These become as hard and as brittle as the petrified stumps. Pieces of wood that have strewn the ground for years are as hard as flint. They will break and chip under the sharp blade of a knife, but no shavings can be whittled from them.

While the days are warm the nights are deliciously cool, but dews and fogs are unknown. Judge Castello, and the Judge won't lie, told me that he built a fire in a stove every day, except the Fourth of July, for the purpose of keeping the blood of his guests in circulation.

ROCKS WITH SATIN LININGS.

The ledge bordering the valley of the petrified stumps is worthy of mention. It contains layers of stone as thin as a plate and whiter than potter's clay. The stone is as light as a feather, and is easily broken. It is so thin and light that it reminded me of the sun-dried pieces of skulls scattered over the Indian mounds of Florida.[18]

Beyond this geological formation there is another equally remarkable. It is a layer of hard, cream-colored stone. When chipped or broken the grain looks like the finest satin. When shifted in the sun it shows a beautiful luster. Ladies declare that it would be a lovely color for a dress.

There are other groups of rock worthy the attention of geologists; but if scientific gentlemen wait to see the stumps, they can't come too soon, for herders and tourists are fast destroying them, and within five years they may be wonders to be talked about, but not seen.

NOTES

1. As noted in the introduction to this section of this book, the judge's name is James Costello, not Castello. Until 1876, St. Louis and St. Louis County were the same.

2. I could not verify that Mr. Costello had been a sheriff in St. Louis. However, the 1870 federal census does list the fifty-six-year-old James "Costello" as a resident of Fairplay, Colorado. He lived with his spouse and three children, ages twenty-four, twenty-one, and twelve. Costello was born in Kentucky, his wife in Pennsylvania, and all three children in Missouri. In 1870 his occupation was "land officer," his real estate was assigned a value of $1,500, and his personal estate was said to be $500.

3. Anthony Hartman was the justice for New York's Fourth District and was active in New York City politics, at times with the Tammany Democratic Party organization. He was well-known to Amos Cummings.

4. The distance from Florissant to Fairplay is about seventy-six miles; by trail it would have been much longer.

5. Presumably, the three were Amos and Frances Cummings and the driver of the buggy or wagon they were traveling in.

6. "Don't know," which is not Standard English, is probably a deliberate quote from Judge Costello.

7. The hubs on the wagon or buggy wheels.

8. In the United States in the mid-nineteenth century, foolscap was generally 8½ × 17 inches.

9. Zebulon Pike actually happened upon "Grand Peak" in 1806 when he was a lieutenant in the United States Army. The mountain later received his name. Eventually, he was promoted to captain, later colonel, and, in 1813, brigadier general.

10. Francisco Vázquez de Coronado indeed explored the southwest United States from 1540 to 1542 and reached the Great Plains, but not Pikes Peak.

11. This individual was Major T. O. Bigney (note spelling), a Civil War veteran who was with the *Colorado Daily Chieftain* in 1873 and later became editor of the *Huerfano Independent*. Among other things, he authored the book *A Month with the Muses: Colorado Tales and Legends of the Earlier Days, in Verse, and Some Fugitive Rhyming Lines*, which was self-published in Pueblo in 1875. It is one of the earlier books published in Colorado.

12. It actually had been 330 years since Coronado was in the western United States.

13. As noted in the introduction to this section, Marshal D. Swisher was co-owner of a livery stable in Manitou that also provided stagecoaches to take tourists around the area. He is listed as Marsh Swisher in the 1870 federal census. A native of Virginia, in 1870 he was thirty-two.

14. Most likely, Cummings was referring to the pre-Columbian Hohokam canals in Arizona, such as those near the Pueblo Grande site near Phoenix. They had been widely described in newspapers in the United States by the late 1860s. The name "Hohokam," however, was not in use until the early 1900s. I am grateful to Todd Bostwick of the Pueblo Grande Museum for this information.

15. "Mound-builders of the West" was a rarely used term. I think that Cummings was likening the "mysterious" builders of pre-Columbian earthworks in the West to the equally unknown (to the general public in 1873) mound-builders of the East. In both areas of the United States there was much speculation about who had built the ancient earthworks that could be seen across the landscape. The connection between those works and the ancestors of the American Indian societies who lived here in the nineteenth century had not been made.

16. The South Park locality is just southwest of Fairplay in the Rocky Mountains, about sixty-five miles west-southwest of Denver. Archaeologists have found that petrified wood from the fossil deposits there was chipped into tools by Native Americans. "Parks" are grassy basins found at various locations in the Rocky Mountains. South Park provided the name for the Emmy award–winning animated television show broadcast on Comedy Central and (as noted in the previous article) based on the town of Fairplay, Colorado.

17. The corner of Nassau and Fulton streets is in the center of Lower Manhattan two blocks from City Hall Park.

18. Earlier in 1873, Cummings had visited several Indian archaeological sites in the central St. Johns River Valley and Cape Canaveral areas of east Florida and witnessed the results of people haphazardly digging into them as they looked for relics.

THE TOWN IN THE DESERT.

A LASTING MONUMENT TO GOOD OLD HORACE GREELEY.

*On the Road to Utah—In the American Desert—
The Dinner at Delmonico's—Horace Greeley's Delight—A Fight
with Rumbirds—Land Secured—Dumped upon a Desert—
Curses and Lynch Law—All Hands Ahoy—Adobe House—
Uncle Meeker's Fate.*

Correspondence of The Sun.

CHEYENNE, Aug. 8.—In the fall of 1869 Horace Greeley[1] sent N. C. Meeker[2] to Utah to write up that Territory for the *Tribune*.[3] When Meeker arrived in this city he heard that there had been heavy snows in the mountains, and was told that it would be almost impossible for him to reach Salt Lake. He took [a] stage, and ran along the base of the Rocky Mountains down to Denver. Vast treeless plains swept away to the east like a boundless ocean, while the snowy range turreted the sky on the west. The land was as dry as ashes, and dotted with cactuses. It was seamed by three or four little streams that gushed from

193

great clefts in the mountains. A few cottonwood trees marked the course of these brooks, and nutritious grasses were rank upon the bottoms. The water descended from the mountains at a grade of a hundred feet per mile. Meeker had been an Illinois farmer. He had drawn in the theory of irrigation from the lips of Horace Greeley. He saw at a glance that the arid plains within a hundred miles of the Rocky range could be easily flooded by the water which was running to waste in the mountain streams. The land appeared to be entirely unproductive, but there were two or three ranches between Cheyenne and Denver, and Meeker's agricultural heart throbbed with joy as he gazed upon the great turnips, beets, and other vegetables exhibited by the ranchmen. The climate was delicious, and the distant mountain scenery unsurpassed. The nights were cool, the days were warm, there were no dews, and sickness was unknown.

A DINNER WITH HORACE GREELEY.

Meeker went East, determined to settle in Colorado. The odd sections of the land through which he had journeyed were a portion of the Denver Pacific Railroad grant. The even sections were reserved for preemption. After his return to the *Tribune* office Meeker thought that if he could get twenty or thirty persons to go out to the new Territory and all chip in together, the railroad land might be bought much cheaper and the expenses of building reduced. Of course he wanted none but sober, industrious folks, with a little ready money. While Meeker was thrashing around the *Tribune* office and expatiating upon the agricultural merits of the great American desert, Horace Greeley accidentally heard of his scheme. He invited Meeker to dinner at Delmonico's,[*] and listened to his plans over a bowl of mush and milk. Horace's weakness for colonies was well known. He had repeatedly tried them, and they had invariably failed; yet his faith in their ultimate success was never shaken.

"Meeker," said he, "I hear that you're going to start a colony out West. That's right. But don't have any fences or rum in it."

The idea of a colony based upon his pet theory of irrigation filled the old Chappaqua[5] farmer with delight. He rubbed his hand over his mush and milk, and horoscoped a wonderful agricultural future.

"Go ahead, Meeker," he continued. "Go ahead. Write an article showing what you purpose to do, and I will back it up in an editorial. You can have all the room you want in the *Tribune*, but don't have any fences or rum in it."

HORACE AT WORK.

Meeker went ahead. The next *Tribune* contained his programme. Here is an extract:

> I propose to unite with proper persons in the establishment of a colony in Colorado territory.
>
> The persons with whom I would be willing to associate must be temperance men, and ambitious to establish good society.
>
> My plan would be to make the settlement almost wholly in a village; all the lots of the village should be sold, that lands may be obtained for making improvements for the common good, such as the building of a church, a town hall, a schoolhouse, and for the establishment of a library. Adjoining the village, the outlying tracts could be apportioned, by lot or otherwise, in size according to distance from the village centre.
>
> Persons wishing to unite in such a colony will please address me at the *Tribune* office, stating their occupation and the value of the property which they could take with them.
>
> N. C. MEEKER.

Horace followed with one of his editorial ten-strikes,[6] in which he cautioned them to have "no fences or rum in it," and the scheme was fairly started. Meeker's faith was not very strong. He never expected more than twenty-five or thirty associates; but Horace kept banging away with wonderful effect, and pigeons began to drop in all directions. Letters poured in like an avalanche. From fifty to a hundred per day were received. They came from all sections of the Union. Even the British Empire was represented.

THE COOPER INSTITUTE[7] MEETING.

The iron got so hot that it became necessary to weld it. A meeting of the proposed colonists was called. It was held in room 24 [at the] Cooper Institute, Dec. 23, 1869. Over 150 persons were present. They came from within a radius of 300 miles, and most of them were strangers to each other. Horace Greeley presided, and made one of his characteristic speeches. He lauded the object of the association, but wanted the colonists not to have any fences or rum in it. Meeker followed in an enthusiastic address, and after him came Gen. Robert A. Cameron[8] of Elmira.[9] A colony was organized upon the spot. Meeker was chosen President, Cameron Vice-President, and Horace Greeley Treasurer. Members were required to pay $5 down for current expenses and to pledge themselves to come down with $150 for a purchase fund on the call of the Treasurer. The money was to be refunded if the land was not settled within a reasonable period. Fifty-nine members enrolled their names, and chucked $5 apiece into Horace's old felt hat. An executive committee was appointed to prepare the constitution and by-laws, and the colony was upon its legs.

The articles of association provide for a locating committee. Horace Greeley was to purchase and hold the lands in trust for the colony. The lands were to be deeded to the members whenever they entered upon them in good faith. None of them should sell any rum. This was to be specified in the deeds. It was to be generally understood that fences were a nuisance. Six hundred and forty acres of land were to be centrally located, and divided into business and residence lots. Ground was to be reserved for a public square, schools, churches, and other institutions. A town lot was to be sold to each member at a fixed valuation, and the proceeds devoted to improvements for the common welfare. Lands adjoining the town were to be divided into farms of five, ten, twenty, forty, and eighty acres, according to their distance from the town, and deeded one to each member, as they might choose or the committee direct. This was all there was of the scheme. The colony wanted only to control a large body of land by purchase and sale. After that every man was to attend to his own business, sell his land, improve or neglect it, just as he pleased; but no rum nor fences.

THE COMMITTEE ON THE PLAINS.

Meeker, Cameron, and H. T. West[10] were the locating committee. On Feb. 3, 1870, they set out in search for the promised land. Over 600 families had joined the colony, and 400 more were on the fence. The committee found that they would require more land than they had anticipated. From the time of their first entry into Colorado they had their eyes upon the site of the town of Greeley. It was near one of the finest little streams in the Territory, and the lay of the land was favorable for irrigation. But there was a drawback. The Denver Pacific Railroad had been built from Cheyenne to Evans,[11] a point on the Platte River,[12] four miles south of the coveted land. Like all border railroad towns it was a hard nut. Its admirers called it a small hell. Gov. Gilpin[13] offered to give the Greeley colony a large tract of land west of the railroad if they would drop down at Evans. The Governor knew that the colonists were sober, industrious people, and that their settlement would greatly increase the value of the land. They smelt rum and fences, and rejected the offer. A few of the people of Evans, hearing that the colony intended to locate upon the present site of Greeley, ran some preemption shanties on wheels over a ridge of land separating the two towns, and made locations. They knew that the Greeleyites would found a large town. They wanted to be on hand to sell them what was left of their stock of goods and liquors after the railroad had crossed the Platte and left Evans high and dry.

RUM BIRDS BARRED OUT OF PARADISE.

The Greeley committee sloped from the place. They floated down to the Fontaine-qui-Bouille, seventy-five miles south of Denver. They examined the land around Colorado Springs, and it was given out that they had finally determined to settle there. The Associated Press telegraphed a report over the country, and everybody in Colorado believed it. Thereupon the Evans skinners swore like troopers, drank up their remaining stock of whisky, and ran their wheeled shanties back to their little hell. Meanwhile the committee slipped back to the Platte, and purchased from the Denver Pacific Railroad, through the National Land Company, 9,324 acres of land for $81,058 cash. At the same time they took up 60,000 acres of Government land, paying the preliminary fees. This included the section that had been deserted by the Evans sharpers.

The trick was skillfully played. I presume that the Greeley committee greased the Government officials. Certain it is that the land office was suddenly filled with clerks, who began recording the claims of each individual member of the colony. These clerks worked in shifts night and day for seventy-two hours. During this time a shower of letters poured into the land office, but the officials were so busy that they could not get time to open them. After all the Greeley claims had been recorded and the preemption fees had been paid in, the letters were opened. They were written by the Evans sharps. These gentry had dropped upon the spot selected by the committee, and were putting in their claims by mail, hoping to secure some rare slices. Too late. The job was complete. The rum birds were shut out of the Greeley paradise, and the colony was ready for business.

THE FIRST SETTLERS.

The town was located on the 5th of April. The colonists were informed of the location by telegraph. Young Ralph Meeker, the son of the old man, began to distinguish himself. He had never been to Colorado, but he had heard his father speak of its beautiful mountain scenery, and he naturally supposed that the new town was a garden of Eden. He sat down in the *Tribune* office, and wrote a circular, which was scattered broadcast throughout the country. Young Ralph made large drafts upon his imagination. He spoke of the crystal brooks and cool mountain grottoes, and rung the changes upon the green meadows carpeted with delicate flowers of every hue and shade. He pictured whispering groves, silver-throated birds, and murmuring streams, swarming with speckled trout. The consequence was that the colonists began to rush for the glowing Utopia.

The first man on the ground was J. F. Sanborn.[14] He pitched his tent on the bank of the Cache-la-Poudre on April 18. On the following day the first lady stepped upon the soil. She was Mrs. Agnes A.G. Benson. Meeker immediately returned to New York to settle up his business preparatory to a final removal. Within two weeks over two hundred colonists arrived. Many of them came without tents or blankets, and were dumped upon a desert, without shelter. The winds of centuries had blown off the light soil, leaving a gravelly coating over all the surface not covered with grass or cactuses. There was but one building in the place and but one well. There was no protection against the cold night air.

TALK OF TAR AND FEATHERS.

Not a tree could be seen away from the banks of the river. Mountain scenery was abundant, but it was sixty miles away. The wind sifted the white dust into the eyes of the new comers, and occasionally one of them sat down upon a cactus, which had hardly a soothing effect. If the colonists had been left on the sands of the Sahara they could not have been more disappointed.

In vain they looked for young Ralph's crystal brooks and mountain grottoes. They pointed to the fields of prickly cactuses, and wanted to know if these were the green meadows and whispering trees. None of them understood irrigation. Their indignation flamed out in bitter charges of fraud and deception. It was fortunate for poor Meeker that he was absent. Lynch law was threatened, and old Horace himself would have been furnished with a coat of tar and feathers if he had made his appearance. Many of the colonists spent a day upon the ground cursing and swearing and departed by the next train. Some took one look at the scene and left without getting off from the cars. Fifty left in one day, cursing at every jump. Old Gen. Cameron was the only officer on the ground. He was a broad-shouldered philosopher, and stood a fearful amount of reviling. He told the discontented ones that it was his business to select the land, and it was their business to make the town. He got some of them to work upon a ditch to supply the soil with water. This ditch was nine miles long and twenty feet wide on the bottom.

ALL HANDS AHOY.

But there was a scarcity of building materials. Lumber was worth almost its weight in silver. Bricks could not be obtained at anything like a reasonable price. Some of the party bought a few deserted shanties in Evans, and toted them up to Greeley on wheels.

Meeker did not arrive until weeks had passed. He had been detained in New York by the sickness of a son.[15] He brought the invalid with him, but the poor boy soon wasted away. It was the first death in the little town. The father is a man of tireless energy. He appreciated the situation, and saw what was wanted. His advice was "stop growling and go to work." He himself set the example. "If we can't buy brick," said he, "we must make them." The big ditch was soon completed, and the pure water began to dance through the flume. Meeker went to puddling in the mud. He began to turn out sun-dried brick. He worked night and day, and a fair adobe house began to rise from the ground. The people caught his spirit. The cry was, "All hands ahoy!" Houses sprang up like magic. The town was laid out a mile square, with streets a hundred feet wide. They were flanked by ditches of clear water and broad sidewalks. Young trees were planted everywhere—along the streets and sidewalks, in private gardens and on the public square. A town hall was built. Before the end of the year a second ditch twenty-eight miles long was completed, and water was plentiful. Two artificial lakes were formed. The cactuses were uprooted, and beautiful gardens turned their faces to the sun. Nor were the farmers idle. Their fat flocks grazed on the rich bottoms, while they were ploughing up the virgin soil and putting in their crops, and building their barns and houses.

THE RESULT.

Three years have passed. The trees are branching into beautiful shade trees, and the town is certainly the handsomest little place in Colorado. It contains over 2,000 people. All the land is taken up, and $96,000 has been paid in by the colonists for land alone. Much more has been spent, however. The ditches, mostly built the first year, cost $60,000. A mill-power canal, a mile and a half wide, has been dug at a cost of $8,000, and a fine mill erected. The logs are cut in the mountains, and are floated down the river. Every farm and each village garden has its little irrigating ditches, all fed from the big canals. The whole colony, forty square miles, is fenced in, and the place is thriving like a green bay tree. In 1872 the colony produced 50,000 bushels of wheat alone. Many of the farmers produce thousands of dollars worth of butter and cheese. The most of them own houses in the town. After their crops are gathered they move from the farm to the town, and spend their winters in listening to lectures and in dancing and other social amusements. One winter Horace

Greeley visited them, and was overjoyed to find neither rum nor fences. The land has greatly increased in value. The Union Pacific is building a railroad between Julesburg and Golden,[16] which passes directly through Greeley, thus opening to them the Colorado coal beds. The track at this point is already graded. There are seven or eight churches in the place, all erected on land given by the colony.

THE RED HOT AUGERS.

The ditches can irrigate 60,000 acres of land. Water may be taken from the artificial lakes in case the Cache-la-Poudre runs short. The farmers generally turn the water upon their land in the fall and let it stand. The soil is plowed in the spring, and produces better crops on account of its soaking. When the lakes were filled from the river, thousands of fish were swept into them. The fishing is now said to be excellent. In the winter the river is nearly dry. It is at its flood in the heat of summer, when the water is most needed. This is owing to the melting of the snow in the mountains. Rain occasionally falls during the summer. The storms are of fearful grandeur. I was caught in one of them. The Rocky Mountains became as black as ink and vivid bolts of lightning flew about their summits. It looked as though a legion of devils were boring into the ledge with red hot augers. A dozen showers could be seen chasing each other along the foot of the mountain. Finally they concentrated in the valley of the Cache-la-Poudre, and swept down upon us at the rate of three miles a minute. The heavens were opened, and for three hours it rained pitchforks. The Cache-la-Poudre gets its name from the fact that some United States soldiers hid several kegs of powder along its banks during an Indian war years ago.

MEEKER'S TROUBLES.

Of course there was trouble in the Greeley paradise. Some men didn't like Meeker, and some didn't like the other officials. The officers resigned twice, and new elections were held. A lady told me that she couldn't bear the Meekers because Mrs. Meeker and the girls dressed so queer. "Why do you know," said she, "that I've seen them out summer nights, going to a lecture, wearing heavy winter clothing. I can't bear such people." The trouble seems to be that the Meekers are a hard-working family, with a way of openly expressing their opinions. Sometimes this is done so bluntly and plainly, and hits so hard, that a few of the colonists imagine they have been punched in the head, and want to get up on their muscle. All, however, agree that Meeker has been strictly honest. His is far from being the best plot in town. In fact he has been too honest for his own good. He has nearly run himself into the ground, and is worth much less than he was when he first came out to Greeley. The colony does not feel his influence so much as at first because they can get along without it. His house is very plain, and his garden was choked with weeds. I was told that he had actually been forced to leave the colony that he had created and go to work in New York City to earn sufficient to keep himself going. The family are all great workers.

One cause of the old man's weakness was his support of Horace Greeley for President. He went in for honest Horace with all his soul, and the columns of the *Greeley Tribune*[17] sparkled with Horatian fire. But his colony went back on him. With all their hatred of rum they liked Grant[18] better than Greeley. A new paper—the *Greeley Sun*[19]—was started in opposition to Meeker's paper. Its editor was W. B. Vickers,[20] a friend of Senator Morton,[21] and formerly editor of the Indianapolis *Journal.*[22] Vickers made the fur fly. Young Ralph[23] was in his element, and scratched back. Since that time the air has been filled with music, both of them holding their own. Meeker's newspaper, however, lost caste by its support of Mr. Greeley. It still keeps its feet, but the Grantites cannot forgive it, and have transferred their patronage to THE SUN which shines for all.[24] The Meekers are full of backbone, and are determined to fight it out to the last.

INJUSTICE OF CORRESPONDENTS.

Greeley people complain of the injustice of newspaper correspondents. Not one in twenty of the correspondents visit the place. They look at it from cars, and then write letters lampooning the little town unmercifully. Even Nordhoff[25] gazed only at the lumber yards on the east, and then claimed to know all about it, writing a report that the people say disgraced himself more than the town. The Colorado newspapers are eternally making fun of Greeley. The impression that it is a city of long-haired fanatics and free lovers, though general, is a false impression. Passengers on the Denver Pacific look at each other and laugh when the brakemen shout "Greeley." All sorts of stories are afloat. A man told me that Meeker rang a big bell at noon, and the colonists all assembled in the Town Hall. Meeker then read several chapters from the "Tribune Almanac," a white-coated fanatic sang a hymn, and a strong-minded woman delivered an address. Each member was then served with a bowl of bran and milk, after which the party went to the sidewalk to discuss social problems.

The truth of the matter is that the people of Greeley are honest, hardworking, intelligent people. I didn't see a lazy man in the place. They own the finest hall in the territory. It was the only town I visited in which nobody attempted to swindle me. The hotel gave me a better dinner than I could get in Denver, and at one-half the price. The village was shady and pleasant, and the people affable and obliging. I saw no rum and but few fences. The farms were groaning with grain, the cattle fat, the butter was good, the cream unsurpassed, the beets were of enormous size, the flowers of the sweetest perfume, the girls beautiful and neatly dressed, and the men highly intellectual and entertaining. No tourist should leave Colorado without visiting Greeley. It is an easy thing to reach the mountains in the vicinity of Long's Peak, where there is the finest scenery in the Rocky Mountains.

THE SUN did well in dropping the proposed monument to good old Horace Greeley. In time to come the noble city of Greeley will be his statue. It will be a living monument, and one as lasting as the fame of the lamented philosopher himself.

NOTES

1. Horace Greeley, son of a Vermont farmer, had considerable national clout prior to his death in November 1872. In that year he was both the Liberal Republican Party's presidential candidate and the Democratic Party's candidate. Even so, he was trounced by Ulysses S. Grant. He died prior to the counting of Electoral College votes.

2. Nathan Cook Meeker (1817–1879) was Greeley's agricultural editor at the *Tribune*. He died in Colorado while serving as agent to the White River Ute Indians. The Indians killed him after Meeker plowed under a horse racetrack the Utes had been using.

3. Greeley's newspaper, the *New York Tribune*, was a rival of Cummings's *New York Sun*. Cummings, as noted in the introduction to this book, had worked for Greeley at the *Tribune* early in his career as a journalist.

4. Delmonico's was New York City's most famous restaurant for nearly a century. Its location in Manhattan changed several times before it finally closed in 1923, a victim of Prohibition.

5. Greeley's home was in Chappaqua, New York, north of New York City in Westchester County. He was known to commute to Manhattan to the *Tribune* office. Today Chappaqua is the home of Senator Hillary Clinton and former president Bill Clinton.

6. This term is taken from bowling and means a remarkably successful act.

7. The building, part of Cooper Union, is in east Greenwich Village in New York City. It is listed on the National Register of Historic Places.

8. General Cameron (1828–1894) was a veteran of the Civil War, serving in the United States Army. He also was involved in the founding of Colorado Springs and Fort Collins.

9. Elmira, New York, is about thirty miles west of Binghamton in Chemung County.

10. Henry T. West.

11. Evans, founded in 1867 in Weld County, was named for Colorado territorial governor John Evans (1814–1897). He served as governor from 1862 to 1865.

12. Evans is on the South Platte River.

13. William Gilpin (1812–1894) was Colorado's first territorial governor, during the period 1861–1862. He was, of course, no longer the sitting governor at the time of the Greeley colony.

14. John F. Sanborn, who is credited with laying out the town, later ran a life and fire insurance business in Greeley. He died in 1876. He is not connected to the Sanborn Map Company, maker of maps for fire insurance purposes.

15. His son, George Meeker, had contracted tuberculosis back in Ohio, probably while his family was living in Trumbull Phalanx, another utopian community.

16. Julesburg is in northeastern Colorado, and Golden is west of Denver. The railroad from Julesburg, a station on the transcontinental Union Pacific Railroad, to Greeley was completed after Cummings was in Colorado.

17. Founded in 1870, the *Tribune* is still published today.

18. U. S. Grant, as noted above, defeated Greeley in the 1872 presidential election.

19. The *Sun*, in various guises, continued into the early twentieth century before ceasing publication.

20. William B. Vickers later was the author of *History of the City of Denver, Arapahoe County, and Colorado* (1880).

21. Oliver P. Morton (1823–1877), a Republican from Indiana, served in the United States Senate from 1867 until his death. From 1861 to 1867 he had been Indiana's governor.

22. The *Journal* later was merged with other papers. Its modern-day relative is the *Indianapolis Star.*

23. Ralph Meeker, Nathan Meeker's son.

24. "It shines for all" was the slogan on the *New York Sun*'s masthead.

25. Charles Nordhoff (1830–1901) wrote for the *New York Evening Post.* He also wrote books, including *Communistic Societies in the United States* (1875), which focused on utopian communities.

Underlying Wealth

OLD! A DECADE AFTER THE FORTY-NINERS RUSHED TO California, the fifty-niners descended on the gulches of Colorado. In the mid-nineteenth century, stories of gold and silver, even rumors, did more to bring people to the West than did any guidebook or chamber of commerce tourism campaign. Fueled by the gold rush, the Front Range of Colorado's Rocky Mountains changed overnight as mining camps and towns with names like Golden and Gold Hill sprang up. Some lasted, but others faded away, leaving decrepit buildings to be turned into theme ghost towns for modern tourists. Not only did

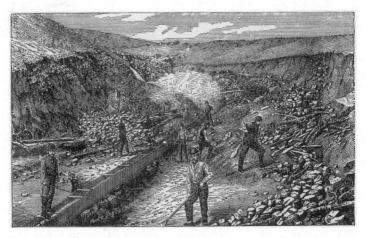

INITIALLY IN COLORADO, GOLD WAS MINED BY DEPOSITING GRAVEL IN SLUICES
(GULCH MINING). (FOSSETT, *COLORADO*, 202)

prospectors head for California and Colorado, they also sought
wealth in Montana, Idaho, Utah, and Nevada.

Fourteen years after the initial discovery of gold in Colorado,
Amos Cummings arrived on the scene, intending to hear and
see what all the hullabaloo was about. In 1873, both in Colorado
and in Utah, it was difficult to ignore the tales of gold and silver
strikes and lost prospectors, as well as the longer, more complicated stories about mining operations, claim jumpers, court
suits, crooked judges, greedy bankers, and corruption. Gold and
silver were on everyone's mind, sometimes causing investors to
leap before they looked.

The gold rush in the Rocky Mountains initially was not as
fiscally dramatic a phenomenon as in California. In Colorado,
placer mining—panning for gold in gravel deposits in rivers—
paid fewer rewards than in California. Both Colorado and Utah
miners faced a much more arduous task: smashing, heating, and
treating tons of rock to separate out the precious gold and silver.
As Cummings relates, it was hard work. Partially smelted ore
from Colorado and Utah was even shipped as far as the United

MOST MINING, HOWEVER, WAS COMPLEX WORK AND REQUIRED SMELTING ORES. THIS IS A SMELTER AT LEADVILLE, COLORADO, ONE OF THE BOOMTOWNS BUILT ON MINING. (FOSSETT, *COLORADO*, 427)

Kingdom where the smelters could extract the metals. Grizzled prospectors with a mule and a tin pan did not last long in parts of the West. Even so, fortunes in gold and silver were indeed made.

In the three articles in this section Cummings focuses on prospectors, prospecting, and mining. The first article, date-lined Colorado Springs, July 1 (1873), recounts a long story told to Cummings by none other than Wilbur Fisk Stone. Stone, at the time a resident of Pueblo, Colorado, was born in Connecticut. He received a law degree in 1858 at Indiana State University at Bloomington.

Like many other adventurers in 1860, Stone was drawn to Colorado and the stories of gold. He did not find much success as a miner but stayed to pursue other interests, including serving as a newspaperman. At the time he was interviewed by Cummings in 1873, Stone was an editor with the *Pueblo People* newspaper, which he had helped to found in 1871. The paper, a source of heavily Democratic news and commentary about Colorado, continued to be published in Pueblo until 1875. Stone, for a time, also was an editor on the staff of the *Pueblo Chieftain* newspaper in that same town.

As Cummings notes, in addition to his journalistic activities, Stone practiced law in Pueblo. His professional advertisements appear in many issues of the *Chieftain*. Stone also was a pillar of the Pueblo community, serving on the school board as well as representing the town's and county's interests in various political endeavors.

Stone eventually became a major figure in Colorado. Among other things, he was elected to the Colorado Supreme Court. Stone also was a prolific author, sometimes writing under the pseudonym "Dornick." He is best known for his four-volume *History of Colorado*, published in 1918. That major contribution to Colorado's past remains a mainstay for historical research. Stone died in 1920.

Stone's lengthy anecdote relates the adventures of Robert McGonigle, whom Stone says he first met in 1860 in Colorado. Stone tells Cummings that "Mack," as McGonigle was known, may have been from Ohio and that he had received a degree from Oberlin College in Oberlin, Ohio. I checked with Tammy L. Martin of the Oberlin College Archives Office, who said nothing could be found showing that Robert McGonigle ever attended or graduated from that institution. She pointed out that in the 1850s there were several technical/trade institutions that were not affiliated with Oberlin College but were also located in Oberlin, Ohio, including the Oberlin Business College.

I also checked the federal census records to see if I could find Robert McGonigle's family in Ohio (or elsewhere; although McGonigle is not a common name, there are a number of McGonigle families listed in the 1870 federal census in the Midwest and East). I located several families or groups of families that may have been McGonigle's relatives. The first is the McGonigle families living in and around the unincorporated southwest Ohio town of McGonigle in the mid-nineteenth century. The town, named for Philip McGonigle, is in Butler County, home to Miami University. Thinking that Robert McGonigle may have been from that locality and attended Miami University, rather than Oberlin, I checked with officials there. But they have no record of such a person. The second possibility, in Ashley, Ohio, in Delaware County, was headed by fifty-three-year-old Robert McGonigle. Mr. McGonigle was a farmer whose net worth is listed as $17,230, no small sum at the time. However, it is unlikely, but not impossible, that that particular individual and his wife (Almira, age fifty at the time of the census) were Robert's parents. In 1870 they had two other boys, ages twenty-two and nineteen, and it seems doubtful that they would have had another son who was in his thirties in that year.

Another candidate for Robert McGonigle's family is the one listed in the 1870 census (but not the 1860 census) from Wisconsin. In 1870 the McGonigle family headed by John McGonigle (age sixty) lived in Grant County. I also found records from 1861 telling of a Robert F. McGonigle living in Lancaster in the same county who enlisted in the U.S. Army that year. According to Civil War documents, Robert served in Company F of the Third Wisconsin Infantry and was captured in 1862 in Virginia. In 1864 he was back in Wisconsin and mustered out of the army. Could he be the Robert "Mack" McGonigle whose adventures Wilbur Stone relates in Cummings's story?

"The Story of Little Emma," the third article in this section, was written while Cummings was in New Smyrna (now New Smyrna Beach), Florida, in spring 1874, having returned from his western trip four months earlier. As he notes in the article, he had visited Salt Lake City the previous August, when he heard firsthand about the scandals surrounding the Little Emma mine (actually a mining district). Like the other articles written from Florida in 1874, Cummings wrote about Little Emma under his pseudonym, "Ziska."

I believe Cummings was prompted to write the article after having read an earlier article in the April 8, 1874, issue of the *Sun* titled "The Yield of Little Emma; Honest Miners' Camp Sympathetically Described," attributed to the "Washington Correspondence of the Inter-Ocean." The *Inter-Ocean* was a newspaper published in the last quarter of the nineteenth century in Chicago. A copy of that article is pasted in one of Cummings's scrapbooks in the New York Public Library. By the time the *Inter-Ocean* article appeared, there also had been coverage in other newspapers and magazines of Little Emma and the mine's role in fleecing unwary British investors.

Two years after Cummings's article appeared in the *Sun* the United States Congress would hold hearings on the scam perpetrated on those unwitting British investors involved with the Little Emma mine. By that time the mine in the Little Cottonwood mining district east of Salt Lake City had become infamous as an example of the illegal lengths to which mining speculators went to induce investors with deep pockets to part with millions of dollars (or British pounds). The lure of silver, like that of gold, put stars in the eyes of people seeking to get rich quickly.

Having read the Little Emma article in the *Sun*, and probably having seen other newspaper coverage as well, Cummings may have felt that he had additional firsthand information about the mine and the scandal that people would want to know. He was right; Little Emma was big news. Some historians, such as Hubert Howe Bancroft, have labeled Little Emma one of the biggest mining swindles in U.S. history.

That Cummings was able to write the story while in Florida suggests both that he received copies of the *Sun* while in Florida (via the U.S. mail?) and that he had his notes from the western trip with him. Perhaps he already had written part of the story.

Cummings was careful to protect his source for the Little Emma article. The person he interviewed was said to be "the only man . . . in Salt Lake City . . . [who was there from the beginning] and can give a connected and accurate account of Emma Mine." After completing my initial annotations on the Emma article, I set out to identify that person. Based on Charles L. Keller's comprehensive 2001 book, *Lady in the Ore Bucket*, I drew up a list of three suspects, one of whom was Joseph Wilde.[1] Then I surfed the Internet to see if I could get more information. Bingo! My search quickly led me to an auction house notice from 2003 that offered for sale a certificate for 1,000 shares in the New York and Utah Prospecting and Mining Company. The certificate was issued to Abram Quereau in 1867. That company, incorporated in New York, as well as the name Quereau, figures in Cummings's account, in which his informant calls the New York and Utah Prospecting and Mining Company "our organization." And the signer of the certificate? It was the president of the mining company, none other than Joseph Wilde, who was a New Yorker and one of my three candidates for interviewee. So Wilde was Cummings's source in 1873 for the story.

Wilde apparently was not a full-time resident of Salt Lake City or even Utah. I could not find him anywhere in Sloan's *Gazeteer* [*sic*]. However, some of the other principals mentioned in Cummings's article were local Salt Lake City residents or they lived elsewhere in Utah and their names are found in that directory. Apparently, Wilde just happened to be in Salt Lake City at the same time as Cummings.

The first of the three articles in this section, "The Fate of a Gold Seeker," was published in the *Sun* on July 28, 1873, whereas the second, "In the Golden Gulches," was in the same paper on July 31, 1873. "The Story of Little Emma," written much later, appeared in the *Sun* on April 30, 1874.

NOTE

1. I also use Keller's book to identify other of the principals mentioned in the article on the Little Emma mine. Another useful source

was *Gazeteer [sic] of Utah and Salt Lake City Directory, 1874* (compiled and edited by Edward L. Sloan and published in that same year; a copy is on microfilm in the New York Public Library). Cummings's account of the Little Emma mine contains additional details about the ins and outs of the history of early mining in the Little Cottonwood/ Alta locale.

THE FATE OF A GOLD SEEKER.

Surprising Adventures of an Oberlin Graduate.

Lost in the Rocky Mountains—The Discovery near Fort Garland—Ho, for the Rio Grande—Fighting Death by Inches—The Humane Ute—Starting for the Great Canyon of the Colorado—The Gold Diggings in the Crater of a Volcano— Disappearing in the Deserts of Arizona.

Correspondence of The Sun.

COLORADO SPRINGS, July 1.—I received the particulars of the fate of Robert McGonigle from the lips of Wilbur F. Stone of the *Pueblo People.*[1] Mr. Stone is a lawyer. His legal duties forbid his writing poor McGonigle's history. Believing that the story of the life of this extraordinary man will interest the readers of THE SUN, I give it as it was told me in Mr. Stone's little law office, a block above the Lindell Hotel in Pueblo.[2] The day was very hot, but the office stood in the shade of a few thriving cottonwood trees, and a cool breeze poured into the room through the open windows. Mr. Stone sat with his heels upon a square table. After listening to the shrill piping of a Mexican locust,[3] which had alighted upon the door sill, the lawyer said:

HO, FOR THE LAND OF GOLD!

"You have been in Colorado long enough to know that Fifty-Niners[4] are the salt of the Territory—the old *noblesse* of the country. Citizens look upon them with awe; at least the '59ers think they do. I'm no Fifty-Niner, I crept over the plains with an army of Pike's Peakers in the spring of 1860. If you remember, gold was first discovered on Cherry Creek, the site of the city of Denver.[5] I shoved for the Cherry Creek diggings. Everybody flocked there who came across the plains. It was a prairie sea-port town, where the gold seekers hauled down their sails after a long voyage and awaited a favorable wind. I got there in the latter part of April. Such a crowd I had never seen before. It was gathered from all parts of the earth. The new comers were crazy after gold. Their lips grew feverish, and a fitful light danced in their eyes when they talked about it. Many of them slept upon the plain wrapped in their blankets. Some lived in holes covered with logs, brush, and dirt. Others had tents. A few aristocrats owned log cabins, plastered and roofed with mud. At that time the main diggings were located in Gregory Gulch, where Black Hawk[6] is now situated; in California Gulch, over near Oro,[7] around the head of the Arkansas; Tarryall,[8] in South Park; and on Blue River, west of the snowy range, in Summit County, near Breckinridge.[9] The Cherry Creek diggings had petered out when I reached them. I had been there about five days when I first met Robert McGonigle.

WHO McGONIGLE WAS.

"I can't positively say where he was born, but I think it was somewhere in Ohio. His parents were Irish. He had a magnificent education, and was a man of marvelous ability. I know that he was a graduate from Oberlin, for I have his diploma. He told

THE TOWN OF BLACK HAWK IN GILPIN COUNTY, COLORADO, GREW UP AROUND
GREGORY GULCH, WHERE GOLD WAS DISCOVERED. (FOSSETT, *COLORADO*, 302)

me that he had been teaching school down in Tennessee. His
abolition tendencies had offended his patrons, and he was forced
to return North. I can't remember how we became acquainted.
We were both suffering from the gold fever. Mack had it bad. He
had spent his last cent in getting to Pike's Peak, but was not dis-
couraged and seemed full of hope. I had mighty little money—
two or three hundred dollars or so. The crowds at the diggings
were boiling over with excitement. They were stirred up by all
sorts of gold reports. The air was full of rumors. Each story
drew off a little knot of miners, and they began to scatter over
the Territory. A vague hint of discoveries of surpassing richness west of the headwaters of the Arkansas created a stampede.
We naturally supposed that the new mines were near the Grand
River, or on Rock Creek and Roaring Fork, both tributaries of
that stream. Grand River rises at the western base of Long's
Peak, flows down the Pacific slope in a south-west direction,
and enters Utah about the middle of the boundary between the
two Territories.[10] It runs many hundred miles through a country
at that time entirely unknown, and empties into the Colorado
near the Arizona line. It is west of the snowy range of the Rocky

Mountains. This is called the main range, and can be crossed only in summer. To this day there are no roads in the Grand River country, and but few if any Indian trails.

OFF FOR THE NEW EL DORADO.

"Well, we heard the most glowing reports of these new diggings. A half-dozen miners had discovered a valley sprinkled with free gold, and were keeping it all to themselves. They were taking out thousands of dollars a day. It was a wild story, but everybody took stock in it. Mack started at once. His first objective point was Tarryall. I had blindly invested a small amount of money in a few claims near that place and hired two men to develop them. I accompanied them, and overtook McGonigle on the way. He had associated himself with a bright young fellow from Boston, and both were afoot pegging for Tarryall with all their might. As my claims looked scaly[11] I went with Mack and his partner. They were bound to cross the range, and drop upon the rich gold fields that the mysterious miners were working. The Bostonian put off on the instant, without waiting for Mack, who had no outfit.[12] I never knew what became of the Boston man. I have even forgotten his name. Alive or dead, he never turned up. He was either starved to death or scalped. The next day Mack ran against an Irishman named Brady,[13] who was hot for the shadowy diggings. I told Mack that I would furnish him with an outfit, and he could join Brady. I was to go snacks[14] in any discovery that was made. Mack snapped at the offer. I procured his outfit, and he and Brady were off without delay. I was to await their return in Tarryall. My claims were worthless, and before they came back I was earning my victuals by the day's work.

THE SEARCH FOR GOLD.

"McGonigle's outfit was a pick, a shovel, prospecting pan, blanket, an old oyster can with a wire bale,[15] eight or ten pounds of bacon, and a dozen pounds of flour. That was all. No gun, no pistol, no coffee, even no matches. I lent him a sun glass,[16] and with that he used to light his fires. He toasted his bacon on a stick which he held over the coals. He mixed his flour in the old oyster can, flattened the dough with his fist, cut it into strips, wound the strips around a stick the same as a hunter would wind a rag around a ramrod, and then baked them in the fire. Well, they left Tarryall about the 1st of June, crossing the snowy range below Mount Lincoln, over 17,000 feet above sea level,[17] and descended into California Gulch. They next climbed the range dividing the waters of the Atlantic and Pacific, and made for the Grand River. There were neither roads nor paths. Day after day they stumbled over rocky mountains and crept through gloomy cañons, panning for gold. They reached the Grand River Valley and scratched the beds of all its streams and brooks, but found no gold. They explored the rough country about Gunnison River,[18] and went as far west as the Uncompahgre Mountains.[19] They searched every gulch and bar, hoping to discover the miners who were taking out thousands of dollars a day, but they never found them. Everywhere they sifted dirt with the same unvarying result. You must remember that they were not the only prospectors looking for the hidden mines. Probably a hundred men were roaming over the vast area beyond the main range. The majority were wandering on their own hook. Each was eager to unearth deposits that would astonish the world, and wanted to keep their whereabouts a secret as long as possible. Occasionally two, three, yes, a half dozen miners were banded together pledged to share each other's luck. Some fell sick and died. Others, with plenty of game around them, starved to death. Two parties were ambuscaded in Dead Man's Gulch[20] and scalped by Indians.

LOST IN THE ROCKY MOUNTAINS.

"Well, Brady and Mack examined the country to their satisfaction. It was evident that the whole thing was humbug. Their

CANYON OF THE UNCOMPAHGRE RIVER IN SOUTHWEST COLORADO. AT THE TIME MCGONIGLE WAS THERE, THIS RELATIVELY ISOLATED REGION ALREADY WAS ATTRACTING MINERS. (FOSSETT, *COLORADO,* 533)

provisions were exhausted, and they headed for the plains. The dividing range was recrossed. Through pathless valleys and over snow-capped mountains they struggled, subsisting on wild berries. They lost their reckoning, and had but little idea of their position. I presume that they were some distance north-west of the Saguache Mountains.[21] Brady thought that by bearing off to the left they might find a stream that emptied into the Arkansas. If so, they could follow the creek to its outlet, and reach the plains through the Arkansas Cañon.[22] He wanted to strike out across the ruggedest and most forbidding mountains in quest of such a stream. McGonigle objected. He believed that they were further south than they imagined, and if they kept to the right he was sure that they would run upon a trail or road that would lead them to Fort Garland.[23] That would be near the New Mexican boundary, about forty miles west of the Spanish Peaks.[24] Both men were starving, but they could come to no agreement. When Brady got the lead he sheered to the left, and when McGonigle was in front he edged to the right. Starvation was bad enough, but they encountered another hardship. They were caught in a snowstorm, and narrowly escaped freezing to death. Over a week had they lived upon berries and stumbled toward the plains when Mack became very sick. They had slept on a mountain near timber line, and he was chilled to the bone. On the previous day he ate a great deal of snow and chewed roots dug from the ground. This gave him violent cramps in the stomach. Eight days they had gone to bed supperless, and risen without breakfast. The strain upon Mack's constitution was too much, and he gave out.

THE STRUGGLE FOR LIFE.

"That morning he unrolled himself from his blanket in a pitiable plight. He was doubled up with pain, and could scarcely move. Brady seems to have made up his mind that his comrade was going to die. He looked at him for some minutes as though undecided whether to abandon or stick to him. Finally he threw his blanket over his shoulder, and moved over the hill. As he reached the summit he looked back at his suffering friend and shouted, 'Come on, Mack!' Ten seconds later his head disappeared behind the mountain, and poor Mack was alone. Brady had his own way at last. He sagged to the left, and shoved for the head waters of the Arkansas. Well, in about an hour Mack began to recover. The cramps ceased. He got upon his feet; left pick, shovel, and pan behind him; and staggered over the hill. The sun came out warm and bright, and a healthy glow drove away his chilliness. He shouted for Brady, but received no answer. Thinking his partner lost, he spent several hours hallooing and endeavoring to find him. The truth dawned upon him at last. Brady had deserted him. Then Mack went his own way. He bore to the right and struck for the Fort Garland trail. Toward evening he got into a cañon and followed it several miles. His passage was barred by a wall of rock several hundred feet high. There was no outlet, and he was compelled to retrace his steps. He found no berries that day, but afterward he told me that he didn't feel very bad about it because he had no appetite. That night he slept between two rocks at the entrance of the cañon. Up early in the morning, he clambered a steep hill, and saw the sun rise a little to the left of a high mountain capped with snow. The air was very clear, and the mountain appeared to be but a few miles away. Mack determined to climb it, thinking that he might catch a glimpse of the plains from its peak, or see some brook or road that would lead him to civilization. He found a few berries during the day, but it was night before he began to ascend the mountain. Long after dark he rolled himself in his tattered blanket, sleeping in a windfall on the side of the range.

THE DISCOVERY NEAR FORT GARLAND.

"You have seen windfalls—where the wind has blown down acres of trees in the mountains. The trees are all dead, and all lie in one direction. They are common enough to this country. As I was saying, Mack passed the night in this windfall. By daylight he was again pushing his way to the top of the mountain. He reached the peak about noon. A glorious valley lay before him. It seemed to be about a hundred miles long and from forty to fifty wide. It bore a large lake upon its bosom. Mack had heard of Saguache lake.[25] He knew that it was in the San Luis Park.[26] The park and the lake were below him. He had been told that there was a road leading from Fort Garland to the San Luis Valley. If he ever reached the fort it must be by that road. So he went down into the valley.

"What happened after that," said Mr. Stone. "I don't know. Mack himself couldn't remember. All that is certain is that eight days after he and Brady had separated Mack was picked up in the San Luis Valley, sixty miles from Fort Garland, in a dying condition. He was found by a party of United States officers who were on a hunt. One of them heard moans along the road, and sent a soldier to ascertain the cause. Mack was borne to the fort and received the best attention. It was several days before he recovered consciousness. His first inquiry was concerning the gold mines. The fever was burning in his veins as fiercely as ever. The report of rich discoveries west of the Arkansas had reached the fort, but rumor located them at the source of the Rio Grande, hundreds of miles south of the Grand River. McGonigle was all on fire in an instant. He wanted to fly to the Rio Grande. He told the officers of his adventures in the Grand River Valley, and drew a map of the country through which he had passed. His intelligence and earnestness so impressed them that they gave him a new outfit. He took with him a supply of writing paper, intending to keep a diary and give the world the benefit of his researches. As he was a splendid botanist and geologist, he was able to collect trustworthy and valuable information.

OFF FOR THE RIO GRANDE.

"You ask why he didn't carry a gun or pistol, so that he could shoot game when he ran out of provisions. He looked upon them as so much unnecessary weight. Every ounce counted. All that he could bear besides a pick, shovel, prospecting pan, oyster can, and blanket, he carried in bacon and flour. If he took firearms he would be compelled to burden himself with powder and bullets. He said that he could lug away bacon and flour enough to last him a month, but I always doubted it. He left Fort Garland for the head of the Rio Grande about the 7th of July. He was alone, but full of hope and enthusiasm. Hitting the Rio Grande a few miles above the Rio Trinchara,[27] he followed it up to its source, over 150 miles west of Fort Garland. He sought for gold, but found none. He was chasing an *ignis fatuus*.[28] I verily believe that he was at that time the only European west of the range. He saw neither trace nor track of a white man during the entire journey. You inquire if he was not troubled by wild animals. Once in a while he ran against a grizzly or a cinnamon bear, or saw a Rocky Mountain lion, but the beast was generally more astonished at

Mack's appearance than Mack was at the beast's, and the brute always gave him a wide berth. Mack told me that he was frequently alarmed by the howls of wild animals, and that he used to climb trees and tie himself to the branches, sleeping in that position until daylight. Hordes of wolves gathered beneath him and kept up a terrible racket until dawn, when they would slink away. When he could build a fire he never slept in a tree. He depended upon the sunglass for his cooking, and if the day was cloudy, or if he did not happen to strike dead wood before sunset he went without a fire. If the sun shone in the morning he collected a bunch of dry grass, covered it with sticks and splinters, ignited it with the sunglass, toasted his dough and bacon, and refreshed himself with water from a creek. He was then ready for a day's tramp. At times his supper was raw bacon and dough. Wherever he went he panned for gold. Oftimes he fetched color,[29] but never discovered the metal in paying quantities. He mapped the country and kept full notes of all his observations. I have a map which he drew while on the mountain overlooking the San Luis Valley. The course of every stream is accurately set down, and the whole thing is as correct as though it had been drawn by a Government surveyor.

ONCE MORE ON THE VERGE OF DEATH.

"Well, McGonigle learned that the wonderful Rio Grande diggings were on a par with those of Grand River. There was no foundation for either report. He slumped to the north, and began prospecting at the foot of the Saguache range. Again he ran out of provisions, and a second time lit out for Fort Garland. Berries became as scarce as gold. He came across a swarm of grasshoppers. They were a godsend. He roasted them on his shovel, and afterward declared he had never tasted anything more palatable. In crossing a range south of the Saguache chain he came very near freezing. Considerable snow lay upon the ground, and the night was bitter cold. He could build no fire, and was afraid to shut his eyes lest he should never open them. All night long he kept in motion. When the sun arose he was so cold that he could hardly stir. He drew out his sunglass. There was plenty of wood, but no dead grass to start a blaze. He had but one substitute. That was his diary. It was like tearing out his heartstrings to use it. The closely-written sheets were heaped upon them, the sunglass was brought to a focus, and a cheery blaze ran up the side of the log.

THE HUMANE INDIAN.

"The work of days was gone in a moment. He saved two small sheets of notes, but they were disconnected and of little value. When thoroughly thawed, Mack got over the range, but recognized no landmarks. It was certain that he had again lost his way. As he had eaten nothing for three days, his energies were directed more toward securing something to eat than toward reaching Fort Garland.

"Worn down by fatigue and faint through want of food, he was staggering aimlessly over the mountains when he heard a human voice. 'Stop!' it said. McGonigle turned about. There stood a Ute Indian with a drawn bow. 'Stop!' the savage repeated. It was the only English word that the Ute had learned, and it was used in a peremptory tone. Mack obeyed orders, and by signs made known his sad condition. Pressing his hand to his stomach and pointing to his mouth, he excited the sympathies of the Indian. The Ute took him by the arm and led him to a field where berries were plentiful. Nor did the Indian's kindness stop there. He boosted the gold hunter on his pony, conducted him to his camp, filled him with meat, gave him a bed of buffalo hides, and cared for him like a Christian. McGonigle spent three days recuperating in the wigwam. Then the Indian lent him a pony, and after twenty-four hours' travel placed him on the road to Fort Garland. Mack entered the fort thirty-one days after he had left it.

THE FATE OF BRADY.

"He stopped there to recruit, and started on foot for Tarryall during the second week in August. Following the old Government road through the Sangre de Cristo pass round to the foot of the Greenhorn Mountains[30] this side of the Spanish Peaks, he took the trail northwest to Cañon City. It was then a new settlement containing a half dozen log houses. Mack made it in three days from Fort Garland. Cañon City, you know, is up the great cañon of the Arkansas, nine miles from where that river emerges from the mountains. While stopping there over night McGonigle heard two hunters say that they had just brought in a man on the point of starvation. The man was lying in a rude cabin but a few rods distant under the care of a doctor. Mack visited the hut, and looked at the sufferer. It was Brady, but so changed that he was hardly recognized. His elbows protruded from the skin, and his face was as thin as a hatchet. He had been crazy for weeks, and incessantly raved about gold diggings and raw bacon. The hunters found him in a deep cañon formed by one of the tributaries of the Arkansas. He was squatted upon a sandbar, almost naked. Suddenly he plunged into the water, and ran his hand into a hole beneath the bank. The hunters spoke to him, but could not attract his attention. The glare of insanity was in his eyes, and his beard and hair were matted with mud. Again he dashed into the water and ran his arm into the hole up to the shoulder. Hunger had driven him to this extremity. He had apparently seen a muskrat enter the hole, and was determined to catch it. Brady had gone seven weeks without provisions. His hardships had unsettled his reason, but he clung to his prospecting pan through all his trials, and clasped it to his breast, fearful that his rescuers intended to tear it from him. Notwithstanding the intensity of his sufferings he rapidly recovered, and I believe that he is now doing business in St. Louis.

OFF FOR THE GRAND CAÑON OF THE COLORADO.

"Two days afterward, McGonigle arrived in Tarryall. He was the worst-looking man I ever saw. His coat was in tatters, and his shirt had literally rotted from his back. Nothing was left of his pantaloons but the lining. Somebody at Fort Garland gave him an old pair of army shoes, and his feet were in passable condition. He lost the sunglass the night before he got into Tarryall. It was a serious loss for both of us, as none could be procured this side of the States. I went to work sewing up a suit of clothes for him. He boiled his old rags in salt and water to kill the vermin, and spent but one day in patching them up before he was off again. He had found out that the mines were all a humbug, but his confidence in the future was unbounded. He always wanted to do a big thing, and had his head filled with all kinds of chimerical projects. The Utah troubles had set him to thinking. He proposed to find the head of navigation of the Colorado River, lay out a town at that point, and open a road to Salt Lake City. This would make the Gulf of California and the Colorado River a base of supplies for the territories. Impressed by the idea that the development of this project would make him independently rich, he laid in bacon and flour and departed from Tarryall. It was about the middle of August.[31] Going down through Cañon City he pushed for the grand cañon of the Colorado by way of Fort Garland and the San Luis Valley.

THE SAN JUAN EXCITEMENT.

"While in the valley he met parties who had joined the famous Baker expedition to the San Juan region.[32] Baker was a man well-known throughout the Territory. Some old Mexican told him that the San Juan country contained extraordinary deposits of gold, and he repeated the story. The report circulated among the miners exaggerated at every step until they believed that Baker had found the richest diggings on the continent. Baker organized a large party and marched for the San Juan mines, situated in a park of the Sierra la Plata Mountains,[33] in the southwestern corner of Colorado, about three hundred miles from Denver. The gold-seekers trooped after Baker from all parts of the Territory. They struck across the range by scores, with nothing but compasses to point them the way. McGonigle joined one of these expeditions. He led the party back to Fort Garland, went south from Garland to Taos, then over by the Ojos Calientes[34] to Abiquia,[35] and from there to Santa Fé. From the latter place they packed mules up the valley of the Rio la Plata[36] and found the new diggings in the mountains at the head of Animas Park.[37] The mines were in the crater of a large extinct volcano, probably forty miles in diameter.[38] There was great excitement. Over a thousand of the most lawless men in Colorado were gathered in this crater. Provisions could not be procured at any price. There were no roads, and all the pack mules in New Mexico could not have supplied such a crowd. Winter was approaching, and the weather was icy and cold. Worse than all, the diggings were many thousand feet above the level of the sea, and not very rich. The gold hunters were terribly enraged. They angrily denounced Baker, and he narrowly escaped lynching. He saved his life by clearing out at night. He had told them nothing but the truth, however. Gold was there in paying quantities, but the miners wanted something better.

THE DARK DAYS OF NEW MEXICO.

"It got to be the last of September or the first of October.[39] A heavy fall of snow scattered the adventurers in all directions. They drifted into Utah, slopped over into Arizona, and poured down into New Mexico like a pack of hungry wolves. A few reached California and Nevada, but hundreds lost their lives while prospecting the sandy deserts of Arizona and the alkali plains of Utah. That was a dark winter for New Mexico. The desperadoes ruled the Territory with an iron rod. Law and order were set at defiance. The innocent Mexicans were robbed and murdered with impunity. If one of the gang fancied a herder's wife or daughter, he took her, and shot the husband or father on the slightest resistance. Horses were stolen, cattle slain, and vast flocks of sheep stampeded. The ruffians filled all the little towns, and sanguinary fights occurred daily. Taos, Albuquerque, Abiquia, and Las Vegas were as good as given up to pillage. A few of the gang dropped down to El Paso, and ransacked Chihuahua and Sonora[40] for gold. McGonigle began the winter by teaching school in Taos. It was like educating Hottentots. After six weeks he broke up his institute, and began roaming over the Territory. His knowledge of the dead languages endeared him to the Catholic priests, and they always extended him a hearty welcome. The high-toned Mexicans, military men, Government surveyors, and others recognized his scientific attainments, and he was at home in their company. He became so well acquainted that he was known throughout New Mexico as "the schoolmaster." Along toward spring he opened a school in Mesilla.[41] By that time war had broken out between the North and the South. Mack's Union sentiments were offensive to the Secesh[42] paper in Mesilla, and the editor raised a mob intending to lynch him or drive him from the country. Mack was cornered in the plaza by an armed mob, but didn't quail. Tearing his shirt from his bosom he called his assailants cowards and assassins, and dared them to fire. He offered to take them one by one and whip them in a fair stand-up fight, but the challenge was not accepted. Mack then made a speech in which he secured the sympathies of the mob, who came near venting their indignation upon the rebel editor causing the trouble.

HUNTING FOR GOLD, AND FINDING DEATH.

"While teaching the Mexican children in Mesilla, McGonigle received a letter from an old friend and schoolmate who had settled down near San Diego, California, and was raising grapes and oranges. The letter gave a glowing account of the soil, climate, and fruits of Lower California. It so impressed Mack that he resolved to go to San Diego, preempt land if he could find any, and plant an orange grove. He determined to walk across Arizona. Filled with this new project, he went to Santa Fé and got all the information he could obtain from priests and the Government officers concerning that country. In the fall of 1861 he left Albuquerque on foot and alone, deaf to all warnings from Mexicans and others, intending to follow Viela's and Whipple's trail across Arizona.[43] I got a letter from him dated the day before he started. It was the last letter he ever wrote. The distance to San Diego is about 700 miles. The intervening country is, as you know, a vast desert of red sand. There are a few streams and rivers, but they have worn channels thousands of yards below the surface, forming terrible cañons and making it almost impossible to secure a supply of water. It never rains, and the earth is destitute of vegetation. Even the cactus gives up in despair and fails to secure nourishment. McGonigle never reached San Diego. At Tucson and Fort Yuma[44] no tidings of him were ever received. Whether he perished with thirst, or whether his scalp adorns the lodge of some Apache warrior, is purely a matter of conjecture.

"Some years ago, however, I met two old miners who had spent the fall of 1861 prospecting in Eastern Arizona. They recounted their sufferings, and told me of their hairbreadth escapes from the Indians, but what interested me the most was what they said about a white man. They had been wandering over the sands for days, and had seen not a living thing. While asleep in their blankets one dark night a man stumbled over them. Half awake, they heard him utter an apology, and beg to lie down between them, as he was very cold. Satisfied that he was not an Indian, they drowsily moved apart, and the stranger crept in the middle. When they awoke in the morning he was gone. They had no idea who he was. I have always thought he was McGonigle, for it was just like Mack."

Here Mr. Stone finished his story and dropped his legs from the table. The fate of McGonigle was an unknown death. It is certain that he was a most remarkable man, and it is doubtful whether Dr. Livingstone[45] or any other explorer ever passed through so eventful an eighteen months.

NOTES

1. As noted in the introduction to this and the two other Cummings articles dealing with mining, this is Wilbur Fisk Stone.

2. The three-story Lindell Hotel at Santa Fe Avenue and Fifth Street was a Pueblo landmark.

3. This grasshopper may have been the Rocky Mountain locust (*Melanoplus spretus*), which became extinct about the end of the nineteenth century.

4. The Colorado gold rush began in 1859, a decade after the California gold rush.

5. Many stories place the initial discovery of gold at the confluence of Cherry Creek and the South Platte River. That, however, is just that: a story. The first important gold strikes were elsewhere. Today, Cherry Creek is still a prominent natural feature in Denver and the immediate vicinity.

6. Black Hawk, in Gilpin County west of Denver, was founded after the 1859 gold was discovered by John H. Gregory, setting off the Colorado gold rush. In the 2000 federal census, Black Hawk's population is listed as 118, making it the smallest town in Colorado. That number, however, belies the number of people who visit the town every day to gamble. Once known for gold, Black Hawk today is known for the millions of dollars taken in by the town's casinos.

7. In 1860, gold was discovered by Abe Lee in what became known as California Gulch. Four months later the newly founded Oro City had more than 5,000 miners working in a five-mile section of the gulch. California Gulch and Oro City soon gave way to the mining settlement of Leadville in 1878. By 1880, Leadville's population had reached nearly 15,000.

8. Gold was discovered in Tarryall Creek, a tributary of the South Platte River, in 1860. The town, in Park County, was east of Fairplay, whose name came in response to the belief that many of the

early settlers in Tarryall claimed more land than they could ever mine. Today, Tarryall is a small unincorporated settlement.

9. This location is northeast of Leadville and about sixty miles west of Denver. The river flows northward along the western mountain slope and intersects the Colorado River. The town of Blue River is south of Breckinridge.

10. Longs Peak, rising to 14,255 feet, is north of Denver in Rocky Mountain National Park (Boulder County). The Grand River is now called the Colorado River.

11. "Scaly" here means "poor."

12. "Outfit" refers to the equipment needed for mining, as specified below in the article.

13. Based on the 1870 federal census for Colorado, I came up with two possible candidates for Brady, both Irish-born miners named James. One, forty-three years of age, was in the town of Granite, then in Park County about ninety miles southwest of Denver in the Rocky Mountains, and the other, age thirty-two, lived in Oro City in Lake County about fourteen miles north of Granite. Once a flourishing mining town, Granite today is often billed as a ghost town whose population is said to be nine.

14. "To go snacks" means "to share the profits."

15. Typically, an oyster can was a one-gallon can in which shucked oysters were packed in brine (resembling a modern paint can in size and shape). Most often packed in the Chesapeake Bay region, some cans were as small as eight ounces and others as large as five gallons.

16. A magnifying glass.

17. Mount Lincoln in Park County actually rises to an elevation of 14,286 feet. It is just east of the Continental Divide. Some information I found credits Wilbur Stone with being the first person to reach the summit of Mount Lincoln in June 1861.

18. The Gunnison River flows from eastern Gunnison County to the southwest, west, and northwest before joining the Colorado River at Grand Junction. It is a spectacularly wild river, flowing through the fifty-three-mile-long Black Canyon, a portion of which is in Gunnison National Park.

19. Uncompahgre Peak is the highest in the San Juan Range in southwestern Colorado (with an elevation of 14,309 feet). Telluride is one of the better-known local towns.

20. There is more than one Dead Man's Gulch in Colorado. I believe this may be the one near Gunnison. Some people believe that victims of Alfred (Alferd) Packer, the infamous "Colorado cannibal," are buried in the gulch. The name "Dead Man's Gulch" was used in a dime novel (Joseph E. Badger's *The Rival Red-Hat Sports; or, The Shady Gambler's High Haul: A Story of the Miners of Dead Man's Gulch*, published in 1895) and the 1943 movie *Dead Man's Gulch*, starring Don "Red" Barry.

21. More commonly known as the Sawatch Range, these mountains on the Continental Divide in south-central Colorado contain several of the highest peaks in the Rocky Mountains.

22. The upper Arkansas River flows between the towering Sawatch and Mosquito ranges, running south and southeast through rugged canyons. The river would have taken them to Cañon City in Fremont County northwest of Pueblo.

23. Fort Garland was established in 1858 in what was then the northern part of New Mexico. From 1866 to 1867, Kit Carson and a unit of volunteers were stationed at the fort. The fort was abandoned as a military facility in 1883. Today the site of Fort Garland is in Costilla County, Colorado, about thirty miles north of the New Mexico–Colorado border. The fort has been reconstructed and is open to the public.

24. In south-central Colorado in the southern Rocky Mountains at the western edge of the High Plains, the two Spanish Peaks (East, which is 12,683 feet high, and West, at 13,626 feet) have also been called Twin Peaks, Dos Hermanos (Two Brothers), and the Mexican Mountains.

25. Saguache Lake today is called San Luis Lake.

26. San Luis Park (today almost always known as San Luis Valley), another of Colorado's grassy high-elevation basins and valleys, is on the eastern side of the Continental Divide in southern Colorado and extends south into New Mexico.

27. Trinchera (note spelling) Creek flows west from the Sangre de Cristo Mountains past Fort Garland into the Rio Grande twelve miles south-southeast of Alamosa, Colorado, just north of the New Mexico–Colorado border.

28. An illusion.

29. Saw traces of gold.

30. Greenhorn Mountain is in the Wet Mountains about twenty-five miles southwest of Pueblo, Colorado, at the eastern side of the Rocky Mountains.

31. Still in 1860.

32. In 1860, Charles Baker and other miners discovered gold near modern Silverton, north of Durango in southwestern Colorado.

33. That park, another high-elevation grassy valley, became known as Bakers Park. La Plata Mountain is northwest of Durango in the San Juan Mountains about forty miles north of the New Mexico–Colorado border.

34. Warm mineral springs located southwest of Taos generally called Ojo Caliente.

35. Abiquiu—note spelling—is twenty miles southwest of Ojo Caliente.

36. Silver Creek, the modern name for Rio la Plata, runs out of the San Juan Mountains.

37. About thirty-five miles north of the original gold strike, which was near modern Silverton. Animas Park no doubt took its name from the miners' settlement of Animas on the Animas River. The river, named El Rio de las Animas Perdidas ("The River of Lost Souls") by Spaniards in the late eighteenth century, flows south past Silverton and Durango. It is another of Colorado's magnificent rivers.

38. Animas Park is not the crater of an extinct volcano.

39. It was still 1860.

40. In northern Mexico.

41. Mesilla is west of Las Cruces, New Mexico, on the Rio Grande.

42. "Secesh" is short for "secessionist." In 1861 and 1862, Mesilla served as the capital of the Confederate Territory of Arizona.

43. On orders from the U.S. Congress, army lieutenant Amiel Weeks Whipple led an expedition that left Fort Smith, Arkansas, in July 1853 and arrived in Los Angeles in March 1854, marching across Texas, New Mexico, and Arizona. The purpose of the exploration was to survey a possible route for a railroad to the Pacific. I was unable to discover who Viela was.

44. Fort Yuma was on the west bank of the Colorado River in California, opposite the location of modern Yuma, Arizona.

45. This is, of course, David Livingstone, famed for his missionary work and explorations in Africa beginning in 1840. He died in 1873 just prior to Cummings's leaving New York on his journey across the West.

IN THE GOLDEN GULCHES.

THE WONDERFUL REVELATIONS OF THE ROCKY MOUNTAINS.

The Golden Sands of the Platte—Gregory's Discovery—What He Sold for $7,000—Green Russell's Extraordinary Luck—A Nail Keg Filled with Gold—An Enormous Waste of Capital—Scientific Asses and Poor Miners—The Dark Days of '64—Trails of a Yankee Professor—The Dawning of a Fortune.

Correspondence of The Sun.

SPANISH BAR,[1] **Colorado, July 15.**—Old miners say that John Gregory[2] found gold in the Platte during the fall of 1858. Gregory was a Georgian. He had dug the precious metal from the mountains near Dahlonega,[3] and knew the difference between quartz and surface mining.[4] Californians who flocked to Colorado thoroughly understood gulch mining,[5] but could hardly tell a gold-bearing lode from a side of sole leather. They panned the river sands and washed out the mountain gulches without looking for the source of the deposits. Gregory, satisfied that the flaky gold of Platte River came from the mountains,

167

determined to discover its origin. He branched from the Platte to Clear Creek,[6] and found fair surface diggings within the edge of the foot hills, twelve miles from Denver. The winter was spent washing sand near the site of Golden City.[7] With the approach of spring Gregory worked up through Clear Creek Cañon in the direction of Gray's Peak.[8] He climbed Bald Mountain,[9] and saw on his right an immense natural basin, the center of a circle of peaks. The whole country was covered with pines. John declared that the Platte River gold came from that valley. The basin was seamed by gulches. The Georgian descended into one of them and shook his pan. A golden sediment settled upon its bottom. Rich nuggets were uncovered, and a genuine gold field was found.

THE GOLDEN GULCH.

Overjoyed with his fortune, the prospector staked his claim, and put for Denver for supplies. He dropped hints of his discovery, and when he left that city was followed by Capt. A. C. Smith[10] and a score of miners. The new diggings were known as Gregory's Gulch.[11] They were the richest that had been discovered in the Territory. Gold seekers poured into them by hundreds, and many gathered fortunes before the gulch petered out. Gregory, however, paid but little attention to surface mining. He trailed up the mountain in search of the vein from which the gold had been driven, and found it not a thousand feet from the gulch. It proved to be one of the most magnificent lodes in the Rocky Mountains. Nearly $2,500,000 in gold ore has been taken from it since the Georgian drove his pick into the lead. It is called the Gregory lode. I am told that the discoverer sold it for $7,000, and spent years vainly hunting for a mine as rich.

THE GOLDEN NAIL-KEG.

The pioneer miners of Colorado were Georgians. One of them was Green Russell,[12] a thorough quartz miner. Green, however, believed that he could do better in the gulches than on the mountains. After sloshing around Gregory's Gulch for a few days he went in partnership with four native Georgians, and struck out for new diggings. They found them in a ravine, a few miles from the Gregory discovery. The ravine was filled with gold pockets. Capt. Smith says:

"I went up to Russell's Gulch a few days after Green and the boys had got to work. It was nigh dark when I got there, and they had got through for the day. Green was sitting in the doorway of his little log cabin. 'What luck, boys,' says I. 'Well,' says Green, kind of sad like, 'we h'aint had much luck to-day. There it is under the bed. You can see for yourself.' So I went to the bed and stooped down. They had their dust in a nail keg. I caught hold of it and tried to pull it out, but I couldn't budge it. So I just raised up the bed and looked into the keg. I hope I may be shot if it wasn't three-quarters full of nuggets from the size of a No. 6 shot up to a filbert. I want you to understand that there wasn't any stealing in those days. Folks was honest. Why, those fellows would go out to work every day and leave that keg of gold under the bed with the door unlocked, and nobody would think of touching it until the boys were ready to divide up."

Green Russell's party were in clover. They took out over $300,000 before the winter snows covered the mountains. Russell's share was $92,000. With this money he returned to Georgia and bought a cotton plantation well stocked with Negroes. The war broke out during the following year, and plantation, negroes, and cotton vanished in the smoke of Sherman's guns. After peace was declared, Green returned to Colorado. Rich gulch diggings were played out and he was tired of prospecting. He founded a colony of Georgians south of Pueblo,[13] and is said to be doing well. He is a genial, whole-souled man of strict integrity, and when the gigantic monopolies that rule the Territory are crushed, Russell ought to find a seat in Congress.

THE GOLD-MILL FEVER.

The Pike's Peak emigrants at first hovered about the streams on the plains. Old trappers and Indians asserted that there were but two or three openings through which a man could possibly enter the mountains. Gregory dispelled this illusion, and the miners covered the peaks like grasshoppers. Gregory's Gulch felt the impetus. Within eighteen months a good wagon road was completed and the flourishing city of Central[14] sprang up among the pine stumps. The trappers and Indians were astounded. Lode after lode was struck, and the mines of Gilpin County[15] capped all other discoveries. As long as the surface digging lasted money was abundant. The city was irrigated with gold, and it grew in proportion to the irrigation. In 1864 the deposit of free gold was exhausted, and nothing remained but refractory metal.[16] Nobody knew how to treat it. Financial clouds gathered above the mountain city and dark days followed. Inventors came from the East loaded with money and erected dozens of mills, but they did not understand the treatment of the ores, and their mills were disastrous failures. Over $3,000,000 was wasted in the erection of these buildings. There are probably at this moment fifty vacant mills within ten miles of Central City of no more use to miners than so many soap factories.

TAKEN IN AND DONE.

Many Eastern men had accumulated fortunes by the war, and were anxious to invest their capital. A swarthy Italian, or crazy Frenchman, or metaphysical German would gain their confidence. He claimed to have discovered the secret of separating ores by electricity, or of extracting silver and gold by the concentration of starlight and nitric acid. Forthwith a company was formed, the capital stock paid in, and away the foreigner sailed to the Rocky Mountains to stick up his machinery. After hundreds of thousands had been spent and a magnificent machine shop erected, the whole scheme would fizzle out. The starlight did not affiliate with the nitric acid, or the electricity of Colorado was not so strong as the electricity of Hoboken,[17] and the ore resisted all attempts at amalgamation.[18] The stockholders would get sick of eternal outlay with no dividends, and the company would dissolve, leaving a huge pile of brick and cog wheels as a testimonial to their affection for the inventor. In some cases houses were built for the workmen, and a gothic mansion constructed for the use of the superintendent. This gentleman sometimes amused himself with fast horses, and drank champagne at every meal. He wore large diamonds, and absorbed the company's money faster than the inventor. When all was gone mining operations stopped, and a deserted village slept in the mountains. I have seen a half dozen empty towns in Gilpin, Boulder, and Clear Creek counties.[19]

THE SHARP CAPITALISTS AND
THE INNOCENT MINERS.

A few Eastern capitalists invested in lodes on the representations of poor miners who appeared in Atlantic cities with long black beards, tobacco-stained teeth, nugget-gold breastpins, buckskin breeches, and cowhide boots. The capitalists went in with a rush. They built their mills before their lodes were developed. If the fissure was rich when they made the purchase, it failed after a few tons of ore were removed. More frequently it turned out entirely barren. You can find in Clear Creek Cañon alone over a dozen decayed mills squatting in front of worthless holes at the foot of craggy mountains. Occasionally the poor miners retained an interest in a lode. The company sent out a scientific gentleman who examined the mine before the purchase was made. If it was unusually rich he would so report. A bargain concluded, the poor miners were sent in to work the lode. They would tear out a few tons of fat ore, but the quality would gradually decrease until apparently nothing but quartz or granite remained. Stock depreciated, and the scientific gentleman again trotted to the hole. Sure enough, the mine had played out. He could see it for himself, and he secretly conveyed the information to his friends. They chucked their shares upon the market, and a panic ensued. When the breeze blew over all the stock had been saddled upon the nearly heartbroken miners at a low figure. The capitalists grinned with pleasure because they had succeeded in saving something. The poor miners, then sole proprietors, quietly resumed their digging, and in a short time the lode would be pouring out hundreds and perhaps thousands of dollars a day. The secret was quickly explained. The innocent miners had hoodwinked the scientific ass by slowly slanting into the rock at the side of the vein, thus giving him the impression that the lode was exhausted.

THE SPECTRE OF HUKILL GULCH.

A Philadelphia company bought a mine in Hukill Gulch, a mile above Idaho Springs.[20] They built a mill near the top of the mountain. Over $100,000 was spent upon it. When the machinery was all in place, and the stockholders had their hands extended to catch the gold as it oozed from the furnace, they found that they could procure no water. The mountain was as dry as a Fourth Ward politician on the morning after election.[21] If the mill had been planted in the Sahara desert it would scarcely have been more useless. It stands on the side of Hukill Gulch to-day, rearing its smoke stack in the sky, like a giant spectre.

THE DARK DAYS OF COLORADO.

Such has been the condition of things in the mountain regions. For years wealthy fools in England and on the Atlantic coast stood upon their tiptoes and tossed their money into the Rocky Mountain cañons. Common business prudence was cast to the winds. The stories of the veriest scalawags were accepted as gospel truth, and the confiding capitalists were swindled out of immense sums in the simplest manner. The effect upon Colorado was disastrous. Men of money were alarmed. When a really

179

deserving enterprise was brought to their attention they turned it a cold shoulder. The gold mines were declared a humbug, and as for silver, the idea was preposterous.

Yet gold and silver are here in extraordinary quantities. Twenty years from now the Rocky Mountain mines will be acknowledged the richest in the world. I have seen piles of ore sold for $6,000 a ton. Responsible men assure me that they have known it to bring much more. Nor were these isolated cases.

No prudent man will buy anything "unsight unseen." If capitalists want to invest in a mine, let them come here and see it; search the records for a clear title; take the ore from all parts of the crevice and have it assayed; or lease the lode for a given time and develop it. If a New Yorker intends to erect a mill to carry out a new process for the treatment of ores, let him come to the Territory and secure ore from all the mining districts, tote it to New York, make his experiments at home, and be sure that his mill will do all that is expected of it before he buys a brick or board.

TRIALS OF A YANKEE PROFESSOR.

One of the earliest and most successful smelting establishments in Gregory Gulch is Prof. Hill's reduction works.[22] For a long time it was the only mill in Colorado that could handle the ores. Without it the miners would have been flat on their backs, unable to stir. It would have taken them years to recover from the depression of 1864. Hill was a professor of chemistry in a New England college. He spent three or four years in the mining districts and two winters in Great Britain before he began his works. Satisfied that the mineral was rich and abundant, his next study was its treatment. He went to Swansea[23] and spent some months in the great reduction works there. Swansea was then the centre of the smelting world. It had two hundred furnaces, and treated ore from the Bobtail[24] and other lodes, and had it ox-teamed six hundred miles across the plains to Atchison.[25]

It was shipped down the Missouri and Mississippi rivers to New Orleans, and from thence to Swansea. There the ore was readily reduced, and the metals separated. This was in 1866. The shipment alone cost Mr. Hill $14,000, but the information gained was worth hundreds of thousands. The following year the Professor completed his works. He was backed by Eastern capitalists under the guise of the Boston and Colorado Smelting Company. Skilled workmen were imported from Wales, among them a German superintendent who had had twenty-five years' experience in Swansea.

THE RESULT OF COMMON SENSE.

When Hill's works began operations there were over twenty mills in its vicinity representing millions of capital, but not one of them could treat the ores. Hill was a theoretical but practical man. He found out exactly what was wanted, and got it. His mill was a success from the start. It has reduced over 40,000 tons of Gilpin County ore, averaging $117 per ton gold and silver, including tailings or refuse of the mines. The average purchase price has been $75. Last year 10,000 tons were treated. The mill has averaged thirty tons per day, though the Professor says he has handled seventy-five tons on a pinch. Mr. Hill reduces the ore to copper matte.[26] In other words, he drives out all the baser metals and concentrates the gold, silver, and copper. The matte is shipped to Wales, where the precious metals are separated. It averages $1,500 per ton. The freight is $40. The Swansea men retain five per cent, for their trouble, and the Professor gets the remainder. Last year he sent a million dollars in matte across the ocean. The Hill reduction works are the largest in Colorado. They run three furnaces.

CENTRAL CITY AND BLACK HAWK.

Yesterday I visited Gregory's Gulch. It is now the site of the second largest city in the Territory. The town is several hundred feet wide, and two or three miles long. Its population is between 7,000 and 8,000. The gulch is thin, and the houses look as though they had been accidentally dropped into it. The streets are narrow and crooked, but the inhabitants are broad and straight. The buildings are mostly pine. There are two daily newspapers, but no fire engine. One of these days the city will be wiped out by conflagration.[27] Water is very scarce. It brings from fifty to seventy-five cents per barrel. Central is the only city in the United States that supports water carriers. Citizens never go to bed without locking up their wells. The trees have all been chopped from the mountains, and shafts and tunnels dot the hills like prairie-dog holes. Black Hawk is the Mackerelville of Central.[28] It is near here that some flighty genius proposes to run a twelve-mile tunnel through the range, provided he can raise the capital. He is ready to tunnel the moon on the same terms.

THE BOBTAIL.

I entered the Bobtail tunnel. It passes from the road 1,200 feet into the side of the mountain, striking the Fisk[29] and Bobtail lodes several hundred feet below the surface. It cost $25 a foot. The Fisk and Bobtail are wonderful mines. They are near the Gregory. The Bobtail has produced nearly $3,000,000 in gold. Water runs into the mine at the rate of 250 gallons a minute. Mr. Rogers, the foreman, has invented a huge pump worked by a steam engine at the further end of the tunnel, which will throw out 500 gallons every sixty seconds. There is nothing to prevent the miners from following the crevice down to China if their pumps are big enough. The mine received its name from a patient bob-tailed ox that used to draw the ore down the hill before the tunnel was put in. Imagine a hole from eight to ten feet wide, 600 feet deep, and 1,500 feet long, covered over with dirt like an immense sewer, and you will have an idea of the Bobtail mine. The tunnel strikes it the same as a tunnel run from the Broadway Bank would strike Beach's pneumatic tube.[30]

The shaft is sunk a few feet below the level of the tunnel, then a drift is run along the vein, and the metal is taken out over-head. The latter operation is called "stoping." Shafts are sunk, drifts run, and stoping continued until either the ore gives out or water stops work.

FITZ JOHN PORTER'S FAILURE.[31]

It would not do to leave Central City without visiting Hill's reduction works. They are in Black Hawk. The valley is filled with their stifling smoke. On my way there I passed a great stone building covering as much ground as your County Court House. It is known as "Fitz John Porter's Failure," and was erected by that celebrated general after his dismissal from the army. The company burst before Porter could get in his machinery, and the huge structure is now a railroad depot. I found Professor Hill buying ore from a miner. A thousand tons of ore were heaped about his building. The place reminded me of one of the big coal yards along the North River. The Professor wore a chip hat,[32] plain gold studs and watch chain, and a business suit through-out. His chin was clean shaven, but a brown moustache sat upon his upper lip. There was a small shaft in his right cheek. He smokes, and is a fast talker. Mr. Hill conducted me through his mill and explained his various processes.

ROASTING THE ORE.

Three or four layers of pine wood are placed upon the ground, covering a space of twenty or thirty square feet. A wooden shaft, ten feet high, arises from the centre of the block. Raw ore is then piled upon the wood in the shape of a pyramid. The mass is fired through the wooden funnel. The ore takes the fire like so much hard coal. But the operation must be conducted with the greatest care. If the draught is too heavy the pile will melt and run over the yard. If the fire is smothered too much the mass will fuse and become as hard as a rock. It would have to be blasted before it could again be used. For two months the golden pyramid smolders. Its top and sides gradually become encrusted with sulphur and arsenic. The fumes arising from it are horrible. When the sulphur has been expelled and the iron reduced to an oxide the fire goes out and the ore is thoroughly roasted. It is as brittle as coke. The gold, silver, and copper are concentrated in the centre of each fragment. The roasted mineral is crushed, and is then ready for the furnace. At least twenty of these huge piles of ore were smouldering in Mr. Hill's yard.

CONCENTRATING THE METALS.

"The grand secret," said Mr. Hill, "is in charging the furnaces. The operator must understand the character of his ores, and mix them accordingly. All ores are different. Ore from one mine must be melted with ore from another to ensure success. The Georgetown[33] ores are very difficult to work. They need a certain percentage of lime before they are cast into the furnaces. If the charges are properly made they will melt within six hours. The least fault will throw them over to eight hours. That would make a difference of $75,000 a year to the company. We require no more than six hours. If the charge is bungled the ore will not concentrate, and workmen will be compelled to chisel it from the furnace."

The furnaces are so constructed as to force a hot flame over the face of the ore. The mineral seems to be all afire, and is stirred about with enormous scrapers until it begins to melt. The base metals, quartz, and silicate of iron float to the surface like oil upon water, and are drawn off in the sand. The melted copper, gold, and silver having settled to the bottom of the furnace, are then tapped, and become copper matte. Nineteen-twentieths of the charge is slag. The matte is bagged and sent to Wales, where the metals are separated. Mr. Hill's treatment is simple, but one that will fail unless the workman is conversant with the nature of the ores.

177

THE GREAT RED CLOUD.[34]

We passed several piles of raw ore, marked "Red Cloud." "The Red Cloud," said the Professor, "is a remarkable gold-bearing lode. That is its second-class ore. I paid $1,200 a ton for it. I have paid as high as $5,000 for a ton of ore from that mine. I buy the tailings for $50 a ton,[35] and clear money from them. I get the second-class ore in large quantities. It will go forty ounces of gold and 250 ounces of silver to the ton. The ore of the Red Cloud is tellurium. It is the only place in America where telluride of gold and silver is found. In the Hartz Mountains[36] they have picked up a few cabinet specimens, but for genuine tellurium the Red Cloud stands alone in the world. You can see that the ore is very rich. It is easily treated."

The Red Cloud mine is at Gold Hill, eight miles from Boulder City.[37] It is owned by the officials of the mint in Denver and by its original discoverers.

UP SHE GOES.

As the Swansea Company no longer separates matte at five per cent, Mr. Hill is about to put up machinery, and turn out his own gold and silver. Heretofore the rate of wages in Wales has defied competition. The capital stock in Boston and Colorado Company was originally $300,000. It has been increased to $500,000. A portion of the original capital, however, has been paid in during the last seventy days. Mr. Hill owns a quarter interest. The German superintendent gets $3,000 a year and a percentage on the profits. None of the stock is on the market, and none can be bought at any reasonable price.

So much for the gold region of Colorado. I did not see the Leavitt[38] and Kansas[39] lodes, but I am told that they are as rich as any in the district. They are said to be turning out from $15,000 to $18,000 a month.

NOTES

1. Spanish Bar was a mining town just west of Idaho Springs in Clear Creek County, west of Denver.

2. John H. Gregory is also mentioned in note 6 in Chapter 6, "The Fate of a Gold Seeker." Most sources say Gregory's discovery was in 1859. Gregory, so important in the history of Colorado mining, remains somewhat unknown (see Caroline Bancroft, "The Elusive Figure of John H. Gregory," *Colorado Magazine* 20, no. 4 (1943):121–135; for more on the early days of mining in Colorado, see James E. Fell Jr., *Ores to Metals: The Rocky Mountain Smelting Industry* (Lincoln: University of Nebraska Press, 1979).

3. Dahlonega is in northeastern Georgia in Lumpkin County. From as early as 1828, gold was mined in Lumpkin and nearby Georgia counties. U.S. and later Confederate gold coins were minted in Dahlonega from the gold.

4. Miners discovered that gold deposits were often found with below-surface quartz veins. Shafts and tunnels were used to reach the quartz deposits, a much more difficult way to mine than looking for gold in surface deposits of quartz.

5. Miners used water to pan for gold in gulches. Sluices were also used to look for gold flecks washed into the gulches from elsewhere.

6. As noted in "A Canadian in Colorado," Clear Creek runs across Jefferson County west of Denver.

7. Golden, today a suburb of Denver, is the county seat of Jefferson County.

8. Grays Peak, elevation 14,270 feet, is in Clear County (extending into Summit County), immediately west of Jefferson County.

9. Just under 14,000 feet, Bald Mountain, in Summit County, is fifteen miles southwest of Grays Peak.

10. I am uncertain who A. C. Smith was. He may have been Abnah Smith, a miner who was in the region at the time.

11. Gregory's Gulch, named for John Gregory, is also mentioned in Chapter 6.

12. William Green Russell (1818–1887) was married to a Cherokee Indian woman. It is claimed that he learned about Colorado gold from Cherokee Indians who also were headed west to California.

13. In Huerfano County in south-central Colorado.

14. Central City, in Gilpin County, was a true boomtown, growing to a population of 3,000 in only months, and as many as 6,000 by 1860, when it was the largest town in Colorado. In the 2000 census Central City's population was 515.

15. Gilpin County is northwest of Denver.

16. Metals with extremely high melting points, which make it difficult to extract precious metals from them.

17. Hoboken, New Jersey, is on the Hudson River just west of New York City.

18. Amalgamation refers to a method used in mining to separate precious metals from ores using mercury. Cummings is using the word here simply to mean separating out the metals.

19. These counties are west and north of Jefferson County.

20. Idaho Springs is still another of the mining towns founded at the time of the Colorado gold rush. Today, with a population of about 2,000, it is the largest town in Clear Creek County.

21. In 1873 the Fourth Ward in Lower Manhattan in New York City was a working-class district that fronted the East River across from Brooklyn. Today, that part of the city is cut by the Brooklyn Bridge. I believe Cummings is suggesting that on election day local politicians who were running for office bought drinks for voters, but the next day the politicians' largesse dried up.

22. Nathaniel P. Hill, a former Brown University professor, managed the Boston & Colorado Smelting Co., beginning in 1867. Later the operation was moved to Denver. Hill was elected to the U.S. Senate and served from 1879 to 1885.

23. Swansea is both a port city and a county on the south coast of Wales in the United Kingdom.

24. The Bobtail lode, discovered in June 1859, was near Gregory Gulch.

25. Atchison is on the Missouri River in northeastern Kansas.

26. Copper matte, a slag-like substance, was a by-product of the smelting process. The matte Cummings is referring to here contained gold, silver, and copper along with sulfides and other impurities and had to be further refined through additional processing.

27. The "second largest city in the Territory" was, of course, Central City. The town was devastated by a fire that started on May

21, 1874, destroying about 150 buildings. Cummings's comment about the lack of a fire engine and his conflagration prediction were not as prophetic as they might seem, however. In January 1873 an earlier fire had wiped out sixteen buildings.

28. In 1873, "Mackerelville" was the name given to the neighborhood located on the east side of Manhattan in the vicinity of Twentieth Street. It was a very tough area known for poverty, gangs, and lawlessness. Central City, a Colorado mining town, had expanded to the point that it had encompassed Black Hawk, another mining town, which shared the same reputation as Mackerelville. Today, long after the mining boom supporting Central City's growth subsided, the two towns, both known for gambling casinos, are about one mile apart.

29. Another mine near Black Hawk and Central City in Gilpin County, Colorado.

30. In 1869, Alfred Ely Beach had a 312-foot-long, 9-foot-diameter underground tube built in Manhattan to house a pneumatically propelled subway. The one-car subway ran under Broadway from Warren to Murray streets (today on the west side of City Hall Park in Lower Manhattan). It opened in 1870 as a curiosity, but was short-lived.

31. Major General Fitz John Porter, a U.S. officer during the Civil War, was court-martialed in 1863 and found guilty on several charges related to disobedience of orders and misconduct in the face of the enemy during the second battle of Bull Run. Drummed out of the army, he moved to Colorado, leaving there in 1865 to relocate to New York City, where he served at various times as commissioner of public works, police commissioner, fire commissioner, and cashier of the New York post office. In 1886, after reviews of the court-martial and the charges against him, Porter was recommissioned as a colonel in the U.S. Army. He then retired.

32. A hat made from plaited straw or split palm fronds.

33. Another mining town about ten miles southwest of Black Hawk and Central City.

34. This particular Red Cloud mine (there were several mines with that name in the West, including at least one other in Colorado) was in what today is Boulder County just northwest of Boulder.

35. Tailings are the refuse left after the metal is extracted from the ore.

36. A mountain range in Germany.

37. Today Boulder.

38. I believe this is the Vasa Leavitt vein, which also is in the Central City–Black Hawk area.

39. Another mine in the Central City–Black Hawk area.

THE STORY OF LITTLE EMMA.

In the Silver Pockets of the Wasatch Mountains.

---

*A Scene in the Streets of Salt Lake City—The Quiet Chat beneath
the Locust Trees—A Doctor's Adventures in Little Cottonwood
Cañon—The Pahranagat Aladdins—A Terrible Winter—The
Wonderful Silver Mines—Financial Vultures on the Scent—The
Battles in the Utah Courts—A United States Senator with Two
Legs on Three Sides of a Fence—San Francisco Bill after Nevada
William—Where Bob Schenck Was Roped In—Millionaires
Spring to the Surface Like Mushrooms.*

Correspondence of The Sun.

NEW SMYRNA, Fla., April 10, 1874—Public attention is
again drawn to the Little Emma Mine[1] by an alleged attempt
to freeze out its British stockholders. Any new light that may be
thrown upon the subject will prove interesting. Last August I
visited Salt Lake City. Becoming acquainted with United States
District Attorney Carey,[2] I made some inquiries concerning the
mine and its legal troubles. So intricate were its complications
that even so good a lawyer as Mr. Carey would not attempt
to unravel them. While we were conversing in front of Zion's
Cooperative Institution,[3] a handsome young man in clean white

THE ZION'S COOPERATIVE SIGN IN SALT LAKE CITY. (WILLIAMS, *PACIFIC TOURIST*, 137)

linen approached us. He wore a Ceylon hat,[4] with a broad black ribbon. His cheeks were rosy, his moustache sloped gracefully, and his movements indicated active business pursuits.

"There is the very man you want," said Mr. Carey. "He is the only man I know in Salt Lake City who pretends to begin at the beginning and give a connected and accurate account of Emma Mine. It's worse and harder to understand than the Schleswig-

Holstein snarl[5] or the Erie troubles under the Jim Fisk dynasty,[6] but I think that young fellow can give you some idea of it."

BENEATH THE LOCUST TREES.

At my request Mr. Carey introduced me to the gentleman. I found him a glib talker. He laughed at the idea of taking in the story of Little Emma at one sitting, but readily promised to do what he could for me. He made a proviso, it was that I should not print his name as the author of the history. "Not," said he, "that I am afraid to father the truth, but because I am financially interested in the Little Cottonwood mines, and if I should happen to tread upon the toes of some of the great silver moguls they might turn in and scorch me. You understand?"

I nodded assent. It was just after dinner. We sat down in two arm chairs beneath the trees shading the sidewalk in front of the Townsend House.[7] I laid my note book upon my knee, and the young man opened his budget as follows:

"It was in the spring of '65 that Dr. Orville H. Congar[8] went to New York to sell mining property in Bingham.[9] I was doing business in New York at that time, and the Doctor had a letter of introduction to me. Silver had been found in Utah as early as 1863, but nothing big had been developed. Wall street was suffering from a relapse of the Colorado and Montana excitement,[10] and I wouldn't touch anything in the shape of mines. I told the Doctor that he couldn't sell a clean-developed diamond gulch for fifty cents. The best thing to do was to get up a prospecting company."

"What is a prospecting company?" I asked.

"A company of fellows who all chip in and furnish grub and an outfit for old, broken-down miners to go out prospecting," the young man answered, and continued his story.

THE TRAMP TO LITTLE COTTONWOOD.

"Well, we got up a prospecting company, Mailler & Quereau, of 108 Wall street,[11] and several others were in it. Dr. Congar was

TOWNSEND HOUSE,

SALT LAKE CITY, UTAH.

JAMES TOWNSEND, - - - Proprietor.

☞—Leading House in the City. One hundred and fifty Rooms, elegantly furnished, neat, clean and airy. The popular Resort for Tourists and the Traveling Public. The head-quarters of Excursions to the Lake, the Mountains and the Mines. Opportunities and facilities for becoming acquainted with representative men in the City, and the prominent business enterprises of the Territory. An old established House, only two stories high, with first-class accommodations in every respect. It is convenient to the Tabernacle, Churches, Theatre, and business portion of the City.

Omnibus and Street Car Lines to and from the House, with Livery accommodations near by.

☞—Every attention paid to the wants of Guests. Charges reasonable.

THIS ADVERTISEMENT FOR THE TOWNSEND HOUSE SHOWS THE SHADED SIDE-WALK WITH CHAIRS WHERE CUMMINGS CONDUCTED HIS INTERVIEW. (WILLIAMS, *PACIFIC TOURIST*, BACK PAGES)

sent back to Utah as our agent. Here he met Silas Braine[12] and B. C. Nicholls,[13] two old prospectors. They had banged around Nevada and Montana until they had knocked the scabs off from their backs, and knew a good thing when they dropped on it. Dr. Congar was told that they had found fair surface indications in Little Cottonwood. They had located what they called the North Star, Chicago, and St. Louis leads,[14] and were making considerable music over them. Congar listened and went with them. Our company furnished the outfit, and we were to have an equal share of whatever was discovered. The Doctor accompanied them to Little Cottonwood. It was hell getting there then. There was no road, and the cañon was choked with chaparral and boulders. Well, they prospected. The veins of ore were there. Cougar took everything running northwest, including the North Star, already located, and Braine and Nicholls everything running southeast. It was agreed that Congar should have the privilege of locating and driving stakes at the initial point. Where the ore cropped to the surface they made nine different locations. These covered what are known as the Emma, Pittsburgh, Chicago and St. Louis. Things looked so well that they formed a mining district and called it the Mountain Lake District.[15]

A FORTUNE, BUT OUT OF THE WORLD.

"The ore was there, but it was out of the world. You must bear in mind that at that time there was no Pacific Railroad, and no road had been built up to the cañon from the Salt Lake Valley. Everything had to be packed up on a man's back or by burros (Spanish donkeys). It would eat up the ore to team it to the Missouri River. Our only hope was in a furnace. Miners then had a limited idea of what they could do with furnaces, and it would cost almost its weight in gold to get one out here. We hadn't the money to spare, but fortune smiled on us. In the winter of sixty-five we sold the old North Star location—on the same ledge as the Emma—to Brunner[16] of Philadelphia for $35,000. There were a thousand feet of it, running northwest. This gave us capital to work upon. Meanwhile prospecting continued. We broke into Emma Hill, taking up eighteen locations, all running northwest. The locators deeded them to the Utah Prospecting and Silver Mining Company of New York—our organization—complying with all mining and other laws. With our capital we began to develop our property. The mountain chaparral was cleared away, and with great difficulty we ran a road down through the cañon. The following year we went in with Brunner and put up a furnace. Its ruins can still be seen on the banks of the Little Cottonwood, below Alta.[17] The ideas of the builder were crude, and the furnace never amounted to anything, because no one understood exactly what was wanted. Our capital was exhausted. Under these circumstances there was but one thing to do. It would not pay to cart the ore to the Missouri, and our furnace would not reduce it. We resolved to suspend operations until the Pacific Railroad reached Salt Lake.

THE PAHRANAGAT ALADDINS.

"In the summer of sixty-eight two men named Woodman[18] and Chisholm[19] were knocking around Pahranagat,[20] down in Nevada, above sixty miles from Pioche.[21] Woodman was a butcher doing a little business with the miners, and Chisholm was a sort of prospector. Through some means they heard of our operations in Little Cottonwood. They came up and jumped the Braine and Nicholls locations and several others, claiming that they were abandoned. They formed a new district, and called it the Little Cottonwood Mining District. Among other things they relocated the Pittsburgh, Chicago and St. Louis claims, consolidated them, and named them the Monitor. This was our property. I wrote to James E. Lyon,[22] a New York member of our company, about it. Lyon came on, and we went to see Woodman and Chisholm. They held on to the locations, but told Lyon if he would furnish capital to develop the mine, they would let us in. We agreed to it. So they located Lyon and myself the same as themselves, and Lyon promised to raise the money for development."

"What did the members of the Utah Prospecting and Silver Mining Company of New York think of this arrangement?" I inquired.

"Oh," replied the young man, with a laugh, "they didn't know anything about it. Such things are all square and legitimate in mining camps so long as you're snug and nobody drops on it.

SWEET LITTLE EMMA.

"Well, as I said, Lyon and myself were planted in with them. Afterward they relocated for Lyon, calling his claim the Sherman. It was the same thing, you know, only under a different name. An arrangement was made to put down a shaft fifty feet at

$3 a foot. It was then down about ten feet. Lyon left for New York after contracting with Snyder[23] and another man to aid Woodman and Chisholm in sinking it fifty feet. All four of them were as poor as the devil. Winter was upon them, and a regular Wasatch snow storm raging. They boarded with old man Reich.[24] He was a Dutchman, with mighty little money. Woodman and Chisholm hadn't a cent, but the old man caught the mining fever and took their promises to pay. More than that, he bought buckets, picks, and shovels, and packed their powder and provisions up to the mine waist deep in the snow. In return they located him with the rest of us. So Snyder and all hands kept singing the shaft. They worked all winter and had taken out sixty or seventy tons of ore when the vein pinched. In going down after this pinch the seam would widen out four or five inches, and then pinch in again until it was as thin as a hair. At one time it was lost altogether, but was afterward found under a bed of trap rock. At the depth of ninety feet they began to strike large bodies of ore. It assayed over a hundred dollars to the ton. Someone nicknamed the mine the Little Emma. I have heard that it first got this name from a daughter of Woodhull,[25] whom Woodman and Chisholm employed as assayer. She was a sweet little child. There had been sharp practice, however, before the large bodies of ore were discovered. Where the vein widened after a pinch they found rich quantities of desulphurized silver. They kept quiet, and first and last made a good deal of money out of it. Lyon and I never found it out until a long time afterward.

ROUGH ON OLD MAN REICH.

"Well, they kept at work, slowly lowering the shaft. The mine grew richer and richer. During 1869 they ran it down to a depth of 120 feet. The Pacific Railroad was completed, and the cars were running. It was evident that it was going to be a big thing all around. In February 1870, Woodman and Chisholm did a smart piece of business. They slyly relocated the mine, and called it the Emma. In the relocation, Lyon, myself, and a man named Crocker[26] were chucked overboard. It was some time before we found it out. But the meanest thing of all was their treatment of old man Reich. They stuck him clear off on the tail end of the mine, and made him believe that he was segregated from them on ground not worth a damn. It was rough on the old Dutchman, for if it hadn't been for him they would at one spell have abandoned the thing altogether. He stepped in at the final moment and put out his last cent to keep them going. They not only relocated the claim, but the books containing our locations were destroyed, and a bogus set made out containing no record of them. It was a black piece of work.

"By this time news of the richness of the mine began to spread over the Territory. Walker Brothers of Salt Lake[27] took a look at it, and bought up a sixth interest, 400 feet, for $30,000. The Emma Silver Mining Company of Salt Lake was then organized. They opened out the mine and shipped the ore to Swansea. Thousands of tons were sent over the water. The shipments netted $135 per ton over and above all expenses. The claim poured out silver like water, and everybody was talking about it. In the summer Lyon came back from New York and was mad as hell. He applied for an injunction and protested the application for a patent. He slung himself loose around Salt Lake City, and raged like a genuine lion. The application for an injunction was refused. The decision didn't please Lyon in the least. He gathered his papers together, and went for a second injunction, and again the courts turned him off.

THE GATHERING OF FINANCIAL SHARKS.

"That winter the brother of your great New York domino player, Bill Lent,[28] turned up in Salt Lake. He had heard of the big thing up in Little Cottonwood, and knife in hand was after a slice of it. His experts tested the mine, and reported everything was entirely satisfactory. On behalf of certain California capitalists he offered the Woodman party $1,200,000 for the whole claim. They snapped at the offer, but Lyon had raised such an internal row about the title that the Californian was scared off before the bargain was closed.

"About this time I began to pick up the old Braine and Nicholls titles. If you remember, they ran southeast, while the locations of the old Utah Prospecting and Silver Mining Company of New York, in which I was still interested, ran northwest, Dr. Congar having driven the stakes at the initial point. Having secured these titles I took a trip to San Francisco, where I fell in with Joseph W. Haskin,[29] better known as "Old Titles." I sold him the St. Louis, Monitor, and Sherman locations for a thousand dollars and half of what could be made out of them. These locations covered a part of the Emma claim. The latter, to be sure, was the mother vein, and the former were little spurs; but, as they were located first, were valid and valuable, taking in a body of the richest ore claimed by the Emma. Blaine and Nicholls had nine locations in all. One was as good as all, but they made nine so as to be sure and cover everything on the ground. Nobody then had any idea there was such an immense silver pocket below, but when a prospector strikes a lead he wants to gobble all the land he can, so as to have a clean scope for future development.

KEEN NEW YORKERS ON THE SCENT.

"Well, after Haskin and I had secured our Braine and Nicholls titles, Trainor W. Park[30] and Gen. Baxter[31] visited Salt Lake. They came from New York, and were nosing about for quite a spell. They had heard of the big thing and were after it. They went up to Little Cottonwood with their experts, and came back assured that the reports concerning the mine were not exaggerated. The Woodman party offered them half of it for $1,500,000. Meanwhile, Lyon was slashing around in the courts, Haskin was opening his parallels, and the sky looked squally. Park and Baxter hesitated. They carefully examined the legal situation, and slipped back to New York without accepting the $1,500,000 offer. During the winter Woodman sold his interest to Warren Hussey[32] of Salt Lake for $130,000. That let more ready capital into the mine, and tons of silver fairly jumped out of it. Now, I want you to try to understand the lay of the ground from a legal point of view. Haskin was in the courts, standing on the old Braine and Nicholls locations running southeast. Lyon was planted on Dr. Congar's locations for the old Utah Prospecting and Silver Mining Company of New York running northwest, and the Woodman party had possession of the mine, backed by the Woodman and Chisholm claim.

"All this time a steady stream of silver was flowing through New York into Wales, and the Eastern capitalists were beginning to open their eyes. With the return of spring, back came Park, accompanied by red-headed Selover[33] and two or three other Wall Street birds. The Woodman party approached Lyon and proposed a compromise. They offered him $300,000 for his titles. They thought that if they could get him out of the way they could easily sell their half interest to the New York crowd for $1,500,000. Judge Smith,[34] Lyon's counsel, advised him to accept the compromise, but he wouldn't. He wanted $500,000. He grabbed for the biggest bottle on the highest shelf, and fell without getting anything. Had he accepted the offer he would have been $300,000 in the pocket, and the Woodman company would have bagged $453,000. If the Woodman party had closed with Lyon at $500,000 they would have saved $250,000. As it was, the New York roosters gobbled it all.

RED-HEADED SELOVER TO THE FRONT.

"From the beginning it was seen that the New Yorkers meant business. Red-headed Selover was buzzing around like a ring-tailed hornet. Wine flowed like water, and elegant suppers were nightly spread in the Townsend House. Park was aware of the Woodman party's attempt to settle with Lyon, and did everything he could to defeat it. He was authorized to buy a half interest in the mine, and he wanted to get it as cheap as possible. He played a pretty game. He hobnobbed with Lyon and acknowledged the validity of his title, but objected to its purchase because the other party was in possession. He invited the Walker Brothers, Warren Hussey, and other members of the Woodman crowd to a Townsend House supper, and insinuated that he was ready to accept their terms if they could give him a clean title; but he could not think of taking hold of a defective title for $1,500,000. They made repeated overtures to Lyon, but in vain. He thought he was sure of selling to the New Yorkers, and was as stiff as a stake. Red-headed Selover was everywhere. He poured his champagne into the throat of every man who knew anything about the dispute, and kept the thing fomenting until the Woodman party lowered their colors and sold out a half interest to Park & Co. for $750,000. They immediately formed what they called the Emma Silver Mining Company of New York, and stocked it for $5,000,000. As for Lyon, they didn't know him after that. His day had gone by. He had ground his meal so fine that the wind had blown it away.

"About that time Haskin rushed off to San Francisco. The Californians were chagrined to hear that a New York gang had got away with the prize, and gladly received proposals from 'Old Titles.' They organized the Emma Silver Mining Company of San Francisco on the Braine and Nicholls papers. Its leading stockholders were Fry, Ralston's father-in-law,[35] Judge Heidenfeldt,[36] Bill Lent, A. E. Head,[37] George D. Frisbie,[38] Gen. Dodge,[39] Haskin, and others. I would give you the amount of capital stock and the money paid in, with other particulars of the organization, but it might produce hard feelings and get me into difficulty.

FIRST APPEARANCE OF NEVADA BILL.

"The spring of seventy-one opened with preparations for a grand struggle in the courts. Lyon made his appearance early in the summer. He was breathing vengeance, and was backed by Bill Stewart of Nevada[40] and a lawyer named Hillyer.[41] Park and another Vermont lawyer were close upon their heels with blood in their eyes. They represented the New York company. The California crowd ranged themselves under the legal guidance of Earl[42] and Smith[43] and Judge Heidenfeldt. The most of their business, however, was managed by Head. Lyon opened the hall by going for another injunction. The application was made before Judge McKean of the Supreme Court.[44] The Vermont lawyer based his opposition on the claim that the locations on Emma Hill were abandoned when Woodman and Chisholm took hold of them. Hillyer answered Lyon so promptly and effectively that counsel·agreed to leave the case to Judge Curtis of Boston,[45] who was to come out here and decide the law points.

"During the pendency of these proceedings the California Company went to work on the Braine and Nicholls claims, 150 feet northwest of the old Emma shaft. They went down fifty-five feet. Twenty-five feet more would have put them upon a large body of ore, but Head listened to the advice of Bill Stewart, who told him that if he went lower and shouldn't happen to get anything but a small feeder, it would damage his chances in the suit. The fact was that Stewart and Hillyer were afraid that Head would strike a big vein, and they wanted to put him to sleep, if possible, while they drove a compromise between Park and Lyon. Head listened to Stewart and stopped digging. God knows what his lawyers were about. I don't. Stewart was working for himself, and was ready to sell out either side so long as his own prospects were bright. I have no doubt that he and Park had an understanding in the early part of the game.

NEVADA BILL A HUMMER.

"All this time Park was making compromise offers to the California Company. First, he offered everything that the mine would bring over $2,500,000. This was refused. The Californians didn't believe that the mine would fetch the sum specified. Finally Park offered them a clean $750,000 for their right and title. The proposition was accepted. The writings were to be drawn up in New York City, where all parties agreed to meet and sign them. The Californians were joyful. Bill Lent pranced around like a nanny goat. They thought that they had got the thing all settled, and that they had made a good speck out of it. Bill Stewart congratulated them, and it is said, claimed that he had considerable to do with effecting the arrangement. I have heard that he pocketed a round fee, but whether he received it from Park, Lent, or Lyon I don't know. He was Lyon's lawyer, and everything was lovely.

"While dickering with the Californians Park was shrewdly effecting a settlement with Lyon. He wanted a patent for the mine, and Lyon, you will remember, had protested his application. The New York market had rejected his $5,000,000 scheme, and he wanted to float it on the bloody Englishmen, but he could do nothing without a patent, but he couldn't get a patent with Lyon's protest barring the door to the department at Washington. The California Company stood upon Lyon's protest on the interest that I held with Lyon to Dr. Congar's locations for the old Utah Prospecting and Silver Mining Company of New York. If Park could settle with Lyon and get the protest withdrawn he would knock the platform from under the Californians and they would go to grass. Through the medium of Bill Stewart, he accomplished his design. Lyon, by Stewart's advice, gave up his claims for $150,000 or $200,000. They were the same claims for which he had previously refused $300,000. Stewart and Hillyer absorbed the most of the $150,000 in fees. The mask was then thrown off, and Nevada William appeared in his true colors as one of Park's counselors. At one time he seemed to be acting as lawyer for all three of the parties, pocketing fees right and left. Oh, he was a hummer, and no mistake.

CALIFORNIA BILL AFTER NEVADA WILLIAM.

"Well, the arrangement with Lyon was concluded, and his patent protest withdrawn. The prop was taken from under the Californians. They knew nothing of the Lyon treaty, and were not aware of the withdrawal of the protest. The coast at Washington was clear. Park and Stewart slipped off to the Interior Department, and through the latter's Senatorial influence and some hocus pocus in the department secured a patent. The sleepy confidence of the Californians was wonderful. Sharps themselves, they knew they were dealing with the sharpest of sharps, and yet were put to sleep as easily as pap-sucking babies. While Park and Stewart were in Washington snaking out a patent, Bill Lent and A. K. Head were in New York waiting for the $750,000 plum to drop into their mouths. The poor innocents thought the New Yorkers wanted to sign the papers.

"The patent secured, Park and Stewart put out for Europe to slip the scheme on the London market. They were mighty quiet about it, but Lent heard of it two hours before the departure of the steamer. The news was like an electric shock. He felt that he had been sold, and suspected that Park did not intend to fulfill his contract. He knew that something had happened, but had no idea what it was. He was groping in the dark. There was no time to lose. Hastily gathering all his titles and papers, he strapped his baggage, and shot for the steamer. Park and Stewart had not yet come on board. The Californian was on nettles. He watched and prayed, and sure enough the two worthies walked up the gang-plank within ten minutes of the time of starting. Lent lay low. Park and Stewart were as smiling as a basket of chips. On the second or third day out the Californian showed up. Park and Stewart were astonished. They were extremely polite and inquired after Lent's health, but said nothing about the $750,000. Lent delicately broached the subject. Park quietly pulled the patent from his pocket and spread it before the eyes of the astonished Pacific sloper. His voice was child like and bland. 'We have no further use for you, William,' he said. 'You are playing a part in "Love's Labor Lost." You had better stop the first inward-bound steamer and go back to Salt Lake.'

THE WALL OF CALIFORNIA BILL.

"The murder was out. California William upbraided Nevada Bill in terms more forcible than polite. The scales had fallen from his eyes. He ripped and raved, and swore that he would follow them to the ends of the earth but he would have satisfaction. He threatened to fill all Europe with his howls if they didn't come down. He would split the financial centre of the world with his complaints unless he was fixed all right. Park and Stewart consulted together. Lent's advent, of course, was a thing that they had not counted upon. There was no doubt of his power to injure their scheme if they placed it on the European market. So they gave the tearing Californian a dose of soothing syrup. How much he got I don't know. It must have been something handsome. I have heard it estimated as high as $75,000 and $100,000. Whatever it was, William was heard of no more. He dropped the California Company like a hot potato, and shouted every man for himself and the devil take the hindmost.

BOB SCHENCK ROPED IN.

"Well, Park and Stewart began operations in London. They succeeded in effecting a junction with Baron Grant,[46] the swell[47] English financier, and the scheme was finally foisted upon the British market. It was not done without difficulty. The mine was stocked for $5,000,000, and the Englishmen didn't put up the money fast enough. Nevada Bill again displayed his activity. He roped in Bob Schenck,[48] and for a time the American Embassy was a figurehead for the beauties. Bob officially endorsed the project, and cracked it to the skies. Meantime the property was examined by London experts, and pronounced very valuable. Their report, with the American Minister's endorsement, sent the thing along quite swimmingly."

"Did Minister Schenck get anything for his services?" I asked.

"Do you think Bob Schenck is a damned fool?" was the reply. "Of course he got an interest for services rendered. I presume it was a fair-sized plum. I know nothing about it, but I have heard on good authority that he received $50,000 worth of the stock. It didn't amount to much in the end, however, for when the stock was way up in the sky he held on to it, and at last let go when it ran below zero. I suppose he expected that Stewart would give him the cue, but you can't most always sometimes depend on Stewart.

PROF. SILLIMAN ON DECK.

"Well, Park and Grant, and Stewart, and Brydges Williams[49] and Bob Schenck got the stock on the market. While they were floating it, another plan was devised to give it a lift. Prof. Silliman of Yale College[50] was asked to examine the mine and make a report. It was understood that he was to have $15,000 for his services anyhow, and $50,000 if the report was very flattering. Silliman, although an American, had a scientific reputation in England, and the right kind of a report from him would send the stock a kiting. The Professor came out here in a palace car, accompanied by Brydges Williams. Several other Englishmen were along watching operations. They found out what the report was going to be, and telegraphed over to Park and Grant in cipher. The stock was selling at par. The Ring bought all they could get hold of. On the publication of Silliman's glowing report it jumped up to ten or twelve pounds premium. Then Park and his friends sold out, and made a splendid thing of it.

That was the time for Bob Schenck to let go, but his fond friends forgot to give him the cue. Silliman pocketed his $50,000, and quietly sailed back to Yale College.

UNCLE POLAND OF VERMONT TAKES A HAND.

"After the organization of the London Emma, Park bought out all of the old Woodman crowd but Chisholm for forty cents on the dollar. Chisholm held on and got fifty. Now you must remember that Woodman, Day, and Chisholm held on to the old Monitor, Magnet, and Illinois tunnel locations. They were all nothing but the old Pittsburgh and St. Louis locations made by Dr. Congar. The Emma was really an older location than either of them, but the Monitor, Magnet, and Illinois were recorded first. They were located as an east and west mine, whereas the Pittsburgh and St. Louis were recorded as running northwest and southwest. They were, however, the same vein. The new party began to bore the Illinois tunnel so as to tap their locations. While digging the tunnel, they struck a large body of rich ore. Although over two hundred feet from their shaft, this ore was claimed by the London Emma. The Emma applied for an injunction, on the ground that it was the same body of ore as their own. The Woodman party produced experts who swore that there was no connection between the ore deposits. Witnesses for the Park party swore point blank against them. There was a hell of a time, Bill Stewart again showed his face as counsel for the Park crowd. Old Uncle Luke P. Poland,[51] chairman of the House Judiciary Committee, was his associate. The case came before Judge McKean. He promptly granted the injunction, and stopped the Woodman party from getting out the ore. So decisively did McKean favor the Stewart crowd in his rulings that he was called one of their advocates. It was asserted that Park owned him, body and breeches, and more than one man believed it. Well, he sustained the injunction, and actually allowed the Emma fellows to go on and get out the Illinois deposits without giving any bonds. If it had proved a different body of ore there could have been no redress for the Woodman party, because the Emma was an English company and limited. Old Uncle Poland was pleased with the decision. He got his fee and sloped back to Washington.

"The worst part of this whole transaction was the action of Judge McKean. Under the Woodman suit Emma stock had again run down on the London market. Park and his friends took in large quantities at the reduced price. McKean's decision was known in London twenty hours before it was promulgated in this city. The editor of the *Salt Lake Herald* received an Associated Press dispatch from London announcing the decision an hour before it was announced from the bench. Of course the stock rose on the English market, and Park and his boys must have cleared a snug percentage.

THE LAST FIGHT.

"Now go back a little. You remember that Dr. Congar and I were the original locators, on the bill of the old Utah Prospecting and Silver Mining Company of New York. Haskin had bought this company's locations, and had formed a copartnership with Congar and myself. We proposed to consolidate with the Woodman party. The hatchet was buried, and the consolidation was effected after McKean had granted the Emma injunction. An organization was formed under the title of the Emma Hill Consolidated Mining Company of San Francisco. It was a stiff crowd. Park saw that he had a damned hard fight on hand. He had put up $300,000 as a guarantee of dividends and titles for one year to the English company, and he didn't want to lose the money. He must have known that he would eventually be compelled to settle the old Haskin titles acquired from Braine, Nicholls, and others. His object seems to have been to keep them entirely out of the way and everything covered up, forcing Emma stock to the highest price, when he would silently unload and settle the Haskin titles to the best advantage. The Emma Company, not satisfied with McKean's injunction, had brought a suit for damages against the Illinois Tunnel. The Illinois stood up for a fight, but under the pressure of the suit Park stepped in and forced a settlement. He secured all the old titles at a reasonable figure, and the London Emma has now a clean title, with no prospective legal troubles. During the last suit everybody supposed that the English crowd would beat and the stock would go up. Park's final settlement made it stiffer than usual. He took advantage of the rise and pitched a lot of it overboard, giving out that he was buying. He played the thing so shrewdly that the market was broken and Warren Hussy caught on the turn to the tune of $150,000.

YOU MUST ASK PARK.

"Every point in Park's scheme has been made with consummate skill. When stock is up he always gets rid of it. When it's down he always gets hold of it. And he invariably keeps himself in a position where he can send it up or down just as he chooses. He has made at least $1,500,000 out of his operations. Baxter, I think, got away with $800,000. The others more or less, according to their weight of metal. Bill Stewart was oiled from ear to toe, and as sweetly scented as a cucumber bug."

Here the young man lighted a cigar, and stopped talking. His story was finished. After waiting for him to continue the conversation I said, "Emma stock is very low now. What is the reason?"

He shrugged his shoulders. "You must ask Park," he replied.

"Prospectors tell me that the mine has petered out," I observed.

"I know better," he answered. "They lie. The mine is as rich as ever."

"Why doesn't it produce the ore then?" I inquired. "I understand that it hardly pays working expenses."

"I have nothing to say about that," said he. "The managing director and superintendent are men appointed through Park's influence. You must ask Park such questions as that. The mine can produce ore if necessary."

The sun was now about an hour high, and the shadows of the locust trees were lengthening. We had occupied our arm chairs nearly four hours, and our bones were aching. After receiving my thanks the young man crossed the street and entered the office of a mining company.

MR. ATWOOD.

All sorts of rumors were afloat in Salt Lake City and Alta concerning the mine. Some declared it richer than ever. Others said that it was completely gutted. Woodman told me that he believed it to be a true fissure vein, and he understood that they had gone through a stratum of limestone, and struck a granite formation which was perfectly barren. A shrewd operator claimed to know all about it. There was an unusually rich deposit in the lower level, but the mine had been flooded for the purpose of concealing it. In the upper levels the rich leads had been boarded up so as to hide them from the eyes of miners and prying stockholders.

With the view of seeing for myself, I visited Mr. Atwood,[52] the agent of the company in Salt Lake City, and asked permission to enter the mine. Mr. Atwood is an Englishman with a Yankee varnish. He treated me with the greatest courtesy, and regretted that he could not give me a pass. "It is against our rules," he said. I told him that I had visited the Terrible, Pelican, Cariboo, Bobtail,[53] and most of the celebrated mines in Colorado, and had been readily furnished with passes. Their agents seemed pleased to have a newspaper man examine their mines. No objection had been made to my inspecting other Utah mines, and the Little Cottonwood people were especially desirous of a visit from a SUN correspondent. It made no difference to Mr. Atwood. He stood firm, and politely but determinedly informed me that he could not allow me to go through the Emma. However, as I was on my way to Alta, he would give me a letter to Mr. Williams, the Superintendent,[54] and I could look at the jiggers and sluices, and the operations outside of the mine, which would, no doubt, prove interesting to me. It was the best that could be done. I thanked him and took the letter.

THE DOOR BARRED.

I found that the Emma mine perched on the side of a mountain about two thousand feet from Alta mining camp. Two or three long houses surrounded by great dumps of dirt, tramway skeletons, and long files of cordwood marked the entrance of the tunnel leading to the mine. The discovery shaft is not used. Dozens of men were sluicing the dirt piles, and rocking or jigging long boxes containing what was left in the sluices. The Superintendent read the agent's letter and treated me most graciously. He actually accompanied me a hundred feet or more into the tunnel, but stopped when we reached a shaft leading to the levels. He is a shrewd Maine Yankee. When I asked him any questions concerning the condition of the mine he referred me to Mr. Atwood. Although it was the best time of the year for mining operations, there appeared to be but little doing in the Emma. The men were sluicing and jigging surface dirt and tailings. Mr. Williams said that the sluicings brought $60 per ton, delivered in Sandy, a point on the Utah Southern Railroad, about twenty miles from Alta. The jigging averaged $200 per ton. The mine was yielding less than eleven tons per day. The Flagstaff, an English mine stocked for only $1,500,000, and situated on the same ledge as the Emma, was producing 125 tons per day, averaging $90 per ton.

It is only during the months of July and August that the Little Cottonwood mines are entirely free from snow. It was therefore remarkable that things were not more lively in the Emma. I asked the superintendent if they were working the lower levels. "No," he answered. "Why not?" I inquired. "Because there is

too much water in the mine," he replied. If true, this was somewhat singular, as the mine is vertically not over 300 feet below
the highest surface. The mountain brooks were nearly dry, and
the Emma Company had tapped a small stream coming from
Grizzly Flat[55] for sluicing purposes. A large pump was lazily
forcing a little water from the bottom of the mine, but the flow
bore no comparison to that of the Bobtail lode in Colorado.

DARK HINTS.

The superintendent said that there were from 2,000 to 2,400
feet of levels. The greatest depth of the mine on a vertical line
below the floor of the tunnel was 150 feet. This was 260 feet below
the discovery shaft, which is further up on the hill. The lowest
point below the upper surface of the hill was 300 feet. The course
of the vein is northwest to southeast, with a dip in the latter direction fifty degrees from a horizontal, varying occasionally.

Satisfied that I could glean no further information I mounted
my horse and rode back to Alta. Everybody was filled with stories told by men working in the mine, but no two were alike.
Nobody but the superintendent knew anything about it, and his
mouth was sealed. The general belief appeared to be that the pro-
ducing power of the mine was as great as ever, but nearly everybody admitted it was overstocked. I accidentally learned that the
superintendent of the Flagstaff was buying Emma stock at the
low prices, and concluded that he knew what he was about. Dark
hints were thrown out concerning a ring of directors, who were
accused of manipulating the mine for their own purposes. I had no
further means of verifying them and returned to Salt Lake after
ten days. During my stay in Little Cottonwood I visited dozens of
its mines. The Emma was the only one that barred me out.

I met Chisholm and Woodman. Their version of the discovery of the mine differs somewhat from the one above given. It is
worth a separate letter.

ZISKA.

NOTES

1. The Little Emma Mine is located in Little Cottonwood Canyon about twenty-five miles east of Salt Lake City in the Wasatch Mountains, a range in the western edge of the Rocky Mountains. Today the area is well-known for snow skiing.

2. In 1875, William C. Carey led the prosecution of John D. Lee for the murder of 120 people at Mountain Meadows in southern Utah in September 1857. Lee was acquitted at that trial but was convicted at a second the next year. The mass murder and the trials remain controversial to this day.

3. The cooperative, a general store that sold everything from produce and dry goods to wagons and Singer sewing machines, was on the southeast corner of East Temple and First South. Incorporated in 1870, it was governed by a board with Brigham Young as president.

4. The Ceylon hat, or baku, was a fedora woven from straw taken from a Ceylonese palm.

5. Today, Schleswig-Holstein is the name given to the northernmost German state. In the mid-nineteenth century, Schleswig and Holstein were two duchies whose association with either Denmark or the German confederation became contentious following the death of King Frederick VII of Denmark in 1863. With no male heir to the line of succession to the Danish crown and the duchies, a number of political and legal questions arose as to the status of the duchies vis-à-vis Denmark and the German confederation. The situation was resolved through complicated treaties brokered in Vienna and Prague.

6. In the late 1860s and early 1870s, "Jubilee" Jim Fisk, a New York City tycoon (some would say shyster) was involved in a host of unscrupulous shenanigans to try to gain control of the railroads for monetary profit. At the same time, both Jay Gould and J. Pierpont Morgan also were speculating on railroads, such as the Erie Railway. In 1869, Fisk and Gould tried to corner the gold market, setting off a panic. They failed when the United States Treasury Department intervened. Their complicated machinations to make money off railroads and the gold market were legendary.

7. In 1873, the two-story Townsend House, with its 150 rooms, was located at the corner of West Temple Street and First South.

8. It is likely Congar, who was either a medical doctor or a mining geologist, was a friend of James P. Bruner (note spelling; Bruner is also mentioned later in this chapter) or one of Bruner's sons and, like the Bruners, was from Philadelphia (Keller, *Lady in the Ore Bucket*, 123).

9. Bingham, a mining town, was about twenty-five miles southwest of Salt Lake City. In recent times it has been engulfed by a copper mine.

10. The excitement was the discovery of gold. Montana's gold rush began in the early 1860s.

11. Undoubtedly, the prospecting company had ties to the New York shipping line of Mailler, Lord, and Quereau, also of 108 Wall Street in Lower Manhattan, whose Kangaroo Line of ships plied the seas between Australia and New York City.

12. In 1865, Silas Brain (note spelling) was credited with filing the first legitimate mining claim in the Wasatch Mountains.

13. This should be D. C. Nicholls.

14. Leads were individual locations where ores were found on the surface of the ground and for which claims were filed.

15. The Mountain Lake mining district was one of more than ninety districts registered in Utah Territory and filed in the General Land Office in Salt Lake City in accordance with federal law.

16. Philadelphia merchant James P. Bruner, as noted above, was connected to Dr. Congar.

17. Alta, today known for its snow skiing, is at the upper end of Little Cottonwood Canyon. In 1874 it was said to be eleven miles up the canyon.

18. James F. Woodman is credited by some historians with initiating the Little Emma mining boom. Cummings's article offers a different perspective (as does Keller, *Lady in the Ore Bucket*, 116–137). By 1874, Woodman had become a successful mine owner in the area.

19. Robert B. Chisholm.

20. The Pahranagat mining district was in the Pahranagat Valley north of Las Vegas and west of the intersection of Arizona, Utah, and Nevada.

21. Pioche, Nevada, is north-northeast, about twenty miles from the Utah border.

22. Lyon was involved in other mining ventures in Colorado.

23. John Snyder.

24. Reich is probably Fritz Rettich, who later ran one of the early hotels in Alta (Keller, *Lady in the Ore Bucket*, 168, 174, 183, 329, 331). In 1874, there was a Fritz Reich who was the proprietor of the Pacific House hotel in Salt Lake City (Sloan, *Gazeteer* [*sic*], 267). One wonders if all three men were not the same individual.

25. There were three Woodhull brothers: Henry J., William S., and Sereno D. (Keller, *Lady in the Ore Bucket*, 154). Henry was shot and killed in a mining camp in Little Cottonwood Canyon in August 1870. The 1870 federal census, taken in Salt Lake City in May, lists Henry as a resident of that town. The source of the name of the Emma Mine has drawn three explanations. In addition to the one offered in Cummings's article, Keller (in *Lady in the Ore Bucket*, 128) cites documents strongly suggesting that the Emma mining district took its name from Robert Chisholm's youngest child and only daughter. *The Nation*, in an 1873 article (Anonymous, "The True History of a Great Mining Enterprise," 402), offers a third explanation: James Woodman and Chisholm named "it after a lady with whom one or possibly both . . . had been illicitly consorting in San Francisco." Keller's documentation and explanation seem most plausible.

26. An Edward Crocker, age forty-eight, was working in the Little Emma mines in 1884 when a winter avalanche killed him and several other people who had been seeking warmth in the mine boiler room (Keller, *Lady in the Ore Bucket*, 173). I do not know if this is the same individual.

27. The four Walker brothers, Samuel Sharp (1834–1887), Joseph Robinson (1836–1901), David Frederick (1838–1910), and Mathew Henry (1845–1916), were natives of Yorkshire, England. They were extremely successful merchants and bankers in Salt Lake City who were excommunicated from the Mormon Church by the time of their investments in Little Emma mining ventures. Salt Lake City's Walker Center was named for the family.

28. Bill Lent is the San Francisco mining entrepreneur William M. Lent, infamous for some of his dealings in supposed diamond mines. I could not identify his brother.

29. Haskin is listed in the 1864 San Francisco City Directory as operating a "mining stocks" office at 728 Montgomery.

30. Trenor W. Park (note spelling) was a banker with interests in Vermont and New York City and also an investor in railroads.

31. H. Henry Baxter had been adjutant general in Vermont during the Civil War. He then became a financier with interests in Wall Street and railroads.

32. Hussey was president of the First National Bank in Salt Lake City. Keller (*Lady in the Ore Bucket,* 129) records the amount as $110,000.

33. James H. Selover was another New York financier.

34. I believe this was Elias Smith of Salt Lake City, who was a probate judge.

35. John D. Fry's daughter was married to William C. Ralston, founder of the Bank of California. The two collaborated in several business ventures.

36. Solomon Heydenfeldt (note spelling) was a San Francisco attorney whose law offices in 1864 were at 712 Montgomery, just down the street from Joseph Haskin's office. In the 1850s he served on the California Supreme Court.

37. Head was prominent in mining ventures in California.

38. I have not been able to further identify George D. Frisbie.

39. General George S. Dodge was a veteran of the Civil War. He previously had been involved in investment schemes with other of these individuals.

40. Senator William M. Stewart served in the U.S. Senate from 1864 to 1875 and from 1887 to 1905. He speculated in mining stocks.

41. Curtis J. Hillyer also was a speculator.

42. This may have been John O. Earl, whose San Francisco business interests included banking and mining. He knew William Lent and Senator Stewart, among others, and was involved in mining ventures in Nevada.

43. I believe this is Judge Elias Smith of Salt Lake City, mentioned previously in this article.

44. Judge James B. McKean was federal judge of the Third District Court and served as Chief Justice of the Utah Supreme Court from 1870 to 1875. He was well-known for his anti-Mormon views.

45. Judge Benjamin R. Curtis served on the United States Supreme Court from 1851 to 1857 and then resigned over the public controversy

surrounding the Dred Scott case. He returned to Boston to practice law.

46. Albert Grant was an English speculator and financier who, according to *The Nation* (Anonymous, "True History," 403), was an "expert in rigging the market."

47. "Swell," used here as an adjective, probably means socially prominent.

48. Robert C. Schenck, a Union general during the Civil War and four-time U.S. congressman (1863–1871), was minister to Great Britain at the time of the Little Emma scandal. His diplomatic immunity kept him from being charged in England, but he was forced to resign his post in 1876 after congressional hearings were held on the scandal.

49. E. Brydges Willyams (note spelling), a former member of Parliament, had financial interests in mining and banking.

50. Benjamin Silliman Jr., a mining expert and paid consultant, charged according to the "value of his services"; that is, the more glowing the report, the higher the fee. He testified before the congressional hearing into the Little Emma investment fiasco in 1876.

51. Poland, from Vermont, served in the United States Senate from 1865 to 1867, having been elected to a vacancy. He then served several terms in the House of Representatives (1867–1875, 1883–1885).

52. According to Sloan's *Gazeteer* [*sic*], 127, George M. Atwood was company manager for the mine.

53. These are all Colorado mines in Boulder, Clear Creek, and Gilpin counties west and northwest of Denver. There are other mines with these same names both in Colorado and elsewhere in the West.

54. Hannibal Williams was superintendent at the mine (Sloan, *Gazeteer* [*sic*], 127).

55. A small stream flowed through Grizzly Gulch and intersected Little Cottonwood Stream. Grizzly Flat was a short-lived mining town adjacent to the former stream.

I Met a Man with Seventeen Wives: Divorce Mormon Style

THE PUBLIC LOVES A GOOD BREAKUP, especially when it involves celebrities of one sort or another. Thousands of words have been written about Brad Pitt and Jennifer Aniston, Elizabeth Taylor and Eddie Fisher, and Antony and Cleopatra (the latter got back together at the end of Act 4, just in time for Antony to die).

In 1873 the breakup of another couple drew similar attention when a not-yet-twenty-four-year-old woman, Ann Eliza Webb Young, announced she was filing for divorce from her husband of five years. What drew the news media, including our

ANN ELIZA YOUNG, CA. 1875. (YOUNG, *WIFE NUMBER 19*, FRONTISPIECE)

own Amos Jay Cummings, was the fact that her husband was
Brigham Young, the Mormon prophet and titular head of the
Church of Jesus Christ of Latter-day Saints, as well as the first
governor of Utah Territory. Ann Eliza Young was one of at least
fifty-two women joined to Mr. Young in polygamous marriages.

Even more than celebrities, polygamy draws a crowd (which may account for the success of HBO's television series *Big Love*).

Less than fifty years old, the Mormon Church in 1873 was viewed by many Americans as strange, exotic, and, by some, a menace to normal society. After the founding of the new church in New York State in the early nineteenth century, its members, often facing fierce hostility from local residents and authorities, moved first to Ohio, then Missouri, Illinois, and finally Utah Territory where, under Brigham Young's leadership, the Mormons established a successful religious and economic enterprise with diverse business interests. Non-Mormons in Utah often cast envious eyes on the Mormons, and legal and other clashes between Mormons and Gentiles (non-Mormons) in Utah are well documented. Gentile attorneys and judges, among others, did not hesitate to try to use the law to blunt the influence of the Mormon Church. It was not uncommon, for instance, to bar Mormons from juries.

The civil divorce lodged by Ann Eliza Young may have originally been filed for personal reasons, but it soon was caught up in the controversies of the day about the Mormons, their power in Utah, their legal conflicts with the federal government and non-Mormons, the power of Mormon-dominated territorial courts versus federal courts, and the practice of polygamy.

Ms. Young was never granted a divorce. Why? In 1877, the courts in Utah ruled that she was never legally married to Brigham Young. Even so, by that time she had become a cause célèbre both for women's rights and for those who were anti-Mormon and anti-polygamy. In late 1873 she began a national speaking tour, from San Francisco to New York City, usually titling her public address something like "My Life in Bondage." Eventually, she also lectured in Canada.

That same theme is manifest in the 1875 book she authored, *Wife Number 19 or the Story of a Life in Bondage, Being a Complete Exposé of Mormonism, and Revealing the Sorrows, Sacrifices and*

Sufferings of Women in Polygamy. The 605-page book, which is still in print, was a hit with those harboring anti-Mormon views. It provides a history of the early Mormon Church, written from Ann Eliza's point of view, along with the story of her religious upbringing and her marriage and separation from Brigham Young.

Whether Ms. Young actually was Wife Number 19 in 1873 is a matter still debated by historians, and it is dependent in part on how one defines marriage, as well as the number of deaths and divorces among Young's previous wives. Cummings labeled Ann Eliza Young "Wife 17," whereas she said "Wife 19." Other accounts offer still other numbers because some women were "sealed" to Brigham Young only in a church ceremony with no official marriage certificate, and they never joined his household. If one examines a list of the women to whom Brigham Young was married or sealed, ordered by date of the union, most historians would agree that Ann Eliza comes in at number forty-nine or fifty, although Brigham Young did not have forty-eight or forty-nine spouses at the time he married Ann Eliza Young in 1868.

Ann Eliza Webb was born September 13, 1844, in Nauvoo, Illinois. Her parents, Eliza Churchill and Chauncey G. Webb, were both early converts to Mormonism in their home state of New York. Later the two moved to Ohio and then to Illinois where they were married. In Illinois, Chauncey eventually was sealed to another spouse.

Ann Eliza and her parents left Illinois in spring 1846 with other Mormon families bound for California to seek religious freedom. Two years later they instead reached Salt Lake City, recently selected as the new home for the Mormon contingent.

In April 1863, when she was eighteen, Ann Eliza married James L. Dee, a Mormon. The wedding ceremony in Salt Lake City was presided over by Brigham Young. The marriage to Dee was unhappy, and in December 1865, twenty-one-year-old Ann

Eliza Dee was granted a divorce. The divorce decree was signed by Judge Elias Smith, whose name appears in Cummings's article about the Little Emma mine, as well as in articles in this section. Two and a half years later she was married to Brigham Young. According to historical records as well as Ann Eliza's account in *Wife Number 19*, the wedding took place on April 6, 1868 (an erroneous date is given elsewhere in that same book).

The first public inkling that Ann Eliza Young was seeking a divorce came in July 1873 when word reached Salt Lake City newspapers. On July 16, the news was sent (perhaps by telegraph) to the *New York Times*. Headlined "A Mormon Sensation" and with the subheadline "Brigham Young's Seventeenth Wife Leaves—Suit for Divorce and Alimony Probable," the short item appeared on page one of the *Times* the next day:

> Salt Lake City, Utah, July 16.—A great sensation was
> caused here to-day by the announcement in the *Journal* that
> Ann Eliza Webb Young, the seventeenth wife of Brigham
> Young, had forever left him, carrying off her furniture
> and personal effects. Brigham will endeavor to replevin
> the goods. Mrs. Young is at the Walker House, and three
> leading lawyers are about to institute a suit for divorce and
> alimony in a large sum. Great revelations are expected con-
> cerning the inner domestic life of the Prophet. Mrs. Young
> is enjoying the sympathy of the Gentile ladies, and polyga-
> mous Mormons are a good deal disturbed.

Cummings was in Salt Lake City at the time and picked up on the story. He arranged two interviews with Ann Eliza Young and one with Brigham Young. The interviews, published in the *Sun* in late July and early August, were preceded by a fourth, introductory article outlining the basis for the suit. The four articles, reprinted below, are full of tidbits about the Youngs, their living conditions, and the people around them. The articles represent Cummings at his human-interest-writing best. He wrote them with the intention of at least partially sating his

New York readers, who were anxious for the inside scoop on the breakup.

These articles were not the only ones Cummings wrote about the divorce during his stay in Salt Lake City in summer 1873. Six other articles, each datelined Salt Lake City, contain verbatim court documents and testimony related to the divorce, as well as Cummings's account of wrangling and arguments made by the attorneys for the two sides. There also are some observations about the attorneys, judges, and other individuals participating in the proceedings. The six articles were published on the following dates (two were in the same issue of the *Sun*) and under the following headlines, subheads, and readouts (dateline dates are in brackets):

> August 7—The Mormon Divorce Suit. Brigham Young's Wife Swears Her Life against Him. The Legal Documents in Full—Extraordinary Revelations—A Seventeenth Wife Suing for Divorce—Remarkable Legal Productions— Wonders of Salt Lake Grammar [July 31].

> August 11—The Salt Lake Divorce. A Methodist Clergyman Mixed Up in the Suit. Ann Eliza about to Join the Methodist Church—The Origins of the Suit— Remarkable Statement of Judge Hagan—The Lawyers and Gen. Maxwell Cut by Ann Eliza—A Curious Muddle All Around [August 4].

> August 13—Brigham Young's Fight. The Mormon Leader Wins the Preliminary Skirmish. Interesting Scene in the Salt Lake Court House—The Great Divorce Suit—Gov. Young's Counsel Move to Quash the Return of Process— The Argument before Judge Emerson, and His Decision [August 5].

> August 16—The Utah Divorce Case. The Mormon Prophet Cool and Unruffled. The Hon. Brigham Young's Plea against the Jurisdiction of the Court—The Wife Appearing on the Streets [August 8].

August 16—Argument on His Demurrer—A Five-Hour
Speech Boiled Down—Scenes in the Court Room—Major
Hempstead's Brilliant and Affecting Peroration [August 9].[1]

August 19—The Great Divorce Suit. A Gentile Lawyer
Tearing up Mormondom by the Roots. The Clash of the
Utah Courts—Judge Tilford's Reply to Brigham Young's
Lawyers—The Air Filled with Chunks of Logic—The
Eagle of Eloquence Soaring over the Court Room—A
Venerable Negro Paralyzed—Hot Times in Salt Lake
[August 11].

Cummings was certainly not the only journalist to write about the divorce. Other articles were being written by reporters from the Salt Lake City newspapers at the same time Cummings wrote his, and outside reporters came to Salt Lake City specifically to cover the story. Many of the local stories were reprinted in papers well beyond Salt Lake City. At least one *New York Times* article ("Brigham Young's Divorce Suit," published on August 8, 1873) reprinted much of an article written by Cummings that had been in the *Sun* on the previous day ("The Mormon Divorce Suit"). Such "borrowing" was not uncommon at the time.

The *New York Times* also published several other articles on the divorce, as did other New York newspapers. All the articles were relatively short and none as informative as those Cummings wrote for the *Sun*. Western newspapers, such as the *San Francisco Chronicle*, covered the story in greater detail. Somewhat surprisingly, the story of the divorce suit received lesser coverage in the Salt Lake City newspapers at the time.

The various newspaper articles, especially those in the *Sun*, document the basis for the divorce suit and its fate in the courts. Some of the same information is contained in *Wife Number 19*, and I would not be surprised if parts of the book were not written with a collection of *Sun* newspaper articles in hand.

According to the newspaper accounts, Ann Eliza Young's case against Brigham Young was first heard in district court (a federal court) on July 18, 1873, with Judge James B. Hagan presiding. Through her testimony Ann Eliza informed the court that she had lived in Brigham Young's household for a year after they were first married. Then she and her children were moved to one of Brigham Young's farms four miles outside of Salt Lake City at Little Cottonwood where they lived for three and a half years with Ann Eliza's mother. The mother was said to be ill and infirm, in part due to her hard life on the farm, a life made worse because Brigham Young did not provide adequate support for her, Ann Eliza, and Ann's children. At least that was the story related by Ann Eliza.

In fall 1872, apparently after numerous complaints, Young moved Ann Eliza and her children into a house in Salt Lake City. But even there, according to her, he did not provide adequately for their needs. For instance, Ann Eliza maintained she did not have clothes sufficient to reflect her station in life. She testified in court that she suffered illnesses and distress as a result, allegations substantiated by the sworn testimony of friends.

Other accounts note that Brigham Young gave permission for Ann Eliza Young to take in boarders as a way to derive income. In an 1896 talk before the Booksellers' League in New York City (reported in the *New York Times* on January 18, 1896), James B. Pond, who previously had booked Ann Eliza on the lecture circuit (as explained below), recalls that among her boarders was "a Methodist preacher and his wife." That person is certainly the Rev. C. C. Stratton, who figures prominently in Amos Cummings's *New York Sun* article on August 11, 1873 (noted above), featuring the subhead "A Methodist Clergyman Mixed Up in the Suit." The Rev. Stratton and his spouse are both mentioned by Ann Eliza Young in *Wife Number 19*, although it is not clear that they ever boarded with her. As we shall see, Stratton (as well as Pond) may have played much larger roles in the whole affair than even Cummings thought.

SALT LAKE CITY AS IT LOOKED WHEN CUMMINGS WAS THERE. THE TABER-
NACLE IS ON THE RIGHT. (WILLIAMS, *PACIFIC TOURIST*, 133)

Apparently fed up with her situation (and perhaps heavily influenced by the Strattons), Ann Eliza moved out of the house and took up residence in the Walker House hotel in Salt Lake City in April 1873. Through her attorneys she asked the court to require Brigham Young to give her $1,000-a-month support for herself and to pay $20,000 in fees to her attorneys. Relative to average incomes of the time, both figures seem exorbitant.

According to some press accounts, Ann Eliza, intending to move into the Walker House, had the furniture removed from Brigham Young's house in Salt Lake City where she had been living and taken to an auctioneer to raise funds to support herself and her family.

At the Walker House she was supported in part by various non-Mormon friends, including the Rev. Stratton. Through these friends she apparently was put in contact with a cadre of local attorneys, all of whom, as far as I can tell, harbored anti-Mormon views and saw the case as an opportunity to attack

Brigham Young and to earn lucrative fees. Stratton and others also sought press coverage for the divorce suit.

The initial hearing in court was pretty much pro forma, and the judge directed Brigham Young's attorneys to appear in court on August 5 to answer the charges. At that hearing, which was postponed once due to the urgency of another case before the same judge, Brigham Young's attorneys argued that the suit filed by Ann Eliza Young's attorneys should be tossed out because the number of the court district written by the court staff on the document was in error. No such court existed in Utah. The judge's staff—no doubt after uttering a large "Uh oh!"—quickly informed the judge that the same number had been put on twenty other pending cases, not to mention ones already heard. Judge Emerson, presiding in Judge Hagan's absence, eventually ruled a court was a court and opted to over-look the error and proceed.

Before the next court session, rumors began flying that Ann Eliza Young was dropping the suit, perhaps because she had reached a settlement with Brigham Young. Some of her supporters, not to mention her attorneys, were indignant. The latter threatened to go on with the suit without her. But, as Amos Cummings wrote, she ultimately went forward with the divorce.

Once back in the courts, the suit soon became muddled in legalese and questions of jurisdiction, with judges overruling judges and vacating previous rulings. Was the district court the proper court to hear the suit, or should it be in probate court, presided over by Judge Elias Smith, the same judge who had signed Ann Eliza Dee's first divorce decree? After hours of arguments in a hearing that provided an opportunity for the Gentile lawyers to harangue Brigham Young (all recorded by Cummings), court adjourned. The arguments over jurisdiction, however, continued. Ultimately, the case was sent to the Utah Territorial Supreme Court to decide jurisdiction.

In the interim, many months after Cummings had left town, Ann Eliza fled Salt Lake City, purportedly afraid for her life. On November 27, 1873, her father abetted her escape, taking her under the cover of night in a closed carriage to the Union Pacific Railroad station in the town of Uintah north of Salt Lake City. There she boarded a train for Laramie and then Denver. She deliberately chose not to take the train out of Salt Lake City because that railroad line was controlled by Brigham Young.

Once out of Utah, Ann Eliza embarked on a national lecture tour, describing for audiences her life as a polygamous spouse of Brigham Young and revealing, according to the press, what went on behind closed doors in Salt Lake City. Thorough coverage of one lecture (in New York City) is contained in an April 10, 1874, *New York Times* article.

In an interview published in the *Los Angeles Times* on January 30, 1898, Major James B. Pond, who had been awarded the Congressional Medal of Honor for bravery in the Civil War and who at the time was living in New Jersey, recounts the origins of his involvement with Ann Eliza as her agent:

> I was in Salt Lake City at the time working on a newspaper [*Salt Lake Tribune*]. This was at the time of the influx of Gentiles. They came in such hordes that there was no accommodation for them except in the houses of the Mormons. Brigham Young gave his followers permission to take boarders. It so happened that the first Methodist minister to start the crusade against Mormonism was a boarder in the house of one of Brigham Young's wives. Through him and his wife the woman became converted. Her name was Ann Eliza Webb Young, and her revelations of Mormonism caused a sensation throughout America. They were embodied in a book called "Wife No. 19. . . ." My connection with the matter was that I rendered some assistance in the preparation of the book. Mrs. Young was urged to go to Washington and tell her story before Congress. She went and I accompanied her. [Afterward, her name] was on

everyone's lips. It occurred to me that she would be a great
attraction as a lecturer. So I took her on tour.

In 1874, Ann Eliza publicly acknowledged her conversion as a
Methodist.

Pond became a well-known agent, later representing a number of famous people, including Samuel L. Clemens, Thomas Nast, and Booker T. Washington. In the introductory chapter to the 1900 book about his career as an agent and the people he represented (*Eccentricities of Genius*), Pond adds more details to his story about Ann Eliza, noting, among other things, that "our people" (a group of anti-Mormons) saw the public-relations benefits of having Ann Eliza tell her story through lectures (pp. xx–xxii). "Our people" would have included John B. Gough and Mary A. Livermore, both of whom also became lecturers for Pond and each of whom wrote an introductory note in *Wife Number 19* attesting to its importance as anti-Mormon literature.

I suspect that not only Pond but also the Rev. Stratton had a great deal to do with the writing of *Wife Number 19*, which in 1875 and 1876 was widely promoted in newspaper and magazine ads and went through several printings. Livermore and, perhaps, Gough might also have helped in the authorship. Ann Eliza certainly knew both individuals and at times was booked with one or the other for lectures on successive nights in the same town.

The contention that Pond was involved in the production of the book is borne out by the engraving of Ann Eliza Young that appears as the frontispiece in *Wife Number 19*. The engraving is noted to be by J. A. Buttre of New York City, based on a photograph by Thomas Houseworth, who ran a large commercial photography studio in San Francisco. It is probably the original Houseworth photograph of Ann Eliza, if not another by him taken at the same time, that is also published in Pond's book *Eccentricities of Genius* (p. xxi). In the 1875 engraving and the 1900 photo, Ann Eliza is wearing the same outfit, earrings, and hairstyle (the engraving may be a mirror image of the photograph). It is likely Pond had the photo made originally for the lecture tour and passed the image on to the engraver for use in *Wife Number 19*. A quarter century later he used the same image (or another made at the same mid-1870s photo session with Houseworth) in his own book.

The ruling on the question of which Utah court had jurisdiction in the divorce case came down from the Utah Territorial Supreme Court in late July 1874. The court decreed that divorce cases such as the one filed by Ann Eliza Young were the purview of the district court, which was controlled by non-Mormons. It was a victory for Ann Eliza and her supporters. The original divorce case was then reinstated in late August in Salt Lake City, including Ann Eliza's request for $20,000 in attorney fees and alimony of $1,000 per month.

Brigham Young's response asked that the suit be denied, citing three main points. First, the attorney fees were absurd. He was not a wealthy man and he had a household of sixty-three persons to support. Second, it was argued that he was never legally married to Ann Eliza Young because she never had been legally divorced from James Dee, her first husband. In view of the recent Utah Territorial Supreme Court ruling that divorces were to be placed before the district court and not the probate court, it was argued that the divorce from Dee granted Ann Eliza by the probate court was not legal. And third, Brigham Young could never have legally married Ann Eliza because he already was married to Mary Ann Angell, whom he had married on January 10, 1834, in Ohio. He admitted that within the Mormon Church, he and others went through ceremonies approximating a marriage, but he denied such rites were legal marriages under the law.

In February 1875, Judge McKean ruled in favor of Ann Eliza's petition but he reduced the monetary awards. He ordered

Brigham Young to pay $3,000 in attorney fees and $500-a-month support for Ann Eliza, retroactive to the date the suit was originally filed twenty months earlier. The ruling made national news and provided an opportunity for editorial writers to attack Mormon plural marriage. The portion of the ruling that dealt with the legality of the marriage of Brigham to Ann Eliza, however, was not entirely clear. Was it a legal marriage or not?

On March 11, by which time Brigham Young had not paid the attorney fees or alimony required by Judge McKean's ruling, the judge held him in contempt and had him jailed. At the time, Young was seventy-four and said to be in feeble health. The Mormon press in Salt Lake City was outraged. More motions were filed in the case.

In May 1876, Utah Territory Supreme Court judge David Lowe vacated Judge McKean's order requiring alimony, saying alimony could not be ordered until an actual divorce was granted. Questions still existed regarding the legality of the marriage. Then in June, Judge Schaeffer of the district court overruled and said, once again, that alimony could indeed be collected. In July, the same judge reduced the alimony to $100 a month, retroactive to the filing of the original suit, which meant Brigham Young owed Ann Eliza $3,600. Young was given thirty days to pay or an attachment could be made on his property.

To the astonishment of many, when Brigham Young did not pay up, a sale of his goods was held in Salt Lake City on November 2. Most residents were afraid to buy anything, and only a little less than $1,200 was collected.

In April 1877, Judge Schaeffer issued another ruling, one that finally brought the case to an end. He declared the marriage of Ann Eliza and Brigham to be de facto and not de jure. Because it was a polygamous marriage it was declared "null and void." He further ruled that Brigham Young's original marriage to Mary Ann Angell in Ohio was illegal because the person performing the ceremony was not licensed by the state. Ann

Eliza would not receive a certificate of divorce. But because of her relationship to Brigham, according to the judge, she essentially had served him as a laborer, and thus she was entitled to receive payment. The amount of the alimony specified in previous decrees was sufficient.

The ruling meant polygamous marriage was not legal; Ann Eliza Webb had never been Ann Eliza Young. The nonmarriage (and, therefore, nondivorce) of Ann Eliza Webb Dee Young was a victory over polygamy.

The Young vs. Young affair provides an extraordinary window into a significant western phenomenon—polygamy—that caught the attention of the public in 1873 and many times since. Nearly a century after Ann Eliza filed her suit, author Irving Wallace wrote about her life in his 1961 novel *The Twenty-Seventh Wife*. He, like Amos Jay Cummings, knew a good story when he saw it. Although some have called Wallace's book a novel, he did extraordinarily thorough research for the book. Anyone wishing to learn more about Ann Eliza Young and her divorce suit should start with *The Twenty-Seventh Wife*.

And what happened to Ann Eliza? An article in the May 20, 1883, *Chicago Tribune* announced the marriage of Ann Eliza Young to Moses R. Denning the previous day in Lodi, Ohio. The couple went to live in Manistee, Michigan, where Mr. Denning was a "prominent banker." Denning, who had been previously married for twenty-six years, divorced his spouse to marry Ann Eliza. He and Ann Eliza had met in 1881 while she was giving a lecture in the Midwest and fell in love. Prior to her marriage to Denning, Ann Eliza, her mother, and her sons may have considered Lockport, New York, a home base.

After the marriage, Ann Eliza Denning, who is said in the *Chicago Tribune* article to have delivered nearly 1,000 public talks, gave up the lecture circuit and settled into life in Manistee. But the marriage did not bring happiness to her or Moses. Wallace's careful research paints a sad picture of the breakup of the marriage in 1892 and the couple's subsequent divorce the next year.

Once a national figure, Ann Eliza had begun to slip from view at about the time of her marriage, especially after the U.S. Congress, stimulated at least in part by the anti-polygamy stance she and others had taken, passed the Edmunds Act in 1882, which outlawed polygamy and decreased Mormon control over Utah's nonfederal courts.

The period after her divorce from Denning must have been a lonely time for Ann Eliza. Her mother had died in 1884 in Manistee, and tuberculosis killed both her sons. In 1903, her father, still in Salt Lake City, died.

In 1908 a new edition of Ann Eliza's 1875 book was published in Philadelphia. *Life in Mormon Bondage: A Complete Exposé of Its False Prophets, Murderous Danites, Despotic Rulers and Hypnotized Deluded Subjects* was published under her old name, Ann Eliza Young. The book revised and reinterpreted some of the previous information and related what had occurred in her life over the past thirty-three years. The book was not well received and few copies are around today.

At the time the second book was published, both of Ann Eliza's brothers still were alive (Edward Webb died in 1927 in Salt Lake City, and Chauncey Gilbert Webb in 1920 in Chihuahua, Mexico, in the town of Colonía Juárez). Whether she was in contact with either of them is unknown.

After 1908, Ann Eliza slips completely below the radar screen of history. Irving Wallace clearly spent considerable effort trying to discover what happened to her, even tracking down rumors that had her living anywhere from California to New York City. But he was unable to substantiate any of them.

Nearly fifty years after the publication of Wallace's *The Twenty-Seventh Wife*, and armed with a plethora of electronic databases that gave me access to historical newspapers and magazines, census data, death records, and other databases, I felt certain I could unravel the mystery of Ann Eliza's fate. But I failed in that endeavor. I did find, however, an article in the *Philadelphia Inquirer* (December 17, 1899) about the recent death of Emily D. Young, a former wife of Brigham Young, that stated that Ann Eliza, said to be one of Young's two remaining widows, was living in Wisconsin. Unfortunately, I could not find any record of her there. It is perhaps coincidental that Major Pond was a native of Alto in Fond du Lac County, Wisconsin.

In the end, I was unable to add anything definitive to what Irving Wallace has already discovered: the final years of Ann Eliza Webb Dee Young Denning remain shrouded. Perhaps someone reading this book can reveal the truth about her last years.

The four articles by Amos Jay Cummings reprinted in this section were all published in the *Sun* in 1873: "The Seventeenth Wife" on July 31, "The Great Utah Divorce" on August 9, "An Interesting Conversation with Ann Eliza Young" on August 9, and "The Prophet's Divorce" on August 21.

NOTE

1. Hempstead was Major Charles H. Hempstead of the law firm of Hempstead & Kirkpatrick and one of Brigham Young's attorneys.

THE SEVENTEENTH WIFE.

THE PROPHET'S PERFIDY EXPOSED.

A Discarded Woman's Suit for $200,000—Brigham Young's Vast Fortune and Princely Income—An Interior View of the Hideousness of Mormondom.

Correspondence of The Sun.

SALT LAKE, July 30.—The papers in the suit of Ann Eliza Young against Brigham Young have been filed. Mrs. Young complains through her next friend, George R. Maxwell.[1] The following is a summary, in the language of the complaint and affidavits, stripped of legal verbiage: Mrs. Young says that she was born in Nauvoo, Ill., and has been in Salt Lake since 1868. She married Brigham Young in Salt Lake, April 6, 1868. She was then a widow, twenty-five years old, and the mother of two children, one aged four and the other three years.[2] She had no property, and was entirely dependent upon the defendant for the support of herself and her children. Brigham well understood this before he married her. For about a year after his marriage Brigham cohabited with her, and acted with some degree of kindness and attention. During that time he supported her and her children, but not in a manner proportionate to his means or to her station in life. After a year, for some reason unknown to her, Brigham began a systematic course of neglect, unkindness, cruel and inhuman treatment, finally deserting her, and satisfying her that he no longer entertained the slightest feeling of affection or respect for her. Against her remonstrances he removed her to a farm owned by him four miles from Salt Lake. She was forced to live on the farm three years and a half, and compelled to perform manual labor and the most menial services to live.

HER ONLY COMPANION.

The only companion which he allowed her was her mother.[3] Her mother worked until her health was ruined. Then Brigham objected to her mother remaining any longer on the place. During the complainant's forced residence on the farm Brigham rarely visited her; the visits were from a few minutes to half an hour in length. On such occasions he treated her with studied neglect and contempt, telling her that the visits were not for her but for the purpose of supervising work on the farm. The complainant swears that Brigham appropriated the entire proceeds of her labor and that of her mother. She was restricted to the coarsest and most meager fare, and had to dress in a manner wholly unsuited to her position. Her children were compelled to go in rags.

In the fall of 1872 Brigham removed her to Salt Lake City. She lived in his house until she was constrained by her destitution, feeble health, and fear of violence to vacate it.

BRIGHAM'S BAD DISPOSITION.

She says that Brigham has a most vindictive disposition, though she declares he never visited her while she was in his house at Salt Lake. On several occasions, however, she called upon him at another one of his houses in Salt Lake City, and besought him to furnish her with wearing apparel or give her the means to procure it. He answered her entreaties with the most offensive language, and only at most distant intervals since the fall of 1872 furnished her with a few articles. They were not sufficient in quality or quantity for her subsistence and that of her children, and to procure the common necessaries of life she has been forced to constant and severe manual labor.

Mrs. Young further affirms that for the past four years she has been in delicate health, not fit to perform any labor without suffering great pain, and is in constant danger of permanent disease. It was necessary that she should have suitable food and medicines, and the services of a physician. She had repeatedly besought Brigham for medical attendance, but he has always refused to provide it for her; in consequence of his refusal she has suffered great mental and bodily anguish; been compelled to rely solely on the charity of friends. The only medical attendance which she has received since her marriage has been within the last months from a physician whose services were rendered without pecuniary recompense.

THE PROPHET'S WEALTH.

The complainant further asserts that in May last Brigham informed her that he would never again contribute to her support, and she must henceforth rely solely upon her exertions. She alleges that Brigham was and is the owner of vast wealth amounting to $8,000,000, and that he has an income of $40,000 a month. She says that he occupies a very prominent station in the society of the Territory, and holds various positions of trust and honor, among others that of prophet, seer, revelator, and

President of the Church of Jesus Christ of Latter-day Saints. She alleges that she has been compelled to sacrifice such furniture and household articles as she had obtained by her own exertions in order to live. She further alleges that in consequence of Brigham's treatment she has been rendered miserable, and that she and Brigham cannot live in peace and union together, and that their mutual welfare

REQUIRES A SEPARATION.

She swears that she has agreed to pay solicitors and counsel a reasonable compensation for their services, and that she knows of no means to comply with her engagement other than those under the control of the President of the Church of Jesus Christ of Latter-day Saints. She thinks $20,000 is a reasonable sum for their services. She further shows that she is without a home, and stopping at a hotel in Salt Lake. She thinks that it will require $1,000 a month to defray her expenses. She prays that Brigham may be ordered to pay to her during the pending of this suit the sum of $1,000 a month from the date of the filing of her bill, and that he be required to pay her solicitors a preliminary fee of not less than $6,000, and upon the final decree of the Court the further sum of $14,000, as well as the costs of Court. She asks that the bonds of matrimony between the complainant and the President of the Church of Jesus Christ of Latter-day Saints be forever dissolved, and that

A PORTION OF THE ESTATE

of the defendant, amounting to $200,000, be set aside for the benefit of the complainant; furthermore, she wants such other and further relief as the equity of her case may warrant and to the Court may seem meet. She closes by asking that Brigham Young be compelled to appear before the Court at a certain time under a certain penalty, there to answer all questions that may be put to him.

An advertisement for Joslin & Park jewelers, where Malcolm Graham, one of Eliza Young's supporters, was employed. (Williams, *Pacific Tourist*, back pages)

In conclusion, Mrs. Young says that she ever will ever pray.

Malcolm Graham[4] swears that in June and July he frequently visited Mrs. Young and found her sick. She had no servants or attendants, and was not supplied with food or medicine. Occasionally her neighbors would send in a meal, and occasionally Mr. Graham himself bought a little something and took [it] to her. Without assistance he swears she was in danger of actual starvation. He never saw Brigham Young in her house, and never heard of his being there.

AN ARMY OF WITNESSES.

Chas. M. Turek swears that he has known Mrs. Young over six months, and during that time she was always in need of food and medical attendance. On several occasions he had carried food to her to keep her from starving. Three times he sent medicine gratis.

Dr. J. M. Williamson[5] swears that he is a white male over 21 years old, and has been well acquainted with Mrs. Young's physical condition for over six months, and that she has been and is in almost constant need of medical attendance. He has visited her, and never been paid for his medical aid nor did he make any charge therefor.

The Doctor's diagnosis follows. Mrs. Young's complaint is female weakness.

Judge McKean[6] orders that said Brigham Young appear before the court Tuesday, August 6th, 1873, at 10 o'clock, to show cause, if he has any, why he, the said Brigham Young, should not pay to Ann Eliza and her counsel the following sums of money:

First, preliminary counsel fees in the sum of $6,000.

Second, alimony in the sum of $1,000 for each and every month from the filing of this bill.

Third, a sum sufficient to defray the legal expenses of this suit.

Mrs. Young is Brigham's seventeenth wife. The Mormons declare that the whole thing is a put up job on the part of a few needy officials to bleed Brigham.

NOTES

1. George Maxwell, age twenty-eight, is listed in the 1870 federal census as a resident of Salt Lake City. His occupation was "register in land office." Maxwell was a Civil War hero from Michigan who was promoted to brigadier general by war's end. At one time, he served as U.S. marshal for Utah. He was known for his anti-Mormon views.

2. Ann Eliza Young had two boys with her previous husband: James E. (age six in the 1870 census) and Lorenzo (age five). Both were born in Utah.

3. Her mother was Eliza J. Webb, a native of New York State. Her name is listed just below Ann Eliza Young's in the 1870 census. Ms. Webb was fifty-three at the time.

4. Malcolm Graham is identified by Ann Eliza Young in the article "An Interesting Conversation with Ann Eliza Young" (Chapter 11)

as an employee of "Joslyn & Parks Jewelry Store" (the correct name, according to Sloan in his *Gazeteer* [*sic*], 221, was "Joslin and Park"). The store was on East Temple between First and Second streets South. Graham is listed in the same Salt Lake City directory as a watchmaker and engraver. An advertisement for the store (Williams, *Pacific Tourist*) offers "novelties of native productions," and notes there also was a store in Cheyenne, Wyoming.

5. In testimony accepted by the court during the divorce proceedings in late July 1873, Williamson, a practicing physician, swore that he was a resident of Salt Lake County. Charles Turek, mentioned in the paragraph above, did not offer that information in his testimony. In Sloan's directory (*Gazeteer* [*sic*], 295), both Williamson's home and office addresses are listed; Turek is not listed.

6. Judge James B. McKean, whom we met in the previous chapter.

10

THE GREAT UTAH DIVORCE.

An Interview with Brigham Young.

What He Thinks of the Divorce Case—He Will Never Be Blackmailed—Adultery Alleged—The Greedy Federal Officials—Gov. Young Tells Speaker Blaine How to Solve the Mormon Problem—A Man Who Wanted $100,000 in Gold—The Arizona Settlements—Can Gentiles Act Justly with the Mormons?

Correspondence of The Sun.

SALT LAKE CITY, Aug. 1, 1873.—I had a talk with the Mormon Prophet yesterday. I called upon him in his business office in what is known as the Lion House. This building is situated upon one of the cross streets of the city, a few steps from the main avenue. It adjoins the Bee Hive, the enclosure where the Prophet keeps most of his wives. The Lion House, like the Bee Hive, is surrounded by a massive stone wall, about twelve feet high. Sectional walls split the front yard, like the iron fences of up-town granite blocks in New York. A wooden stoop with two long steps fronts the office, or offices, for there are two of them.

Passing through the gateway and up the stoop I entered the door on the left. Neither the Prophet nor either of his sons was in; so I sat down in a cane-bottomed chair to wait for them.

I should think the room was forty feet long and thirty feet wide. A row of yellow pine bookcases, poorly grained, was fastened along the left wall. "They were made in 1857, sir, and they're 16 years old," said a Mormon brother. Some of them contained pigeon holes filled with documents. Others were piled with ponderous ledgers and account books, the business schedules and balances of the Great Church of Jesus Christ of Latterday Saints. The ceiling was lofty. A high little gallery, like the one in Hudnut's drug store,[1] or like those in the Astor Library,[2] encircled the room. It was backed by shelves, loaded with law books. A circular iron railing occupied the centre of the apartment. Through it the Mormon clerks passed on their way to their desks.

BRIGHAM'S RECEPTION ROOMS.

It was about 6 P.M. of a very hot day. I was accompanied by Mr. Sloan of the *Salt Lake Herald*.[3] Sloan is a genial Mormon, with a high mind and forehead, and a pair of old-fashioned gold-bowed spectacles. "I am afraid," said he, before we started, "that you can't see the President. His press of business comes in the afternoon. He goes to his dinner after he gets through. Then right in to prayers."

After waiting a few moments we went out on the wooden stoop. Two handsome women, bareheaded, were walking about the narrow yard. I took them for the President's wives. They were pretty enough to be his handmaids, though it is possible that they were his daughters. Their silvery laughter floated on the air. A fine-looking Mormon seized Mr. Sloan by the arm and whispered in his ear. Sloan majestically waved his hand, and I followed him to a second door. It was the entrance to the Prophet's reception room. I saw the great Religious Chief sit-

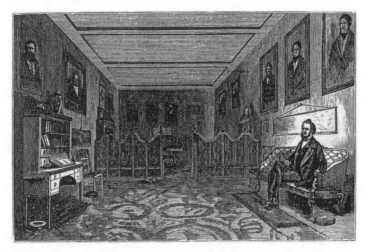

BRIGHAM YOUNG'S SALT LAKE CITY RECEPTION ROOM WHERE HE WAS INTER-VIEWED BY AMOS CUMMINGS. (WILLIAMS, *PACIFIC TOURIST*, 136; WILLIAMS SAYS THE ROOM WAS BRIGHAM YOUNG'S "OFFICE," BUT ITS APPEARANCE FITS THE RECEPTION ROOM DESCRIBED BY CUMMINGS)

ting on a sofa before I entered the room. I recognized him from the pictures that I had seen hanging at the doors of the Salt Lake photograph galleries. He was looking toward the stoop, and evidently expecting me. He kept his eyes fixed upon me as I approached, then he arose, shook hands, politely offered me his seat upon the sofa, and sat down upon a chair at my side. The room was partially darkened. It was furnished in exquisite taste. There was a soft carpet beneath my feet. Elegant ormolu ornaments[4] were negligently strewn over rich little tables. In the further end of the office two of the Prophet's secretaries were seated at their desks scratching away on various docu-ments. Unframed oil portraits of Orson Pratt,[5] Heber Kimball,[6] and other Mormon dignitaries adorned the walls. I recognized among them the sad faces of the martyrs of the Church. All of the heads were life size. A beautiful picture of Horace Greeley occupied a prominent position. Poor Horace looked out of place.

His pleasant face and mild eyes seemed like sunshine among the somber garments, white cravats, and grave countenances of the Mormon divines.

THE PROPHET.

Correspondents generally do Brigham Young an injustice. Their personal descriptions are incorrect. He is not grave looking. His face is far from sensual. Animal passion is certainly more strongly marked in Henry Ward Beecher[7] and other noted English clergymen than in the Mormon Saint. Combativeness is strongly developed. Brigham looks like a religious bull-dog. His clear, blue eyes are not hidden behind glasses, and his bearing, though dignified, is social to the last degree. He wore a white linen coat. A snowy cravat was wound about his neck. Its folds reached his ears. A cloth hat sat upon his head. The underside of the brim was of a green color. At times he laughed heartily. The following was the conversation to the best of your correspondent's recollection:

Mr. Sloan—President Young, I have the pleasure of introducing to you the correspondent of THE SUN.

The Prophet (with a good, hearty grip)—I am glad to meet you, sir.

Correspondent (removing his hat)—I am pleased to make your acquaintance, sir.

The Prophet (without removing his hat)—How long have you been in the city?

Correspondent—About a week.

The Prophet—How do you like it?

Correspondent—I find it very warm. Do you find it so, Mr. Young?

The Prophet (looking into the correspondent's eyes with a meaning smile)—Not particularly so. Do I look warm? I am used to it; you are not.

THE DIVORCE SUIT.

Correspondent—Were the papers served upon you in the divorce suit of Ann Eliza Young?

The Prophet—Yes, I received them.

Correspondent—Did you read them?

The Prophet—Oh, yes, I read them through. They are not of much account.

Correspondent—What did you think of them?

The Prophet (firmly)—Blackmail! Blackmail! It is not the first time that they have attempted to blackmail the Mormon Church, and I presume it will not be the last. We have never allowed them to blackmail us out of a single cent, and we don't propose to allow them to do it now.

Correspondent—I think, Mr. Young, you will acknowledge that THE SUN has always done the Mormons exact justice.

The Prophet (in a musing way)—Well, I don't know. I think THE SUN has been one of the papers that has tried to act fairly by us. I don't remember of any positive injustice. It is very bitter against polygamy; but it seems to understand the political situation here.

Correspondent—Then if it is not offensive to you I would like to ask a few more questions concerning this divorce suit.

The Prophet—Oh, I will answer them, though it's really a small matter. This man Sawyer[8] who sends the press dispatches East has tried to make a great thing out of it; but there is nothing in it to make anything. He is a notorious liar. Nobody here believes a word he says. His own paper acknowledges that it is an attempt to blackmail. The men who are running the suit want our money, and they won't get it. That's all there's of it.

THIEVES AND SCOUNDRELS.

Correspondent—The complaint alleges brutal treatment and desertion. Is the allegation true?

The Prophet (laughing as though everybody knew that it was not true)—Nothing of the kind (shaking his head); nothing of the kind. She was always treated as a wife should be treated. No stipulations were made. She had no cause for complaint. She has had bad advisers, and has taken a wrong step. We were driven from the States by the persecutions of bigoted priests and robbers. Many of us were cruelly murdered and our lands and property seized. We wandered off to this wilderness, and the bigoted priests and robbers are again upon our track. This time they are headed by Government officials. (Suddenly firing up.) They will do well to pause. This is not Nauvoo.[9] God has given us these lands, and they have been consecrated by the sweat of our brows. We will not be robbed of them in silence. It is our land that the thieves are after. This suit is of no account. It is a small attempt to blackmail, but a greater effort will follow. We are a law-abiding people and have always been so. We have been loyal to the Government, and all we ask is simple justice, and we're going to have it. What is law for a Gentile ought to be law for a Mormon.

THE LEGAL ASPECT OF THE CASE.

Correspondent—What answer will you make to Mrs. Young's complaint?

The Prophet—Of course it is a put-up job. The complaint is made in a United States Court, which has no jurisdiction. You don't try divorce suits in United States Courts in New York. The Territorial law confers the power upon the Probate Court alone, and Territorial laws are binding within a prescribed limit until Congress annuls them. Congress has never annulled this law. The Gentiles have brought similar suits in Probate Court. One of their leading lawyers sought a divorce for a lady in the Probate Court some time ago, and afterward married her. Why, McKean's[10] packed Grand Jury presented a bogus indictment against me some time ago for what they called lascivious cohabitation with this very woman. It is a case of unadulterated blackmail, and the complaint itself shows it. As it is a put-up job, I have no doubt but what they will wrongfully entertain the case in the United States Court. But that won't help them.

Correspondent—Supposing the Judge decides that he will hear the case, what then?

The Prophet (lowering his voice)—Adultery. The facts are plain, and there is plenty of evidence.

THE WORK OF GREEDY GENTILES.

Correspondent—Do you think that the United States office-holders are concerned in this suit?

The Prophet—Do I think? Why, the officeholders have tried to fill their pockets ever since they have been in the Territory. They have endeavored to set all our local laws aside. They have packed Grand Juries, and have found any quantity of illegal indictments against us. Scores have been arrested and held in custody on trumped up charges, until the Supreme Court of the United States was compelled to interfere and undo the work of the officeholders. Look at them. They came here puffed with piety and pretended to be horrified at polygamy. Yet there wasn't one of them who wouldn't run to an assignation house within twenty-four hours afterward if he had an opportunity. They have always been a set of canting hypocrites, and they are trying to get hold of our lands and property. In their attempt to do this they have overridden all law. Why should they object to a Mormon upon a jury? It is a fact that can't be denied that the Mormon juries have been more honest and just in their decisions than any juries in the land. Murderers and thieves never escaped when before a Mormon jury. Since these officeholders have got hold of things all kinds of crime is on the increase. Nobody is convicted and you can't even get a criminal on trial. Money will do anything. They are all on the make. The laws are at a dead-lock, and everything is in confusion. The business interests of the Territory are suffering, and we are all at sea.

A MAN WHO WANTED $100,000 IN GOLD.

Correspondent—Who is responsible for this state of things?

The Prophet—The man who makes the Territorial appointments—Grant,[11] isn't he?

Correspondent—I have heard that the Rev. Dr. Newman[12] ran the machine in this Territory.

The Prophet—I suppose that he keeps the loafers and thieves in their positions, but the man who makes the appointments is responsible.

Correspondent—Have you ever been approached by an appointed official who attempted to blackmail you?

The Prophet—Frequently, indirectly and by insinuation. Why, two years ago, when McKean's packed Grand Jury found their bogus bills of indictment, a Pennsylvania politician approached me and offered to fix the thing up all right if I would give him $100,000 in gold.

Correspondent—Was it Wm. H. Kemble?[13]

The Prophet (laughing)—I can't give his name.

Correspondent—What answer did you make to him?

The Prophet (laughing heartily)—I asked him if $100,000 greenbacks wouldn't do as well. (Shouting across the room) Wasn't that what I said, Sloan?

Mr. Sloan, who was talking to Mr. Joseph Young,[14] but who had heard the remark, responded in the affirmative, and we all had a jolly laugh, the Prophet laughing harder than any of us.

BLAINE AND THE MORMON PROBLEM.

Correspondent—Did you see a dispatch sent to the Eastern papers in which Speaker Blaine[15] is said to have fiercely denounced Mormonism while in conversation with you?

The Prophet—Let me see. It appears to me that I do remember something about that (starting up). Yes, yes, I remember now, but I don't believe that Blaine had anything to do with sending off that dispatch.

Correspondent—Did you have any such conversation with Mr. Blaine?

The Prophet—No, nothing of the kind. I tell you that you can't believe anything that the *Telegraph*[16] says about the Mormons. Why, the Speaker came down here and I went with him all around. He thoroughly enjoyed himself. We went down the Southern road and stayed all night, and were together most of the time that he was here. Of course we had a good many little chats together. He said that he had been trying for the last twelve years to solve the Mormon problem. I explained to him the situation, and told him that all the Mormons wanted was to have the Gentiles keep their hands off of them. Congressmen had been puzzling their brains over the Mormon problem, and the more they tried to solve it, the worse they made it. "Now," said I, "Mr. Speaker, when you go back to Washington, just plant your feet on the floor of the House and shout that you have found a solution to the Mormon problem. Tell them that the true solution is this: Let the Mormons alone."

THE TRUE INDIAN POLICY.

Correspondent—Have the Mormons ever had any trouble with the Indians?

The Prophet—But very little. When we make an Indian a promise we never break it.

Correspondent—What do you think of the Indian agents?

The Prophet—With but few exceptions they are the most God-forsaken rascals that ever cursed the country. They promise everything and fulfill nothing. They swindle the Indians from right to left, and the Indians know it. If there had never been an Indian agent the Indians would be far better than they are now.

Correspondent—Did you ever see any of the blankets or things of that kind that were given to the Indians as annuities?

The Prophet—Oh, the agents are a great set of rascals. I think I have seen one or two Indians who had received blankets at some agency, but they were very few. They don't get many blankets.

Correspondent—Were the blankets of good quality?

The Prophet—Well, I never saw enough of them to know. I do know that the Indians are thoroughly disgusted with the agents, and I believe with good reason. The true policy is to make but few promises or treaties, as you call them, and when promises are made to sacredly fulfill them.

THE ARIZONA SETTLEMENT.

Correspondent—Mr. Young, if I am growing tedious, don't let me detain you. I am told that you are generally very busy at this hour.

The Prophet (laughing)—Well, I must say that I have something very important to do to-night, but I can spare you a few minutes longer. I have got to go to the circus this evening, and it is getting toward 7 o'clock.

Correspondent—I will touch upon one more subject. Some days ago I saw a dispatch from here saying that 6,000 Mormons had left their settlements in Arizona and were on their way to Salt Lake utterly destitute.

The Prophet (roaring with laughter)—Well, that is about as big a lie as the press agent ever got off. I think there were a few of the emigrants to Arizona who lost their way and couldn't find the exact spot that they were looking for. They got homesick, thinking of the green trees and broad meadows of the Salt Lake Valley, and turned back. But 6,000—oh, that's a good one—I think there were about twenty wagons in all. Brother McKenzie[17] (turning to one of his secretaries), how many wagons were there in this Arizona expedition? Do you remember?

As Brother McKenzie arose from his desk the Prophet turned to me, saying, "Do you know Brother McKenzie? No, of course you don't. Let me introduce you."

The introduction was made. Brother McKenzie said, "I'm quite sure there were only twenty wagons, but I have the papers in my desk here somewhere, and I'll look them up." As Brother McKenzie was a good-looking Mormon and very busy, I begged that he would not trouble himself. The conversation proceeded.

Correspondent—What is the subject of these Arizona settlements?

The Prophet—Well, some fine land, well watered, has been discovered in the mountains of Arizona. The valleys are unusually rich and fertile. You know that the Apaches and other Indians in that country have been very hostile and have killed a great many whites. We thought that by making a settlement in that country we could materially aid the Government and stop the Apache outrages. We feel it our duty to assist the Government whenever we can do so. You will find no stronger loyalty in any part of the United States than there is here among our people.

SAD EFFECT OF THE INTERVIEW.

After some further talk the Prophet excused himself and walked out. A gentlemanly brother asked me to write my name in the visitors' book, and I gratified him. Uncle Sloan then introduced me to Mr. Joseph Young, the Prophet's eldest son. I expressed surprise to see his father looking so strong and hearty. "They tell me he is 73 years old," said I, "but he don't look more than 55. I never saw a man of his age look more healthy."

"Yes," replied Mr. Joseph Young. "He's healthy. We are all healthy. We think that he has a healthy lot of boys."

"Those that I have seen," I replied, "are certainly remarkable specimens of manly and intellectual beauty."

Then Sloan laughed, Joseph laughed, and I ventured a modest smile. We talked a little longer and stepped out upon the stoop. The Prophet was seated upon one of the wooden steps. The interview had been too much for him. His nose was bleeding and he was endeavoring to staunch the flow of blood with pieces of cotton which he drew from his coat pocket. Mr. Sloan shook hands with him and waited for me to say good-by. I was embarrassed. To attract his attention, I said, "I am sorry you are ill, Mr. Young." The Prophet looked up, saying, "I am not unwell, sir. You are mistaken." He seemed annoyed.

"Then," I said, "allow me to thank you for your courtesy and bid you good evening."

We shook hands and I followed Mr. Sloan without the massive gates as the last rays of the sun were gilding the snowy tops of the Wasatch range.

NOTES

1. The A. Hudnut and Co. drugstore was in the Herald Building at 218 Broadway (at the corner of Ann Street) in Lower Manhattan in New York City. That location today is just south of City Hall Park.

2. The building, which is at 425 Lafayette Street in Manhattan in New York City, today houses the Joseph Papp Public Theater. The Astor Library's collections were incorporated into the New York Public Library in the late nineteenth century.

3. Edward L. Sloan.

4. Metal objects, such as vases, candlesticks, and inkstands, that were gilded with bronze or other alloys to give them a faux gold appearance.

5. Born in Hartford, New York, in 1811, Pratt was appointed historian and general church recorder in 1874. He died in Salt Lake City in 1881. Among other things, he was known for his research in mathematics and astronomy.

6. Heber C. Kimball (1802–1868), a Vermont native, served in Utah's territorial legislature and was a longtime official and leader in the church.

7. Beecher (1813–1887) was a liberal Congregationalist clergyman and reformer. His elder sister was Harriet Beecher Stowe, author of *Uncle Tom's Cabin.*

8. Oscar G. Sawyer, a former reporter for the *New York Herald,* wrote for the *Salt Lake Daily Tribune and Utah Mining News* (later the *Salt Lake Tribune*). The newspaper was anti-Mormon in its editorial

policies and Sawyer was known for his vitriolic personal attacks on Brigham Young.

9. Nauvoo, Illinois, was where Ann Eliza had been born and from where the Mormons had been forced out by anti-Mormon fervor.

10. Judge James B. McKean appears in other of Cummings's articles about the divorce proceedings.

11. A Republican (i.e., a backer of President Ulysses S. Grant).

12. I believe the reference is to the Rev. Dr. John Philip Newman, a Methodist minister and later bishop who in 1870 traveled to Salt Lake City and participated in a three-day debate with Mormon elders about the religious basis for polygamy. He served as chaplain to the United States Congress from 1869 to 1874. His name here may be tongue-in-cheek: President Grant and his spouse attended the Rev. Dr. Newman's church in Washington. Cummings may be suggesting that Newman influenced Grant and the Republican Party to appoint anti-Mormon officials in Utah Territory.

13. Kemble was a Philadelphia businessman and Republican politician.

14. Joseph Angell Young, Brigham Young's eldest son (so identified later in this article), was born in Ohio in 1834. A church official and aide to Brigham Young, Joseph died suddenly in 1875 at age forty-two.

15. James G. Blaine was elected to the House of Representatives from Maine in 1863 and served until 1876, when he resigned to accept an appointment to a vacated Senate seat, to which he was subsequently elected for another term. He was Speaker of the House for the Forty-first, Forty-second, and Forty-third Congresses.

16. Most likely the *Salt Lake Daily Telegraph* newspaper.

17. David McKenzie was a secretary to Brigham Young for more than two decades. McKenzie was a photographer and he was active in the Salt Lake City theater.

11

AN INTERESTING CONVERSATION
WITH ANN ELIZA YOUNG.

*Her Parents Came from Cayuga County—How She
Came to Marry the Prophet—Brigham's Courtship—
Sacrificed to Save a Brother—Mrs. Young's Fears of
Abduction—How the Wives Are Treated.*

Correspondence of The Sun.

SALT LAKE CITY, Aug. 1.—I called upon Mrs. Ann Eliza
Young this evening. I was accompanied by my wife and the
Rev. Mr. Stratton, of the Methodist Episcopal Church in Third
South street.[1] It was through his kindness that I was introduced to the lady. I found Mrs. Young occupying a front room
on the fourth floor of the Walker House.[2] It is a small apartment, but neatly furnished, containing a little lounge, a marble
topped bureau, a sewing machine, a small table, and a common
trunk. Photographs of Mrs. Young's brother, mother, and other
relatives were suspended on the wall. The room contained two

ANN ELIZA YOUNG WAS STAYING AT THE WALKER HOUSE HOTEL WHEN SHE WAS INTERVIEWED BY AMOS CUMMINGS. (WILLIAMS, *PACIFIC TOURIST*, BACK PAGES)

windows. They overlooked a large part of the city, and gave one a magnificent view of the snowy range south of the Great Salt Lake.

MRS. YOUNG'S APPEARANCE.

Mrs. Young is a modest, unassuming woman, apparently about 25 years old. She has evidently been handsome, but sickness and mental suffering have left their footprints upon her countenance. When she married Brigham Young she had a round face and rosy cheeks, but now she is as pale as a ghost. She has blue eyes, regular features, a fair complexion, red lips, good teeth, and brown hair fashionably arranged. She wore a plain black dress, with very little trimming, jet earrings and breastpin, a green neck tie, and simple linen collar and cuffs. Her youngest boy, eight years old, sat at her side.

In a few words I explained the object of my visit. Mrs. Young said that she had been sick for several weeks, and that she was very nervous and troubled, but that she was willing to answer any questions. The conversation proceeded as follows:

MRS. YOUNG'S PARENTS.

Correspondent—Mrs. Young, I believe you were born in Nauvoo. Where were your parents born, and who were they?

Mrs. Young—My father's name was Chauncey G. Webb.[3] He came from New York.

Correspondent—New York City?

Mrs. Young—York State; I believe that's what they call it. Cayuga County.[4]

Correspondent—Were your father and mother Mormons?

Mrs. Young—My parents joined the Mormons when my mother was but sixteen years old. They were among the original members of the Mormon Church.

Correspondent—Was your first husband[5] a Mormon?

Mrs. Young (very sadly)—Yes.

Correspondent—Did he have more than one wife?

Mrs. Young—No.

Here the Rev. Mr. Stratton excused himself, as he had a church meeting to attend. The conversation continued:

Correspondent—How did you come to marry Brigham Young? Did you marry him of your own free will, or were you forced to marry him?

A BROTHER'S TROUBLE.

Mrs. Young (rubbing her forehead as if in pain)—Well, it is a long story. I did and I didn't. In the first place, the leaders of the church controlled everything. Their will was law. If one of them said he wanted a woman, no woman dared refuse to marry him. However much she hated him, she sacrificed herself to her fears. My first marriage was an unhappy one, and my life had been blighted. My brother[6] was in trouble and I thought that by sacrificing myself I could help him. He had a contract with Joseph Young (Brigham's eldest son) to put up a great many telegraph poles. It cost him a great deal of money. The President was concerned in the contract, although his name did not appear. When the work was completed they refused to pay my brother and he dared make no complaint. Every one was afraid of the President, and he did as he pleased without much regard to his promises. The Gentiles got hold of his property, and this made the President very angry. He had intended that Col. Hooper[7] should take possession of my brother's assets.

CONGRESSMAN HOOPER FOILED.

Correspondent (interrupting)—Was this Congressman Hooper?

Mrs. Young—Yes, Congressman Hooper. He is no more of a Mormon than you are, though he pretends to be. He is closely associated with Mr. Young, and is in the church for what he can make. Well, the President was mad because my brother's estate fell into the hands of the Gentiles instead of Hooper's, and he cut him off from the church. It was a terrible blow to my brother, and we all felt it very keenly. He seemed to think that if I married Mr. Young it would help him, and probably restore him to his position. So I sacrificed myself as much as anything else to help my brother.

Correspondent—How did Brigham come to propose marriage to you?

BRIGHAM'S COURTSHIP.

Mrs. Young—We lived at Little Cottonwood, ten miles south of here. The President was down there attending one of his big meetings. When the meeting was out he asked me if he could walk home from church with me. I said, "I have no objection." He took my little boy by the hand, and walked home with me. On the way he asked me if I had thought of getting married again, and whether I had received any offers of marriage. I replied that I had had two or three offers, but had refused them. Then he said, "Let me give you a little advice. Don't marry any man because you love him, but marry some one that you can look up to and respect." That was all that was said about marriage. I had no idea that he was speaking for himself. I looked upon him as a father. Why, he had always known me. He held me upon his knee from the time I was a baby. I didn't imagine that he wanted to marry me. He stayed at our home to dinner, although he had been invited and had promised to go somewhere else. After dinner he took my father [to] one side and

PROPOSED TO MARRY ME.

He said that he had always loved me, and that he had meant to marry me in the first place. He would have done it only that it was about the time that Congress passed the act against polygamy. He thought that it would be dangerous for him to take another wife so soon after the passage of that act. While he was in this quandary, and before he was aware of it, I was married to my first husband. He told father that he didn't wish to force himself upon me against my will, but that he always loved me, and that I had better consider the matter well. He also asked father and mother both to use their influence with me. He left the house without saying a word to me about it.

Correspondent—How many wives did he have at that time?

Mrs. Young—I think fifteen. Let me see, let me count up. I know their names.

Here Mrs. Young began to call the roll, but was interrupted. She afterward resumed her story, as follows:

BRIGHAM'S PROMISE.

"Well, matters went on this way for some time. The President continually flattered my father and mother, and urged the thing upon them. He said that he would give me a house and lot and a good support, with a thousand dollars a year for pocket money. He told my father this, but never said anything to me about it. That was the last I ever heard of it. He never gave me a cent, and never even supported me. He gave me a house to live in, but very little to eat, and that little was poor. My father and mother thought it was best for me to marry him if I could reconcile it to my feelings. My brother believed that it would be the means of reinstating him and of saving him from utter ruin. I felt very badly about it. For weeks I did nothing but cry over the proposition, and it was months before I could bring myself to look upon it favorably. I didn't like polygamy, although I had been brought up in the faith, and taught to believe it right.

Correspondent—I suppose you thought it would be better to marry the highest man in the church, and be well cared for, than to marry some one in an inferior station?

HOW HE LOVED HER.

Mrs. Young—No. I had no such thoughts. I felt that my life had been blighted anyhow, and I might as well make a further sacrifice if I could save my brother, so nearly a year after the meeting I married him. And just six months before we were married he took Mary Van Cott.[8]

Correspondent—Who is Mary Van Cott?

Mrs. Young—She is a woman just about my age, and he has treated her just about as bad as he has me. Amelia[9] is his favorite.

Correspondent—What is there about Amelia that he fancies?

Mrs. Young—Well, she's a woman with a powerful will, in fact, she is a virago.[10] She carries everything by storm, and her will is law. On the contrary, I was mild, and gave in to everything. He supposed that I was the last one that would dare to rebel. I have been told that he says that I could go to the cooperative stores and order what I wanted. He never told me so, and his statement is untrue. Amelia is the only one of all his wives who can walk into a cooperative store and run up a bill. She has everything that she asks for, and when she gets mad and breaks and smashes the furniture he buys her more. Amelia is the second wife before me.

Correspondent—Are you his last wife?

Mrs. Young—I am; but the impression that the last wife is always the favorite is incorrect.

WHY BRIGHAM KEEPS ON MARRYING.

Correspondent—If Amelia is the favorite why did he marry you and Mary Van Cott?

Mrs. Young—Well, we think it's vanity. He just wants to show that if he is an old man he can marry young women; and he isn't the only one in power who does the same thing.

Correspondent—How long is it since he married Amelia?

Mrs. Young—About twelve years ago.

Correspondent—Has she had any children by him?

Mrs. Young—No.

Correspondent—Has Mary Van Cott any children?

Mrs. Young—Yes; she had one born about two years ago. It is the youngest in his family. [It may interest the reader to know that Brigham Young is 78 years old.][11]

AN ALARM.

Here there was a knock at the door. Mrs. Young said, "Come." A gentleman walked into the room and was introduced. After a moment he said that he wished to see Mrs. Young on important private business. She stepped out in the hall and closed the door. In three minutes she returned alone, very much agitated. "Mr. ——," said she, "It is important that I should see Mr. Stratton to-night. Will you be kind enough to go to his house on your way to your hotel, and ask him to step around here after church?" I promised to do so.

MRS. YOUNG'S TERROR.

It was some minutes before Mrs. Young could recover the thread of the conversation. She seemed entirely broken down. She rubbed her forehead, and at one time tears started to her eyes. She had evidently received information that had unnerved her. "You will excuse me," she said, "but I have had so much trouble that I am sick in mind as well as in body. I can't remember what we were talking about." After a few moments she started up and said:

"Would you think they could abduct me from this house?"

Correspondent—Why, no. I have no idea that they would attempt anything of the kind. Do you really fear it?

Mrs. Young (in much agitation)—You don't know anything about them. You don't know how powerful they are. I have taken this room up here hoping to be safe, but I don't know how soon they may attempt to put me out of the way. I dare not let my child go out of the room. It is only within two or three days that I have been out on the street, and then I walked to the Rev. Mr. Stratton's house. When I first came here I went down to the table once or twice, but I was advised that it was not safe, and since then have had my meals served in my room.

JOSEPH YOUNG'S WIFE.

Correspondent—Have any of the Mormons called upon you?

Mrs. Young—One of Joseph Young's wives has been to see me twice. She is a daughter of Mr. Stenhouse, and the third and favorite wife.[12] You have read her mother's book. Every word of it is true. The mother feels terribly over her daughter. When Mrs. Joseph Young called on me she expressed surprise at the course I had taken. I said, "You know that you would have done the same thing if you had been treated as I have been." She replied, "Well, I don't know but what I would." She knew all about my treatment, for she boarded with me several months. The last time she called I felt sure that she had come as a spy.

Correspondent—I think you need have no fear of abduction. The effect upon the country at large would be disastrous to Brigham Young, and he is wise enough to see it. I have been told that Brigham is a very profane man. Is that true?

BRIGHAM YOUNG'S PROFANITY.

Mrs. Young—He uses profane language when in the Tabernacle, and preaching against the Gentiles.

Correspondent—Has he ever used profanity in talking to you?

Mrs. Young—No, I cannot say that he has, but he has used shockingly insulting and extremely vulgar language to me. Oh, he's a vile old creature—well, I shouldn't talk that way, but he can make the most cutting remarks of any man, and he is in the habit of doing so. He treats his wives with the utmost indifference.

"TWIST."

Correspondent—Do they seem to be pleased to see him?

Mrs. Young—Yes, some of them are. They like to have him come around once in awhile—they seem to. "Twist"[13] always gets his dinner for him. He eats only two meals a day.

Correspondent—Who's "Twist"?

Mrs. Young—She's one of his wives. They call her "Twist" because I think her husband's name was "Twist." At all events, she goes by the name of "Twist." The rest of us always call her "Twist," and the President calls her "Twist."

Correspondent—Who gets Brigham's breakfast?

Mrs. Young—Lucy Decker[14] used to get it for him, but now Clara Decker[15] always gets it for him. They are sisters.

Correspondent—Do his wives take their meals with him?

Mrs. Young—Amelia always eats with him, and Eliza Snow. You've heard of her. She's Joseph Smith's widow, and was sealed to both Mr. Young and Joseph Smith.[16]

MRS. YOUNG HORRIFIED.

Correspondent—I am told that Brigham alleged adultery against you.

Mrs. Young (horrified and much affected)—Is it possible? Is it possible?

For a few minutes she could not utter another word.

Correspondent—Do you think that they would manufacture evidence upon this point?

Mrs. Young—If necessary they would induce 2,000 Mormons to swear to anything, and there are plenty of bad Gentiles in this place who would do anything for money. They said that some man brought me to this hotel and is paying my expenses. But (with flashing eyes) it is the work of no one but Ann Eliza Webb.

NOTES

1. The Rev. C. C. Stratton, whose church on Third Street South was between East Temple and First Street South. As noted in the introduction to this section, I believe he played a major role in Ann Eliza Young's filing the divorce suit.

2. The four-story Walker House hotel on South Main Street was the city's best. Sometimes referred to as the "Gentile Hotel," the Walker House was advertised as "the most complete hotel between

Chicago and San Francisco." Among other amenities, it featured a passenger elevator.

3. In the 1870 federal census, Chauncey Webb, age fifty and a farmer, is listed as a resident of South Cottonwood, Utah.

4. Cayuga County is in the Finger Lakes region and extends south from Lake Ontario.

5. James Dee did not contest the divorce action against him and did not show up for the divorce hearing before a judge. After her divorce from Mr. Dee, Ann Eliza lived with her mother and father on a farm in South Cottonwood.

6. Gilbert Webb, who was married, was thirty-five at the time of the 1870 federal census.

7. William H. Hooper was a delegate from the Territory of Utah to the U.S. Congress and served in the territorial senate. He also was one of the superintendents of the Zion's Cooperative Institution.

8. Mary Van Cott married Brigham Young in January 1856, more than three years earlier than Ann Eliza Young's marriage to him. She, like Ann Eliza Webb, was born in 1844.

9. Harriet Amelia Folsom, born in 1838, married Brigham Young in 1863.

10. A domineering woman.

11. Brigham Young was born June 1, 1801, so he would have been seventy-two, not seventy-eight.

12. Clara Federata Stenhouse, born in 1850, married Joseph Young in 1867 in Salt Lake City.

13. Naamah Kendel Jenkins Carter married John Saunders Twiss (note spelling) in 1845 in Illinois. Brigham Young performed the ceremony. Mr. Twiss died four months later, and the next year his widow, who was twenty-four, married Brigham Young.

14. Lucy Ann Decker was twenty when she married Brigham Young in 1842.

15. Brigham Young married Clarissa Decker in 1844 when she was fifteen.

16. Eliza R. Snow married Joseph Smith in 1842. In 1849, five years after Smith's death in 1844, she married Brigham Young. At the time she was forty-five. Altogether, Brigham Young married six of Joseph Smith's widows.

THE PROPHET'S DIVORCE.

How She Came to Prefer the Complaint—Her Story of the Difficulty with Her Lawyers—She Accuses Them of Extraordinary Greediness—A Next Friend Whom She Never Saw—She Exonerates the Rev. Mr. Stratton— She Asked His Advice.

Correspondence of The Sun.

SALT LAKE CITY, Aug. 13.—At the request of Mrs. Ann Eliza Young, I visited the Walker House this afternoon to hear her story of the difficulty with her counsel. It is well-known that the Hon. Brigham Young, through mutual friends, offered to compromise the divorce suit by paying her $15,000. She accepted the offer without consultation with her lawyers. It was reported that the lawyers then threw up the case in high dudgeon. They denied the rumor, and forced the matter to trial at the appointed time, despite Mrs. Young's wish. The complaint was drawn up in such a manner that she could not withdraw it except with the consent of her next friend, Gen. Maxwell,[1] and that of her solici-tor and counsel.

I found the lady in her pleasant little room on the third floor of the Walker House. The sewing machine and trunk occupied their old positions, and the former furnished evidence of the industry of its owner. Looking from the windows I could see rich patches of sunlight chasing the shadows over the snowy peaks of the Wasatch Mountains, while the valley below was carpeted with yellow fields of grain. Mrs. Young looked much improved. She was more composed in manner, and was exceed-ingly gracious. She wore a silver gray poplin dress, made up in the most fashionable style. A little frill of Valenciennes lace surrounded her neck, and merged itself into an elaborate bow in front. I noticed no jewelry except a pair of jet earrings, an amethyst ring on the forefinger of her left hand, and two plain gold rings on her wedding finger. Her blue eyes had lost their sad expression, and her brown hair was arranged *à la grecque*,[2] which was certainly very becoming. In my former interview she had spoken of her husband as President Young, but to-day she called him simply Mr. Young and Brigham.

"I have sent for you," she said, "for the purpose of setting at rest certain reports concerning myself and the Rev. Mr. Stratton.[3] I understand that the men who claim to be my law-yers are spreading derogatory reports concerning us, alleging that Mr. Stratton has officiously intermeddled in my affairs, and that it was through his means that a compromise was effected independent of the men in charge of my case. These reports are unjust to Mr. Stratton, as well as untrue."

THE REV. MR. STRATTON.

"Mrs. Young," said I, "would it not be better to go back to the beginning and give me the history of your negotiations with the lawyers as well as tell me how you came to make the complaint."

"Probably it will," she answered. "But it is a long story. First, I want you to exonerate Mr. Stratton from any blame. He has been a true friend and has never been a busybody in my affairs. Yet the most shocking reports have been circulated concerning his conduct."

"How did you first become acquainted with Mr. Stratton?" I asked.

"I knew Mr. Stratton," she replied, "long before I left Mr. Young. I was introduced to him and his wife by Mr. Sawyer."[4]

Knowing Mr. Oscar F. Sawyer to be an inveterate enemy of the Mormons and the editor of the Gentile organ[5] in Salt Lake City I naturally inquired if she meant him.

"Oh, no," was the answer. "It was another gentleman named Sawyer. I became very well acquainted with Mrs. Stratton and frequently called upon her."

MRS. YOUNG'S BOARDERS.

"You were keeping boarders, I believe, before your trouble with Mr. Young, were you not?" I inquired.

Her eyes lighted up. "The most shameful stories have been circulated concerning that," she said. "He never made any objections. I sent his wife to him—Lucy Decker[6]—to ask if I might take a few boarders and he said that I could. He rather liked the idea. Well, Judge Hagan[7] and his wife came and boarded with me, and Mr. and Mrs. Smith,[8] and Mr. Graham[9] of Joslyn & Parks's jewelry store.[10] Mr. Graham only took day board. He slept at the store nights."

"I have been told," I said, "that Mr. Young thought you acted imprudently with some of your boarders and that he repeatedly reprimanded you. Is that so?"

"Mr. Young frequently urged me to go to social parties and other gatherings," she answered. "'Why don't you go and enjoy yourself, Eliza,' he would say. 'You are young, and I like to see you amused and happy.' Well, I would go to a party or entertainment with some married gentleman and his wife, and the next thing I heard of the most shocking gossip floating through the city. Oh, you don't know the way in which these Mormon women do talk of one another. 'What do you think,' they would say. 'Eliza Young was at such a place last night with Mr. So-and-so, when his wife was home sick—what a shame.' I would hear all sorts of stories and it actually made me feel as though I never wanted to go into society again. Then Brigham would urge me to pay no attention to the stories. He never objected to my going out in society."

"But as to the origin of the suit," I suggested.

HER STORY OF THE ORIGIN OF THE SUIT.

"When I went to Mr. Young," she said, "and made my last appeal for support, he avowed that he would have nothing more to do with me, and told me that I must earn a living for myself and children. I came home sick at heart. Up to that time I had suffered in silence. I had told nobody of the way in which he had treated me. While I was lying upon the sofa utterly prostrated, Mrs. Hagan came in and asked me what was the matter. I was driven to desperation. I told her the whole story. She was shocked. When Judge Hagan came home at night she informed him of the treatment that I had received. I asked him if the law did not provide some relief for a wife who had been so cruelly used. He said that he thought it did, and told me that he would confer with his partners, Judges Smith[11] and Tilford,[12] and see what could be done. This was on a Friday. On Saturday Judge Hagan said that Brigham could be compelled to support me. On Sunday I met Judges Hagan, Smith, and Tilford in Mr. Tilford's house. They sympathized with me deeply, and advised me to go to a hotel. I told them I was entirely destitute, and I hadn't a penny in the world to carry on a suit, or to pay my board in a hotel. They told me that they would pay my board, and trust to the law to get the money from Brigham. They said that they would take the chance of getting a twenty thousand dollar fee from him, and that they would compel him to give me a thousand dollars a month during the suit, besides a large sum when the trial was concluded. They expressly stated that I should have all the money thus obtained, they looking to him alone for their fees and expenses.

HOW SHE CAME TO GO TO A HOTEL.

Here the band of the San Francisco Minstrels[13] passed along the street in a wagon, tooting the brass instruments and filling the air with brazen melody. Mrs. Young went to the window and gazed at the scene with apparent interest. After the negro minstrels had passed she resumed her seat.

"Well," she continued, "Judge Tilford told me that after the suit was commenced he thought Mr. Young would be glad to settle it without allowing it to go to trial. He said he would go to him and give him an opportunity to compromise it, and he had no idea but that it would be all right. They would get their fee, and I would get enough to keep me through life. That Sunday night Judge Hagan went to San Francisco. He was gone a month. He thought it wouldn't look well for his wife to be boarding in Mr. Young's house while he was conducting a suit against him, and so Mrs. Hagan left me. Well, people began to suspect what was going on. I became afraid to remain in the house. I knew what power Brigham had, and I was fearful that he would abduct me or do something else to get me out of the way. When Judge Hagan came back I told him that I felt that I was in a dangerous position; that I might mysteriously disappear some night, and no one would be the wiser. He wanted to know why I didn't go to a hotel, but that was all. I was quite surprised that he didn't say something about arranging for my board, as he and his partner had said that they would see to that when they first spoke of the suit. Well, I finally went to the Walker House. By the request of Judge Tilford, Mr. and Mrs. Stratton went with me to see that I had rooms."

WHO PAYS HER BOARD.

"Mrs. Young," I said, "if it is a fair question, I would like to ask who pays your board at the Walker House."

"Well," she answered, "I have paid my own board up to the present time from the proceeds of the sale of my furniture. But Mr. Wilkins (the superintendent of the hotel) and his wife have been very kind. I wish you would say that I feel very grateful for their kindness. Mr. Wilkins told me to give myself no uneasiness about my board. If I succeeded in the suit I could pay my bill, but if I didn't it would be all right and he would feel just as well satisfied."

A QUEER STORY.

"What occurred after you went to the Walker House?" was the next question.

"I went to the Walker House on July 14," she said. "On the Thursday morning before the suit was to come before the court Judge Tilford visited me. I asked him if he had seen Brigham about the suit, as he had promised when the papers were drawn. He acknowledged that he had not. He wasn't going to Brigham; Brigham must come to him. He said that he had some papers that he wanted me to sign. I looked at them. Their purport was that I should sign off $500 per month of my alimony to the lawyers; that I should bind myself to turn over to them half of what came to me at the close of the suit, and in case of a compromise I should hand them half of what I got. They were to have all this in addition to their $20,000. I was astonished. I didn't know what to do; but I told him that I would give him an answer in the afternoon. He went away, and inside of half an hour I had information from three different sources that Mr. Young wanted to compromise with me, but first it was not yet decided what the offer was to be. I went down to Mr. Stratton's and told him what Judge Tilford wanted me to do. Mr. Stratton said he would confer with some trustworthy lawyer and tell me the result. He afterward advised me to sign no papers whatever. After I got back to the hotel, Gen. Maxwell, who had been put in the complaint as my next friend, came in to see me. It was the first time that I had ever met him. He wanted to know what I was going to do. He said if I was going to fight the thing out to the bitter end he would stick to me to the last; but if I was going to compromise he would drop it then and there and have nothing more to do with it. Judge Smith came to my room in the afternoon, and I told him plumply and plainly that I would not sign the document. He intimated that they would withdraw from the case if I refused, and left me somewhat abruptly. My father soon afterward came in and told me that Brigham had offered me $15,000 to settle the trouble. Father advised me to accept the offer, but told me to keep it to myself for the time being. I agreed to the compromise and promised not to open my mouth until he thought best."

WOMAN VS. WOMAN.

After a short pause Mrs. Young continued as follows:

"In the evening Judge Smith visited me a second time. He again urged me to sign the paper that Judge Tilford had left with me in the morning. I steadily refused. The fact is that I began to be afraid of these men, and I had persons posted in the hall to tell me when they were coming, so that I could prepare myself to meet them. When Mr. Smith found that I would not accede he made another proposal. He agreed to let me have all the alimony—$1,000 a month—but they wanted half of what the court might grant me in the end; or half of what might be got through a compromise, as well as the $20,000 fee from Brigham. I positively refused to sign any or all papers. He then said that he thought he should drop the case. I was welcome to what had been done. I could undoubtedly get other lawyers, and would not have trouble in finding them. He nevertheless took a great interest in my welfare, and wanted to assure me that I should never want for anything if he could assist me. On Friday morning Mrs. Tilford came in. After some general conversation she asked me if anybody had been to see me. I told her no. Then she inquired if I had heard anything about a compromise. I answered in the negative. I knew it wouldn't do for me to tell her. She said 'Good morning,' and shut the door."

ANOTHER QUEER STORY.

"Did you hear from the lawyers again?" I ventured to ask.

"Yes," Mrs. Young replied. "At 2 o'clock that afternoon all three of them, Tilford, Smith, and Hagan, called upon me to get my final answer on signing the papers. I utterly refused to sign anything. Judge Tilford then told me that they had concluded to drop the case. I made no reply, and they departed. An eminent California lawyer had told me that if he could be of any service to me, he would come back to Salt Lake and take charge of the case free of expense. I thought if there was a hitch in the settlement I might better have him than Tilford, Hagan, and Smith. Well, five minutes after the three lawyers had left me Tilford came rushing back, and asked me for the paper that he had left for my signature on Thursday morning. I was foolish, or I would have said that I didn't know what had become of it. I told him, however, that I had left the document at Mr. Stratton's, and added that I would get it when I went down there. He immediately visited Mr. Stratton. He got possession of the paper by telling Mr. Stratton that I said he could have it. The statement was an unblushing falsehood. I never said anything of the kind. Well, the three lawyers waited down stairs for some time, hoping that I would get scared because they had left me, and call them back. At last they went away. If you remember, I was talking with you that same evening. During our conversation Hagan came and called me out into the hall. He asked me if I understood that they had thrown up the case. I said that I certainly did so understand it and that I had so informed Mr. Stratton. 'Well,' said he,

'Stratton or no Stratton, we are going to carry the case through. I told Tilford when we came down stairs that I thought that was the way you understood it.'

THE SITUATION.

"Now," continued the lady, "look at the situation. What am I to do? Tilford that very evening went into the *Salt Lake Herald* office and told Harrington,[14] the press agent, that they had thrown up the case, and Harrington telegraphed it all over the country. At the same hour Hagan was rushing up to me and declaring that they had not thrown up the suit. They went on with the case on the Tuesday following without my wishes, and are now running it on their own hook. They have dismissed themselves, but deny it. If I dismiss them they will fall upon me for any money I may receive in compromise. If Judge Emerson[15] holds that his court has no jurisdiction, the case drops into the Mormon court, and that ends it, for neither party would get a cent in that court.

"These," said Mrs. Young in conclusion, "are the facts in the matter. You can see that Mr. Stratton had no hand in the thing from the beginning. All he has done was to advise me when I asked his advice."

NOTES

1. George R. Maxwell, who also is mentioned in "The Seventeenth Wife."

2. Hair bound in a chignon or bun at the back of the head.

3. The Rev. C. C. Stratton, the Methodist minister mentioned by Ann Eliza Young in the previous article.

4. Howard Sawyer.

5. Oscar Sawyer of the *Salt Lake Daily Tribune* is mentioned by Brigham Young in the article "The Great Utah Divorce."

6. Lucy Decker and her sister are mentioned in the previous article.

7. Albert Hagan was an attorney. I believe he was the same Albert Hagan who was a judge in Santa Cruz, California, from 1868 to 1871. Albert Hagan later was the recorder for the Utah Supreme Court.

8. A "Mr. Smith" was an attorney representing Ann Eliza Young (see note 11 below), but I am not certain if this is the same individual and his spouse.

9. Malcolm Graham, mentioned in "The Seventeenth Wife."

10. As noted in "The Seventeenth Wife," the store's name was Joslin and Park.

11. F. M. Smith. The title of judge may be honorary. In some newspaper accounts his name appears erroneously, I think, as F. N. Smith.

12. Frank Tilford had been a judge in California and also served in the senate in that state. He later practiced law in Nevada, moving to Salt Lake City in 1872. Sloan's 1874 directory (*Gazeteer* [*sic*], 303) contains an advertisement for "Tilford and Hagan, Attorneys." Smith is not listed as a partner.

13. The San Francisco Minstrels actually were from New York.

14. I believe this is William H. Harrington, who formerly had worked for Western Union in Denver.

15. Phillip H. Emerson, First District Court judge from 1873 to 1885.

Strangers in a Strange Land

HE SUNDAY, JULY 14, 1873, editions of the *New York Sun* and the *New York Times* carried a short article datelined the previous day from Salt Lake City. Headlined "The Prophet's Latest Failure" and probably telegraphed to New York from Salt Lake City, the three paragraphs in the *Sun* read:

> The San Francisco [Mountains], Arizona, Mormon mission projected by Brigham Young to settle in that territory and build that section of Tom Scott's Southern Pacific Railway has proved a disastrous failure. The entire colony, more than seven hundred in number, is on the way home to Utah

again. Many have already arrived. Others will remain on the other side of the Colorado River, for the want of the boats, which were lost, to cross.

The emigrants experienced terrible sufferings. The country was utterly misrepresented. It is sterile, and water and pasturage are scarce. Nothing short of the Apache country came up to the representations, and the colony refused to take the chances of a massacre by Indians.

On the return the emigrants were compelled to throw away their stoves and all heavy articles to enable them to reach water and feed for their teams. The condition of the people and the train is extremely bad. The result has shaken faith in the infallibility of the head of the Church as an inspired prophet.

Most likely the article was written by one of the anti-Mormon newspapermen in Salt Lake City, perhaps Oscar G. Sawyer of the *Salt Lake Daily Tribune and Utah Mining News* mentioned in Cummings's article "The Great Utah Divorce."

Amos Cummings, once again smelling a story, wrote a follow-up article about the expedition ("The Arizona Expedition"), which is reprinted in this section and was apparently based in large part on information provided by members of the expedition who returned to Salt Lake City. Cummings later arranged an interview with Brigham Young to gather more information and to see what future expeditions might be planned to plant a Mormon colony in Arizona. That interview also is reprinted here ("The Mormon Pioneers"). By the time of that interview, Cummings knew that early news accounts claiming at least partial success by the colonists were in error. He asked Brigham Young point-blank about the outcome and received an equally direct answer: the expedition had been a failure.

Modern readers might suspect expeditions such as the one to Arizona in 1873 were intended solely to spread the teachings of the Mormon Church, but that would be an incorrect assumption. Like other ventures initiated by Brigham Young and other church officials in the mid-nineteenth century, expansion out of Salt Lake City often was intended to further the economic interests of the church. Historians have documented a host of such undertakings in Arizona, California, Colorado, Idaho, Nevada, and Utah. For instance, the town of Kanab in southernmost Utah, a scenic region that has been drawing movie directors since the 1920s, was initially colonized by a Mormon expedition in 1858 as a place to raise cattle. In the early years the town did not flourish, largely because efforts to negotiate with the local Native American groups, who opposed the usurping of their lands, failed. Open conflicts resulted. Forts were built and rebuilt and settlers came and went. It was not until 1870 that the town, a jumping-off place for the 1873 Arizona expedition described by Cummings, was firmly established. Settling the land was no easier for Mormons than it was for other pioneers in isolated regions of the West.

One catalyst for attempts by the Mormon Church to establish colonies in the West was the outbreak of the Civil War and the addition of new states to the union. Church officials feared their overland access to eastern markets might be cut off. Also, they decried the high costs of transporting cotton and other produce and goods by wagon across the Great Plains and Rocky Mountains. To alleviate the situation Brigham Young sought another mode of transportation, as well as an alternative route to the East: steamboats that would go up the Colorado River to an inland port town. Goods could be off-loaded and then shipped overland by wagons to Salt Lake City and other towns in the West and Southwest.

A first step in carrying out that plan took place in 1864 when an expedition was sent to the Colorado River west of the Grand Canyon. The small outpost of Callville was established, but the colony never succeeded. The attempt was abandoned after the completion of the transcontinental railroad provided the alternative transportation sought by the church. Still, other expeditions were sent out to found new settlements.

The 1873 Arizona expedition has achieved notoriety as one of the more disastrous mid-nineteenth-century attempts by Mormon pioneers to expand the church's economic and religious influence. In reading Cummings's subsequent interview with Brigham Young ("The Mormon Pioneers"), I got the feeling that Young was not at all pleased with the failure of the expedition. In that 1873 interview, Young displays detailed knowledge of Arizona Territory. From his conversation with Amos Cummings, we learn that Young possessed not only what must have been an excellent map but also an understanding of geographical details, such as where the better-watered regions suitable for an Arizona settlement were located.

The Mormon colonists sent to Arizona failed in large part because they had gotten bogged down in the desert, unwilling or unable to move farther south to the wetter areas described by Young in his interview with Cummings. In part they were victims of the seasonal flow of the Little Colorado River. The expedition arrived at the river in a dry season, essentially dooming the ability of the colonists to move farther south and east. Had a significant town been successfully founded in central Arizona, the history of the West may have been quite different.

In his interview with Cummings, Brigham Young suggested that another try to establish a colony in Arizona might be in order. Next time, he said, either he or his son—probably Joseph Angell Young—would head it. If you want something done right, do it yourself!

As an archaeologist I was intrigued by the references in Amos's two articles—"The Arizona Expedition" and "The Mormon Pioneers"—to Indian "ruins." Clearly Brigham Young and other Mormons were acquainted with the numerous ancestral Pueblo Indian sites that dotted southern Utah and Arizona.

One wonders if more detailed information about those archaeological sites exists in church archives.

Members of the Church of Latter-day Saints were not the only people to discover that the West could be an unforgiving land. To easterners the West indeed was a strange land. Mountainous terrain and arid deserts taxed even the hardiest pioneers.

Once the transcontinental railroad was completed, the West became accessible not only to settlers but to casual visitors like Amos Cummings as well. He, too, could marvel at the Rocky Mountains and other natural phenomena like the Great Salt Lake, which he likened to its saline counterpart in ancient Palestine. In his article "The American Dead Sea," the third article reprinted in this section, Cummings provides a firsthand, somewhat wide-eyed account of his visit to that lake. Like many tourists before and since, Amos jumped in to test the fabled buoyancy of the saline sea, proclaiming the experience "novel." It is a charming anecdote. Clearly, the Great Salt Lake could captivate even a well-traveled journalist like Cummings.

"The Arizona Expedition" was published in the *New York Sun* on August 15, 1873. It took only a week for the letter containing the article to be sent by rail in a mail bag from Salt Lake City to *Sun* editors in New York City. The second article, "The Mormon Pioneers," was in the *Sun* on August 18, and the third, "The American Dead Sea," was published September 6.

THE ARIZONA EXPEDITION.

Particulars of the Last Mormon Expedition—The Paradise in the Gadsden Purchase—Terrible Suffering in the Painted Desert— The Prophet Asked for Instructions—On to the Mexican Frontier.

Correspondence of The Sun.

SALT LAKE CITY, Aug. 7.—Some of the members of Brigham Young's Arizona expedition have returned to this city. They are very reticent, but I have succeeded in eliciting considerable information from them. Gov. Young tells me that the main idea of the expedition was to aid the Government in keeping down the Apaches and Navajos. This undoubtedly was one of its objects. Another object was to effect a settlement on the line of Tom Scott's Southern Pacific road.[1] Col. Scott was here some time ago, and held long consultations with the Mormon President. If a strong body of the Saints were located along the projected route the Indians would not be apt to interfere in the construction of the road, and the services of the Mormons in building it would be invaluable. And this was not all. If there are any really fine lands in Arizona the sons of Zion could pre-empt them, and hold them for a rise. The Gentiles declare that Brigham wanted to plant the colony for a place of refuge in case the United States authorities here should drive him from cover. This is nonsense. The Mormon chief is shrewd and nervy. He thoroughly understands the Grant[2] officials and knows how to deal with them when necessary.

TOM SCOTT'S PLANS.

It was supposed that Tom Scott would be ready to begin opera-tions during the coming winter. His intention was to drive through the last Congress a scheme similar to the old Union Pacific Measure, thus securing large grants of land and the credit of the Government to the extent of $30,000,000. His agents had been already at work, and had secured the votes of all but two of the Southern members of Congress in favor of the plan. Everything was lovely and the cars were about to start, when the Credit Mobilier[3] exposé dropped from a clear sky and smashed things into splinters. Our Christian statesmen were seriously injured, and were unable to put their shoulders to the Colonel's wheel. It is now not possible to begin the construction of the Arizona section of the road in under two or three years. The Mormon chief, however, determined to take time by the forelock, and secure a lodgment that will prove valuable when the road is built.

THE PROMISED LAND.

For this purpose he issued a call for 200 volunteers from Salt Lake and the counties north of here. The Mormons promptly responded, and the expedition was quickly fitted out. Over eighty teams[4] and 120 men and five women were in the party.

They were well supplied with bacon, flour, and other provisions. Their objective point was the Mountains of Arizona, six or seven hundred miles south of this city.[5] Reports had located a rich country in the vicinity of an unknown range of mountains. The land was represented as extraordinarily fertile. Water was abundant, and the productive soil could be irrigated without much trouble. Vast ranges of hickory and black walnut forests slept in the shadows of the mountains. They were filled with wild turkeys and all kinds of game. The whole region was a glowing paradise, and it was located on the line of the Southern Pacific Railroad. Such was the picture as it was exhibited in Salt Lake City.

DEPARTURE OF THE EXPEDITION.

The expedition left Great Salt Lake on the 1st of April, and reached Kanab,[6] the last Mormon settlement in Southern Utah, about two weeks afterward. They crossed the Buckskin Mountains[7] and struck the Paria River.[8] Following this stream down to its outlet, they got over the Big Colorado at Lee's Crossing,[9] near the head of the great cañon. Between Lee's Crossing and Call's Landing[10] the river is impassable. The grand cañon of the Colorado cuts through the country for a distance of nearly 600 miles. It varies in depth from 3,000 to 8,000 feet.[11] Its walls are mostly perpendicular. The river can scarcely be seen from above. The distance is so great that it resembles a silver hair. The whole country is of volcanic formation.[12] The party suffered from scarcity of water before they reached the Paria; but they managed to find enough in holes and springs to keep a portion of them on the move. Still many of their mules gave out, and twenty-six of their wagons were abandoned.

Only fifty-four teams crossed the Big Colorado. They spent some time visiting the Moqui villages near the river.[13] The Moquis are the remnants of Aztec civilization.[14] They live in walled towns, and spin and weave. They understand irrigation, and produce fair crops. They wear their hair long, and part it in the middle. Polygamy is one of their innocent amusements, and this endeared them to the Mormons. These Indians were very friendly. They gladly furnished the expedition with fresh vegetables, and urged the Saints to settle down in their country. It was with regret that the party left them, and turned their faces to the south.

WONDERFUL DISCOVERY OF WATER.

Lee's Crossing is at the mouth of the Paria River. On reaching the left bank of the Big Colorado the Mormons found themselves hemmed in by a range of volcanic mountains. They crawled along the base of these mountains, following the course of the Big Colorado down to the mouth of the Chiquito or Little Colorado River.[15] Here the mountains made a turn. The range ran up the right bank of the Colorado Chiquito. The expedition began to move up that river. It was a mass of sand, and nearly dry. As they left the mountain range and entered the Painted Desert,[16] the bed of the river became perfectly dry. The sun was scorching. There were no trees, and the thermometer frequently stood at 120° above zero. The sky was copper-colored, and hot puffs of air chased each other over the burning sands. The expedition was well supplied with water kegs. These were filled as often as possible. At last, however, they ran dry. The mules began to suffer from thirst. When the blazing sun went down there was no water in sight. A feeling of despair settled upon the party. Big holes were dug in the bed of the river in hopes of finding the precious fluid, but the sand was dry down to the very bottom. A hundred persons crept under their blankets that night with parched throats. When daylight came and the hot sun began to crawl above the red sand a shout of joy arose from the waterless river. The holes dug on the previous evening were filled with water. It had oozed into them from beneath the sands during the cool hours of the night. This was an important discovery. It saved the expedition. For weeks the party struggled through the sands of the Little Colorado, digging holes at sundown, which were filled with water during the night. In vain they looked for the promised land. They could not find it. Gov. Young says they lost their way, and I guess the Governor is right.

BRIGHAM ASKED FOR INSTRUCTIONS.

They stayed along the dry river several weeks. The land was all desert, and volcanic. Scores of extinct craters were discovered. At last the expedition halted. They sent a messenger back to Kanab to communicate with the great Mormon chief. Kanab and Salt Lake City are connected by a telegraphic wire. The messenger was directed to report to Brigham, inform him of the nature of the country, and ask further instructions. He departed, but never returned. Whether he lost his way or was killed is uncertain. After waiting some time a party of a half dozen were ordered to Kanab to open communication with the President. They obeyed orders, but returned without any reply or instructions. I suppose that Brigham was absent from Salt Lake City, preaching in some of the outlying settlements.

TERRIBLE SUFFERINGS.

The expedition, however, hesitated to return. They spent some time longer—six weeks in all—in the desolate country between the Big Colorado and the Colorado Chiquito. No word came from Salt Lake. Water became more scarce and brackish. The holes did not fill up as usual. The sun was terrible and the burning sands insufferable. The hoofs of the poor mules and horses were cracked by the heat. When released from the wagons the patient animals threw themselves upon their backs and held their hoofs in the air to cool them off. All the horses were lamed, and many of them died. They were fed upon flour, weeds, and brush. The teams became so weak that three or four spans were put on in front of a wagon to haul it through the sand. The sufferings of the party were intense. Sickness appeared, and the men began to look worse than the horses. The women stood it far better than the men.

THE PROPHET'S INSTRUCTIONS.

The Prophet finally sent them word to scatter and locate somewhere among the settlements in Southern Utah. Before these instructions were received, many of them had straggled toward the Big Colorado. They afterward concentrated at Lee's Crossing. The most of them reached the Mormon settlements, but a few of the plucky ones stuck it out, and have found the promised land. A telegram from Tucson says they have settled somewhere in the mountains between the two rivers. The exact location is not given. There was much sickness in the expedition, but so far as is positively known no lives were lost.

Those who have returned to Salt Lake City inform me that the country between the Big and Little Colorado has the appearance of having once been inhabited. They found lots of old broken stoneware and things of that kind. Occasionally they met Indians, who said that they lived on streams running all the season. The members of the expedition, however, did not credit their story. The Indians wanted the emigrants to stay and build up the country. The Little Colorado and most of the springs dry up every summer. South of the San Francisco Mountains[17] there is a fine country, but it is settled by Mexican ranchers, who are extremely hostile to the whites. They will allow no American to take up land.

A NARROW ESCAPE.

The pioneers are all glad to get home. They say they want Brigham Young to head the next expedition. Several of them were pretty well off before they left Utah. They sold everything to purchase a good outfit, and are now destitute. The most of them were powerful young men, especially chosen by the church authorities for this service. In recrossing the Colorado at the mouth of the Paria their ferryboat was washed away, and many had to cross in Indian canoes. They took their wagons apart, and brought them over piecemeal. The horses swam the river. Many teams were abandoned on the Colorado Chiquito. I am told that but sixteen returned to Utah. The river at Lee's Crossing is about forty rods wide.[18] It is very deep, and the current is swift. The ferryboat was whirled away toward the Great Cañon at a speed of nearly fifteen miles an hour.

ON TO THE MEXICAN FRONTIER.

The result of the expedition is that a very small body of Mormons have effected a settlement in Arizona. The Prophet, however, is not satisfied. He never does things by halves. He knows there is good land in Arizona and is determined to have it. A second party of stout Mormon hearts is to be organized, and before another year has swept over the nation the standard of Zion will be borne to the Mexican border.

NOTES

1. The Southern Pacific, not to be confused with a later Southern Pacific railroad in California, was to be part of a transcontinental line that cut across the southern United States through Texas, New Mexico, and Arizona to California. The railroad, operating as the Texas and Pacific Railroad, was sanctioned by a lucrative federal charter granted by Congress in 1871 that gave the railroad vast sections of land. Colonel Thomas A. Scott, a veteran of the Civil War and former Pennsylvania Railroad executive, was made president of the Texas and Pacific in 1872. As originally envisioned, the railroad line was never completed; a southern transcontinental rail network did not become a reality until the late nineteenth century.

2. Officials in the administration of President Ulysses S. Grant.

3. The story of Credit Mobilier, one of the great financial scandals of the time, was broken by the *New York Sun* in 1872. Amos Cummings had a hand in the exposé. Credit Mobilier, incorporated

in Pennsylvania, was a construction company founded to help build the Union Pacific Railroad. Wealthy stockholders in the Union Pacific contracted with the company—controlled by themselves—to build sections of the railroad at exorbitant prices, thus lining their pockets with construction funds provided by Congress. To stymie congressional investigation of the deal, shares of stock in the company were sold to members of Congress and other officials at a much lower price than they were worth, allowing the buyers to reap huge profits. The scandal even reached into the office of then–vice president Schuyler Colfax, and future president James A. Garfield also was involved. Ultimately, no one was prosecuted.

4. Mule-drawn wagons.

5. A good estimate; the distance from Salt Lake City to Phoenix is 650 miles, as the crow flies.

6. Kanab is about four miles north of the Utah-Arizona border.

7. The Buckskin Mountains are in La Paz County in northwestern Arizona.

8. The Paria River flows down from Utah into Arizona, intersecting the Colorado River at Lee's Crossing, at the beginning of the Grand Canyon.

9. Named for John D. Lee, who crossed the Colorado River there in 1871 and later established a ferry. Lees Ferry marks the location today. Lee was infamous for his involvement with the 1857 Mountain Meadows (in southern Utah) massacre of westward-bound members of a wagon train from Arkansas. The massacre was depicted in the 2007 movie *September Dawn*.

10. The Colorado River landing was named for Anson Call, who was with the Mormon party that attempted a settlement on the river in 1864. As noted in the introduction to this section, the intent of the settlement was to help anchor a route for people and goods to travel up the Colorado River; these goods could then be taken overland to Utah and the Southwest. Today the city of Callville, Arizona, near the Hoover Dam and Lake Mead, marks this location.

11. Cummings's estimates are a little overblown. The Grand Canyon is 277 miles long and its deepest point is 6,000 feet.

12. The rock strata forming the Grand Canyon are actually not of volcanic origin.

13. Likely Hopi Indians, although at times "Moqui" was a term used more generally for Pueblo Indians, including their pre-Columbian ancestors.

14. The Pueblo Indians of the Four Corners region are not related to the Aztec Indians of Mexico.

15. The Little Colorado River drains the Painted Desert, flowing northwest to intersect the Colorado River in the Grand Canyon north of Flagstaff about seventy miles.

16. Stretching southeast from the Grand Canyon in Arizona.

17. The San Francisco Mountains are remains of ancient volcanoes and are just north of Flagstaff. The highest peak is just over 12,600 feet.

18. Equal to 660 feet.

THE MORMON PIONEERS.

ANOTHER EXPEDITION TO MARCH INTO THE ARIZONA DESERTS.

*A Second Talk with Brigham Young—What He Thinks of Adobe
Houses—Reminiscences of New York State—The Old Mormon
Handcarts and Joseph Young's Sad Mistake—The Prophet to
Head a New Arizona Expedition—Not on Exhibition.*

Correspondence of The Sun.

SALT LAKE CITY, Aug. 9.—I dropped in upon ex-Gov. Brigham Young again yesterday. The old gentleman was very busy, but he stopped work and received me rather graciously. He wore a white duck[1] coat and a big snowy cravat but no hat. His son Joseph[2] and several other Mormon gentlemen were in the room. A lady accompanied me.[3] I introduced her to the prophet, and they shook hands, after which he placed chairs for us near the door. He then sat down on the opposite side of the room, and awaited our pleasure. After we had inquired concerning his health and been assured that it was excellent, the conversation proceeded as follows:

Correspondent—It is a very warm day, Governor, but you look remarkably cool and comfortable.

The Prophet (swelling his chest)—Do you think so? Well this house is always cool. Adobe buildings are invariably cool in the summer and warm in the winter.

Correspondent—Then this is an adobe house.

The Prophet—Yes, the most of our houses are adobe. We built nothing else when we first came here.

A TALK ABOUT ADOBE HOUSES.

Correspondent—Had you ever seen an adobe house when you came to Salt Lake?

The Prophet—No, I never had, but I had heard of them, and we put them up without much trouble.

Correspondent—Well, judging from what I saw of them in Pueblo and Greeley, down in Colorado, I shouldn't think they were very durable. The rain seemed to wash them away, and they looked crumbling and shaky.

The Prophet—That is not the case here. The older they are the harder the walls become. Why, down in the southern part of the Territory, at St. George⁴ and other places, you find nothing but adobe houses. You have heard of the Moqui cities down in the Arizona deserts. Well, they are all adobe, and I suppose are centuries old. The walls are adobe, and are as hard as flint. Some time ago one of our brothers settled near some ruined Moqui houses in Southern Utah. He had occasion to cut through one of these walls, and he told me that he actually had to blast his way through it. He would have had an easier job if the wall had been solid rock. You see when we came to this valley it was a desert. There was no timber in sight, and nothing but sage brush. We found the very thing we wanted in these sun dried bricks.

THE RUINS IN THE DESERTS.

Correspondent—Talking of the Moquis, I have heard that after your arrival in Utah you discovered ruined cities of vast size[5] in various parts of the Territory.

The Prophet—Yes, that is true. You will find ancient ruins to-day scattered over the southern part of the Territory. It is no uncommon thing, while traveling through the deserts down there, to run across piles of broken pottery, mixed with red arrow heads and similar things. We have discovered these ruins even as far north as the other side of Salt Lake. But then you find the footmarks of an unknown race all over the continent. Now I haven't been in New York State for a great many years, but they used to have very interesting ruins there when I was young—Indian mounds and pieces of pottery, and stone hatchets, and the same little red arrow heads that I find to-day in Southern Utah and Arizona. And you find the same thing in Ohio and out on the Plains—the same pieces of pottery and red flinty arrow heads.

Correspondent—Is the country as desolate down that way as the alkali country this side of Laramie?

The Prophet—It's volcanic, and a good deal of it is a desert. You will find ruined cities in the most desolate spots. This shows that the whole country has some time or other been thickly populated, and to support such a population it must have been very fertile.

THE MORMON HANDCARTS.

Correspondent—Well, after passing through the alkali country, I can't conceive how it was possible for you folks to drag your handcarts through it and live to reach Salt Lake.

The Prophet—Well, I am not so sure that the handcart system was the best that could have been devised. A great many of our poor people died on the road. My son Joseph here headed one large handcart party. He had been in England on a mission,

THE HANDCARTS PULLED BY MORMONS ACROSS THE GREAT PLAINS TO SALT LAKE CITY. MANY PEOPLE WHO WERE CRITICAL OF THE MORMONS, INCLUDING THE ENGRAVER OF THIS IMAGE, EMPHASIZED THE HARDSHIPS SUFFERED BY THE TRAVELERS. (YOUNG, *WIFE NUMBER 19*, FACING PAGE 210)

and brought them out with him. It was the beginning of winter when they left Missouri. Our brethren there urged them to stay until spring, but Joseph thought they could get through, and they started over the Plains. The snow fell, and it was unusually cold. A great many died—more than need to have died. I never approved of Joseph's coming right through. It was a sad mistake. We heard that they were on the way, and went out to meet them with our teams and brought them in. They were in a heartrending condition, but we saved many of their lives. It was fortunate that we did go out after them, for I don't believe that half of them would have ever seen the valley if we hadn't done so. No, on looking everything over at this time, I think there might have been some better system adopted than the handcart system.[6]

TOTAL FAILURE OF THE ARIZONA EXPEDITION.

Correspondent—I saw a dispatch from Tucson saying that a few Mormons had effected a settlement between the Big and Little

Colorado rivers. So your Arizona expedition this spring was not a total failure after all?

The Prophet—Well, that dispatch is a mistake. No settlement was made. They all came back. You see, some of our parties were down on the Little Colorado last year, and reported that they found some fine lands. Grass was growing, and there was plenty of water for irrigating purposes. This year we organized a band of pioneers, and sent them down there to effect a settlement. Well, they found the sun scorching hot and the river entirely dried up, and they all came back. None of them remained. Now, I know there is plenty of good land there.

Correspondent—They tell me that they want you to head the next expedition.

The Prophet (with much emphasis)—Well, I have no doubt if I had been with them they would have found some good land. I know the land is there. If I had headed the party I should have found it.

STUDYING THE MAP.

Here I arose, faced a fine map of Utah and Arizona, which was hanging on the wall over the sofa, and said, "Governor, won't you please show me where this party went?"

Gov. Young stepped over to my side. Placing his fat forefinger on the map he ran it down the Paria River, down the Big Colorado, and up the Colorado Chiquito beyond the Painted Desert. "That was their route," said he. He then made a circle around the Moqui village in the north-western portion of the Territory, saying, "There's where they went. There's a good land here," pointing to the junction of the Rio Puerco[7] and the Zuni River. Here his finger swooped to the south, taking in the Apache and Mogollon Mountains, the Sierra de Natanes, and the Pinaleno Range.[8] "All these mountains," he continued, "enclose some excellent land. They are filled with Indians, to be sure, but they are a different Indian from the lousy, lazy devils on the plains. They will work as well as a white man if you pay them for it."

WILL THE APACHES WORK?

I rather laughed at the idea of an Apache hoeing corn for a Mormon; but the Prophet was in earnest. "Why," he said, "they plant their own grain already, and weave their own clothes and blankets. You've seen these Navajo blankets. They're worth four times as much as a blanket woven by a white man. It's a mistake to think that an Indian won't work. His work is honest work, and he'll work as well if not better than a white man, if you only faithfully pay him."

The Prophet next ran his finger through the Corn and Antelope valleys,[9] over the Pueblo Viejo,[10] jumped the Peloncillo and the Chi-ri-ca-Hua mountains,[11] and brought up against the Mexican border at the Santa Rita Range, east of Tubac.[12] "All this," he continued, "can be made a good country. In some places there are miles upon miles of grassy plains." Then he pointed out the rivers, the Rio Verde, the Dry Fork, Tonto Creek, San Carlos, Santa Maria, Salado, San Pedro, Arivaypa, San Domingo, Natrosa, the Gila, and all the streams that flow through the mountains,[13] saying, "Tell me that there isn't any good land along those streams, and I tell you, you don't know what you're talking about. We are going to settle that country. It will all lie handy to Col. Scott's road, and a great deal of it is capable of sustaining a large population. Way, even over here," skipping to the western part of the Territory in the Wallapi Valley and Bill Williams Mountains,[14] "there's some good land. This expedition is so far a failure, but you haven't seen the end of it. We shall plant our settlements."

A NEW EXPEDITION.

Correspondent—Are you going to send out a new expedition?

The Prophet (returning to his seat)—We shall settle in Arizona. I did think that since the failure of this last expedition I would wait two or three years until Col. Scott got to work upon his road, but I have made up my mind to forward another company of pioneers this fall. One of my sons will head the party, and it is by no means improbable that I myself may accompany them. There will be no more turning back. I know there is as good land in Arizona as there is in Utah. We shall make our settlement this time without fail. You may be sure of that.

BRIGHAM AND THE LADIES.

Here Gov. Young asked the lady for her signature in his visitor's book. It was the first word he had spoken to her, and the last. I am told, however, that he chats with some of his female visitors in a most nonchalant manner, parrying their little thrusts with the skill of an old stager. A Mrs. Gould, wife of a well-known San Francisco lawyer,[15] was among his recent visitors. Brigham engaged in a lively conversation with her. At length she said, "Well, now, Mr. Young, really, do you know that I should be ever so much delighted to visit your families?"

The old gentleman straightened right up in an instant. "Madam," he retorted, "I'm sorry to be compelled to inform you that they are not on exhibition to-day."

NOTES

1. A tightly woven, heavy cotton fabric.

2. Almost certainly Joseph Angell Young, who also is mentioned in "The Great Utah Divorce."

3. The lady likely was Amos's spouse, Frances Cummings.

4. St. George is in southwestern Utah west of Kanab. The town was founded by Mormons in 1861 to produce cotton.

5. No doubt Pueblo Indian sites.

6. Shortly after setting up the church organization in Utah, Brigham Young and other church officials sought to enlarge their membership by making converts who would then move to Salt Lake City. One field of missionary activity was England. Originally, wagon trains were organized to transport people who emigrated to the United States across the Great Plains and Rocky Mountains to Utah. That was an expensive proposition, so small carts that could be pulled

by hand were proposed. Four groups set out from Iowa in 1856. The system did not work well, and many people died on the way west.

7. The original newspaper article has "Rio Puerso," an obvious mistake. Both the Puerco and Zuni originate in New Mexico and flow in a west-southwesterly direction, emptying into the Little Colorado River near Holbrook, Arizona.

8. The ranges, none as extensive as those farther north in the Rocky Mountains, are in portions of east-central Arizona in Apache, Gila, and Graham counties. The Gila River flows through the region.

9. These particular valleys (other valleys with the same name are found elsewhere in Arizona) probably were the ones in the east-central portion of the state in the mountains north of the Gila River.

10. An area of the upper Gila River drainage in eastern Arizona. Its name likely comes from the Pueblo Indian archaeological sites in the region. Pueblo Viejo was settled by Hispanic pioneers from Mexico. Today the town is called Solomonville and is in Graham County.

11. The Peloncillo and Chiricahua mountains are in Cochise, Graham, and Greenlee counties in southeastern Arizona near New Mexico.

12. Tubac, in southern Arizona, is less than twenty-five miles north of the Mexican border.

13. Brigham Young had a good map. These streams, some large and some small, for the most part are found in the Gila–Salt River drainage in Gila and Graham counties west across Arizona into Maricopa County. The Salado is the Salt River, Arivaypa today is more commonly spelled Aravaipa, and Rio Verde is commonly called the Verde River. "Natrosa" is likely Nutrioso Creek in southern Apache County (near Gila and Graham counties). It flows northward into the Little Colorado River.

14. The Hualapai (note spelling) and Bill Williams Mountains are in Mohave County in western Arizona.

15. Based on San Francisco city directories and genealogical data, I suspect the woman was Charlotte Goold (née Tobin), spouse of San Francisco attorney Edmond L. Goold.

THE AMERICAN DEAD SEA.

Driving through an Alkali Desert—The Stream of Zion—A Sacred Herd of Cattle—The Black Sea Gulls and the Flying Lizards—Swimming in the Great Salt Sea—The Mysterious Worms and the Hidden Whirlpool—A Sad Oyster Experiment— The Mormons to Be Drowned Out.

Correspondence of The Sun.

SALT LAKE CITY, Aug. 28.—Yesterday I visited the Great Salt Lake. But few strangers go to it. A tourist might spend a month in the city before he would find out how to reach it. Probably half of the residents of the Mormon capital have never stood upon the shores of this great inland sea. Black and Profile Rocks,[1] the main points of interest, are twenty miles from the city. Accompanied by the Hon. Standish Rood,[2] formerly of Milwaukee, and a party of ladies, I left Salt Lake City at 6 A.M. We had a fine span of horses. Running out of town through a shady street turning at the Tabernacle, we struck for a moun-

PROFILE ROCK, ALSO KNOWN AS LION'S HEAD ROCK, ON THE SHORE OF THE GREAT SALT LAKE. THE FORMATION WAS FORTY FEET TALL. (WILLIAMS, *PACIFIC TOURIST*, 149)

tain jutting into the lake apparently but three miles away. Its true distance is eighteen miles. The atmosphere is so clear that it is one vast field-glass, making the mountains appear much nearer than they really are. At times they seem to be within rifle range. Occasionally, however, the valley grows hazy and the dark, rocky peaks loom up above the smoke like island cliffs above the ocean.

THE SACRED RIVER.

The road to the lake is intersected by irrigating ditches and the River Jordan.[3] With these exceptions it is as level as a barn floor. For a short distance it is bordered by fields of grain. There are but few fences. The most of the land is a desert. Even the hardy sage brush refuses to grow. The soil is so strongly impregnated with alkali that in many places it looks as though somebody had sprinkled it with pulverized lime. The Jordan is a quiet stream, several rods[4] wide. The water is clear and pure. There are no trees upon its banks. The Mormons look upon it very much as the Crusaders regarded the original Jordan in Palestine. In their eyes it is a sacred river. They declare that the spirit of Joe Smith appeared to Brigham Young upon one of the mountains back of the city, and pointed out to him the Jordan as it wound its way over the valley like a narrow silver ribbon. Joseph told Brigham that the Great Salt Lake basin was the promised land. He selected the site of the city of Zion, and ordered the erection of the temple upon a chosen spot.

THE GREAT SALT LAKE MARSHES.

A dozen miles from the city we approached the marshes fringing the Great Salt Lake. They are miles in extent, and were covered with large herds of fat cattle. These grazing herds are owned by the Church of Jesus Christ of Latter-day Saints. The real foundation of this church is its tithing system. Under this system each saint turns over one-tenth of all his earnings for the benefit of the church. Many of the Mormons pay their tithes in cattle. The church herd is said to include over a million head of stock. It is a source of never failing revenue, for the beeves are of the choicest kind and command the best prices. The herders are appointed by the dignitaries of the church, and the bishops keep a careful account of the stock.

The marshes of the Great Salt Lake are the resort of thousands of wild fowl. They present a splendid field for sportsmen.

Among the ducks and snipe we saw a large white swan paddling up a little lagoon. The grasses are said to be very nutritious. Acres of wild beans are scattered over the marshes. The stalks grow to the height of three or four feet, and bear fragrant pink flowers as large as bolls of cotton just burst from their pods.

THE GREAT SALT LAKE.

As we neared the mountains a thin blue streak appeared beyond the marshes. It was the Great Salt Lake. Gradually the streak expanded until the surface of the sea was spread before us. A strong wind came from the northwest, and caps of foam danced upon the bosom of the waters. They were of dazzling white-ness. The lake, however, was as blue as indigo. In some places it was streaked with green as though veined with streams of sulphur water. We drove along the base of the mountains, which throw their rocky spurs to the shore line. Looking to the north nothing could be seen but the water heaving against a clear sky. It was like gazing upon the ocean at Long Branch.[5] The lake stretches toward the Central Pacific road over a hundred and twenty-five miles. Fifty miles west it washes the borders of the great American Desert. It is a large body of water. Delaware and Rhode Island might be thrown into its depths and there would still be room for a fair slice of New Jersey. On our right was Church Island,[6] a mountain etched with sparkling springs and green valleys, nearly thirty miles long. A similar island arose on the left. The lake is dotted with these mountain islands.

THE SHORES OF THE LAKE.

Profile Rock is a cliff which projects into the lake about twenty miles from the Tabernacle. Black Rock rears its head from the water several hundred feet from the foot of the cliff. The waves dashed against these rocks with great fury, creating a noise not unlike the roar of the ocean surf. The beach is white sand, though in some places it is ridged with pebbles of variegated colors. Along the marshes the action of the water has thrown up breastworks of white sand, which line the shore for miles. All the stories about men riding down to the shores of the lake and shoveling up bushels of clear salt are false. The sand beyond the reach of the breakers has a coating of salt, but it is as thin as a sheet of foolscap. Parties, however, go to the beach and boil down the water in large kettles, getting about 33 per cent of salt; but it can only be used for curing beef and pork. It must be refined before it is fit for table use. The water tastes like spoiled brine, and smells like the seaweed of Long Island Sound at low tide.

THE BLACK SEA GULLS.[7]

Breakers dashed upon the beach in triple lines like the breakers at Coney Island.[8] They rolled in from ten to twelve feet. In spite of all precautions our party got wet feet. Within a half hour our boots were encrusted with salt. Myriads of small flies covered the shore.[9] The sand and pebbles were perfectly black with them. They were the laziest flies in the world. I crushed hundreds of thousands of them beneath my feet. They were caught in the roll of the surf and licked up from the beach by millions, making the water look as though bushels of gunpowder had been strewn over its surface. Black gulls flapped their wings over the waves and rode upon the swells of the lake. They lacked the light, airy gracefulness of the sea gull, and moved more like crows than petrels. They were built like Dutch galliots,[10] broad in the stern, and their wings and feathers were so stiff that one of the party remarked the birds acted as though they had just got out of the glue-pot.

THE FLYING LIZARDS.

The high ground shelving the shores of the lake is covered with lizards. They are called "swifts."[11] They darted over the ground like lightning. A dragon-fly could barely beat them in speed. They are of a dull gray color, and their eyes sparkle like drops of dew. The Indians catch them with sticks curved like the handle of a cane, and eat them. When a Piute[12] sees a swift he extends his stick, and by a dexterous twist of the wrist spins the lizard in the air, catching him in his hand as he comes down. The flesh of these lizards resembles the meat of a bullfrog, and they are said to be even more delicious. As fast as the Indians catch them they string them around their waists and necks, and roast them one by one, as they become hungry.

SWIMMING IN THE SALT LAKE.

There are no fish in the Great Salt Lake. The only living thing beneath its waters is a worm about a quarter of an inch long.[13] This worm shows up beautifully beneath the lens of a microscope. When a storm arises the worms are driven ashore by thousands, and devoured by the black gulls. We found a pure stream pouring into a lake. It was filled with little chubs and shiners. The fish became frightened and were driven down the brook into the briny lake. The instant they touched its waters they came to the surface belly upward, and died without a gasp.

The water is remarkably buoyant. Eggs and potatoes float upon it like corks. Mr. Rood and myself stripped and went in swimming. I dove into the lake from a long pier, which had been built for the use of a small steamboat that formerly plied upon its waters. The sensation was novel. The water was so salt that my eyes and ears began to smart, but so buoyant that I found no difficulty in floating even when the air was exhausted in my lungs. As I struck out for the beach I felt as light as a feather. In spite of all that I could do, my heels would fly out of the water. I found it impossible to stand upon the bottom. The lightness of the water and the surging of the waves forced my feet from under me. A person who could not swim might be easily drowned in five feet of water. His head would go down like a lump of lead, while his feet would fly up like a pair of ducks. The water is as clear as the water of Seneca Lake,[14] so clear that the bottom could be seen at the depth of twenty feet. When we reached the shore and crawled out upon the sand in the light of the sun, our bodies were quickly coated with salt. We were compelled to go to the little stream from which we had driven the chums and shiners, and wash off in fresh water before we put on our clothes. Our hair was filled with grains of salt which could not be washed out. The Mormons occasionally visit the lake in droves for the purpose of bathing. Many of them say that their health is improved by leaving the salt upon their bodies, and dressing without wiping themselves with napkins.

AN OYSTER EXPERIMENT.

I saw no sailboats upon the lake. But few people live near its shores, and probably none of them know how to manage a cat-rigged boat.[15] The steamboat lies hard aground, and is rarely used. It is a one-horse affair, and last year ran between Corinne[16] and the southern shore of the lake. The company collapsed, owing to a lack of freight.

It is a question whether shrimps, crabs, and ocean fish will live in the waters of the Great Salt Lake. The experiment has never been tried. A drumfish or shark thrives in the shallow lagoons of Florida. The water in these lagoons is three times as salt as the water of the ocean. The sulphur in the Great Salt Lake would not kill salt water fish, because such fish live in the sulphur springs of Florida. The fish might fail to secure proper food in the lake, and die of starvation. One thing is certain. If the lake was filled with sea fish it would become one of the most popular resorts west of the Missouri River. As it is, people shun it as though it were a graveyard. Some years ago a gentleman planted a bed of oysters at the mouth of Bear River, one of the tributaries of the lake.[17] The oysters died. Since then nobody has invested a cent in Salt Lake experiments. The only salt water insect living upon its shores is the mosquito, and he grows to an enormous size.

THE GREAT BASIN FILLING UP WITH WATER.

All sorts of theories are advanced concerning the outlet of this vast body of water. Over a dozen rivers of respectable size empty into the lake. Last year a party of explorers claimed to have discovered a whirlpool through which the water was funneled into the Pacific Ocean. The newspapers were filled with their reports, but the whole thing turned out a humbug. Since then some genius has printed a story asserting that a green-ribbed boat was drawn into an unknown vortex while sailing upon the lake, and that the same boat was picked up below the Black Cañon of the Colorado twenty-four hours afterward. This was a little too much for even the Mormons; and now, whenever anybody advances a theory concerning the outlet of the great inland sea, people listen with an incredulous smile. It seems to be settled that the lake has no outlet, and that its water is only kept within bounds through evaporation by the sun.

The water of the lake has certainly risen twenty feet since the Mormons first entered the valley. I have seen Saints who tell me that they used to go in swimming at the foot of Black Rock. The rock is now several hundred feet from the shore, and is surrounded by twenty feet of water. If the lake rises in the same proportion for a hundred years the Saints will be drowned out, and Salt Lake City will be sunk as deep as Sodom and Gomorrah. Over twenty years ago the Mormons drove a herd of church cattle over to Church Island, which proved a wonderful grazing ground. They found a ridge extending from the main land to the island covered by barely three feet of water. For years they drove their herds over this ridge. To-day the ridge is over twenty feet deep, and no beeves have been taken from the island for years. Thousands of wild cattle roam over its valleys and gorges. But one family ever lived there, and that was the family of the church herder. Last year he died, and the island is now deserted. At some time the water has filled the whole Salt Lake Valley. A rim or shore line is visible on the side of the mountains thousands of feet above the city. This rim is so plainly defined that a railroad could be built on the side of the range for miles at a stretch without excavating a ton of rock.

A MORMON JUDGE AND HIS FAMILY.

Jeter Clinton[18] keeps a hotel on the shore of the lake twenty miles from Salt Lake City. It was here that we got breakfast. Jeter is the greatest curiosity on the lake, but he is only on exhibition during the Sabbath. He is the Judge Dowling[19] of Mormondom. All the bummers fear him. He never was known to fine a man less than fifty dollars, and never was known to imprison one less than ten days. I said Jeter runs a hotel. It is a mistake. One of his wives keeps it and turns the money over to Jeter. I am told that the Judge has five wives. The wife that I saw was a well-informed lady, with small black eyes. She kept a neat house, and did the best she could in the way of meals. As she had borne Judge Jeter nine children and was compelled to attend to their wants, a man couldn't expect to find a superabundance of food in the house. The whole family looked happy and contented. Jeter visits the house only on Sunday. He divides the remainder of his time with his wives in the city. If they all do as well as his wife on the Salt Lake, Jeter is the happy father of twenty girls and twenty-five boys, enough to make him feel like a patriarch.

The parlor contained a mineral cabinet and a library that did credit to the literary tastes of one of the Judge's families. A harmonium occupied one side of the room. Among the books were *Paradise Lost, David Copperfield,* and Tennyson's, Eliza Cook's,[20] Mrs. Hemans's,[21] and other poems. They were all well thumbed, and gave one the impression that somebody around the house must do a great deal of reading. Among the newspapers I noticed a copy of THE SUN. This probably accounts for the happiness of the family. The children were well clad and unusually intelligent. In this respect they presented a marked contrast to most of the Mormon young ones in the country, who are dull and ignorant. There are but few schools outside of Salt Lake City.

NOTES

1. Black Rock, on the lake's south shore, was near a popular swimming beach. The Utah Western Railroad, built in 1874 and 1875 just after Cummings's visit, took visitors to Black Rock, said to be 17.5 miles from Salt Lake City. Profile Rock, nearby and sometimes referred to as Lion's Head Rock, is about forty feet high (depending on the water level). The two rocks were famous markers. In his 1877 book, world traveler Alfred Falk wrote, "A peculiar feature of Salt Lake is two rocks: one, a great mass, rising abruptly out of the water, and standing black and desolate, called Black Rock; the other, overhanging the margin, and bearing an indistinct resemblance to a human face, is called Profile Rock" (*Trans-Pacific Sketches*, 44).

2. The Milwaukee City Directory for 1859–1860 (compiled by Franklin E. Town) lists Standish Rood as a clerk in the law offices of Butler, Buttrick, and Cottrill. I believe he was the son of Sidney L. Rood, a prominent Milwaukee businessman. By the time of Cummings's visit to Salt Lake City, Rood was a correspondent for the *Salt Lake Herald*, at times writing under the pseudonym Archibald (Keller, *Lady in the Ore Bucket*, 141). He also had written an article for *Whittaker's Milwaukee Monthly* magazine (August–September issue, 1872; reprinted in Lingenfelter and Dwyer, *Death Valley Lore*, 90–112), and he authored a 28-page pamphlet published in 1866 in New York City by William C. Bryant and Company titled "Report of Standish Rood on the Pahranagat Lake Silver Mines of Southeastern Nevada."

3. The River Jordan drains from Utah Lake into the southeast corner of the Great Salt Lake.

4. A rod is 16.5 feet in length.

5. Long Branch is on the ocean in Monmouth County, New Jersey. At the time, it was a major beach resort.

6. Church Island, about five by fifteen miles in extent, is also known as Antelope Island. Today Antelope Island is owned by the State of Utah and is an important recreational area.

7. The California gull (*Larus californicus*) is the Utah state bird.

8. The beach on the south side of Brooklyn in New York City.

9. Two species of brine flies (*Ephydra* spp.) inhabit the Great Salt Lake. *E. hians* are much more numerous in the southern parts of the lake.

10. A broad sailing vessel used for commercial shipping that was said to look clumsy, but it was a worthy seagoing craft.

11. "Swift" is a common name for the Western fence lizard (*Scelop-orus occidentalis*).

12. Cummings is likely misidentifying the tribal affiliation; the Native Americans who lived in the general vicinity of the Great Salt Lake in northwest Utah in the nineteenth century were Western Shoshone rather than Paiute Indians.

13. Larvae of the brine flies.

14. Seneca Lake is in the center of New York State's Finger Lake district. The town of Watkins Glen is at the lake's southern end.

15. Cat-rigged sailboats have a single mast and sail. Often the mast is set well forward in the boat.

16. Founded in 1869 and known as the "Gentile Capital of Utah," Corinne was on the north side of the Great Salt Lake east of Prom-ontory, where the Union Pacific and Central Pacific railroads met. Corinne's non-Mormon founders thought their town, placed along the new railway by Bear River, could compete with Salt Lake City. It did not.

17. Bear River, the largest tributary of the Great Salt Lake, emp-ties into the northeast side of the lake.

18. Zeder (note spelling) Clinton is listed in the 1870 federal census as the fifty-six-year-old judge of police court. Two wives are listed in the census: Malina, from Vermont, who had six children, and Emma(?), from England, with seven.

19. Judge Joseph Dowling was justice of the New York Police Court. His court was in Lower Manhattan in the Halls of Justice building known as the Tombs. Dowling was a Tammany Democrat and would have been well acquainted with Amos Cummings.

20. In the nineteenth century, Eliza Cook, an English writer and poet, was quite popular.

21. Felicia Dorothea Hemans (née Browne) also was a popular English poet and author at the time.

Lambs and Other Fauna to the Slaughter

SEAS OF SHEEP, JACKALOPE SIGHTINGS AND OTHER TALL TALES, and pistol duels on dirt streets—certainly storytellers, novelists, and Hollywood movies have featured these western phenomena. But did they really happen? Were they truly a part of the old West? The answer, as we shall see in these four Amos Cummings articles, is yes!

The first article, "Mutton Chops by the Million," was written while Amos Cummings was in Pueblo, Colorado, hanging out at the Lindell Hotel. There he met Mr. J. J. Armijo, who, along with his brother, had brought 37,000 sheep to Colorado to

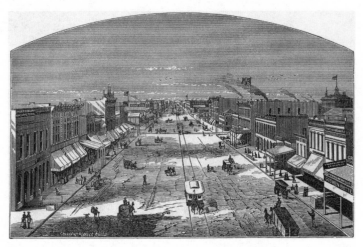

THE MAIN STREET OF DENVER SEVERAL YEARS AFTER P. C. ARMIJO STAYED THERE WHILE SELLING HIS SHEEP. (FOSSETT, *COLORADO*, 34)

sell. By any count, that is a lot of sheep! Amos clearly thought so, too, and once again sensing a story, he interviewed Mr. Armijo. The article that resulted explains how the flocks of sheep were grazed back in New Mexico, how they were driven to market, and how one made money raising and selling sheep.

My initial reaction to reading the story was that Amos had exaggerated. Were there that many sheep grazing somewhere around Denver, a sea of them, and had Mr. Armijo's brother really been a bank teller in New York City before giving up that job to raise sheep? Again the answer to both questions is yes.

As I dug into the story, I first tried using genealogical records to try to identify the Armijo brothers. That effort went nowhere; there were and still are many Armijo families in New Mexico. A Manuel Armijo had served three terms as governor of New Mexico in the early nineteenth century when what later would become a territory of the United States was still a province of Mexico.

Next I turned to Colorado's historical newspapers (especially the *Colorado Springs Gazette, Denver Daily Times,* and *Rocky Mountain News* from mid-1873 to mid-1874). In the pages of those papers I discovered that behind Amos's story was another one. It goes like this.

The Armijos dealt in sheep—a lot of sheep. According to an article in the *Rocky Mountain Times* (dated July 2, 1873), the New Mexico Armijo family, including Don Juan Cristobal and his two sons, P. C. (Pedro) and J. J. (Juan), maintained a herd of 250,000 sheep. Pedro, presumably the younger son, was about twenty years of age in 1873. Earlier he had been sent to Christian Brothers College, a small Catholic institution in St. Louis, and then had taken a job with Northrup and Chick on Wall Street in New York City (where he was known as Pete), before returning home to join the family's lucrative sheep-raising business.

The week before Amos Cummings interviewed Juan Armijo the *Denver Daily Times* (June 16, 1873) carried a short note in its personal section regarding his brother Pedro:

> P. C. Armijo, Esq., of Albuquerque, New Mexico, one of the most extensive sheep breeders in that territory, is stopping at the American House in this city, and will probably remain here two or three months. His flock of sheep now numbers thirty-five thousand, and presents a fine opportunity for purchase in large and small numbers. Mr. Armijo is a very prepossessing gentleman and we recommend those interested to call upon him.

The 200-room American House, located at Blake and Sixteenth streets, was one of Denver's most elegant hotels in the 1870s. Advertisements touted its brick construction and gaslights, among other amenities.

At about that same time (on June 17), P. C. placed an ad in the *Rocky Mountain Times.* The ad appeared on June 24 and announced that P. C. was staying at the American House and that he had brought 35,000 ewes, lambs, and wethers (castrated rams) to sell; another 7,000 wethers, also for sale, already were in Colorado. P. C. soon joined efforts with Benito Baca, a member of another prominent New Mexico sheep-raising family, to find buyers for their respective flocks. Over the next several months, from early July into October, Armijo and Baca placed more than 100 advertisements in Denver and Colorado Springs newspapers, announcing that Benito Baca of Las Vegas, New Mexico, and P. C. Armijo of Albuquerque, operating as Baca & Armijo, were "Sheep Dealers . . . ready to supply the Colorado and New Mexico markets with Ewes, Wethers, and Lambs." The advertisements also noted that Dr. S. B. Davis was their agent for Colorado and that he could be found at Charpiot's in Denver.[1] Apparently, selling thousands of sheep was neither an easy nor quick process; it could take months.

Amos Cummings's *New York Sun* interview with J. J. Armijo was published on July 2, and within days copies of the paper with the article must have found their way back to Denver. I suspect no one in Denver had ever considered that something as mundane as selling sheep could be news, yet here was an article on that very subject in the *New York Sun*. Jumping on the sheep-as-news bandwagon, the editors of the *Rocky Mountain News* wrote an article about Amos Cummings's having written an article. The item, which appeared in the paper on July 13, 1873, quoted at length from the *Sun* article and noted that the "Colorado correspondent of the New York *Sun*, who has told some pretty good stories concerning this territory," employed "his inquisitorial auger" in interviewing Mr. Armijo.

About six weeks later, the *News*, perhaps in sheepish recognition of having been scooped by Cummings, sent its own reporter to interview one of the Armijo brothers, this time Pedro, who was still at his hotel in Denver. The August 24, 1873, article, which actually is quite informative, was headlined "Mutton and Wool" and carried seven subheads, each in a different font and two in all-capital letters for emphasis: "The Sheep Kings of New Mexico and How They Thrive"; "Interview with Senor [*sic*] P. C. Armijo"; "Sheep by the Million—Mutton and Wool for the World"; "The Home of the Gentle Ewe and the Prolific Wether"; "HOW TO GET RICH IN FIVE YEARS"; "Interesting Details of One of the Leading Industries of the West"; and "GRADING THE HERDS OF NEW MEXICO."

The writer of "Mutton and Wool" was not as adept a writer as Cummings. The article's first sentence reads, "The growing of sheep in the far west is becoming a matter of vital importance, and at the same time a question that comparatively few of the people of the country thoroughly understand." The closing paragraph was equally lackluster:

> The reporter of THE NEWS was highly entertained with the particulars of sheep raising, as detailed above by Mr. Armijo, and thanked the gentleman kindly for the favor of the information received. The sheep interest is one that is growing rapidly in importance, and we presume that many will be found to enter into the business when they see how large are the incomes and increase of a small investment. We commend the matter to careful perusal.

I assume that P. C. and his brother J. J., along with Benito Baca, sold their respective sheep. The November 12 *Rocky Mountain News* contains a small personal ad headlined "Dissolution of Copartnership," stating that the firm of Baca & Armijo was dissolved by mutual consent. Pedro, and presumably brother Juan, if the latter had not already left town, went back to Albuquerque.

While living in Denver for about five months, Pedro, according to the January 8, 1874, *Rocky Mountain News*, had "lived a fast life" and spent his money "prodigally," because his "liberality exceeded his better judgement." And those were his good points!

But tragedy soon ensued. On the night of January 6, 1874, back home in Albuquerque, P. C. shot himself in the chest with a pistol. He lingered into the next day, dying on January 7 about 11:00 P.M. The suicide was big news. The *News* carried stories about the incident on January 8 and January 21. According to the articles the suicide was over a thwarted love affair. Pedro's mental anguish was "caused by the perfidy of a supposed friend who secretly used his influence to break an engagement of marriage which existed between Mr. Armijo and a beautiful girl—a fair daughter of New Mexico." The woman involved, educated at "Georgetown, D.C.," and spending the winter of 1873–1874 in St. Louis, was said in one article to be the daughter of a cousin of the deceased. In the other she is further identified as Miss Otero, sister of Benito Baca's wife. Most likely, the Armijo, Otero, and Baca families were to be interlinked by marriage ties.

Perhaps the engagement was broken off when Ms. Otero or her relatives heard stories about Pedro's exploits in Denver. And who was the "supposed friend"? It might have been Dr. S. B. Davis, the Denver agent for Armijo & Baca the previous year. On January 22, the *News* carried notice of Davis's own death on January 17, only ten days after Pedro's death. No details were given except to note that Smith did business in Denver and died in Las Vegas, New Mexico. The latter is where Benito Baca lived. Was Smith's death retaliation for telling stories about Pedro? And what happened to Pedro's brother J. J.?

On April 5, 1874, the *Denver Mirror,* reporting on the effects of a severe winter on the sheep herds in New Mexico, wrote that "Don Juan Armijo, brother of the late lamented Don Pedro Armijo," suffered heavy losses among his herds. Juan clearly had taken over the family's sheep-raising business. Three months later ads signed by J. J. Armijo again were appearing in the Denver papers, announcing "Ewes for Sale." Pedro Armijo and Dr. Smith were gone, but the next generations of sheep were headed north from New Mexico to face the same fates as their ancestors.

The second article in this section, "The King of Jack Rabbits," is a classic western tale, one promulgated by Cummings, who presumably heard it from some of the principals involved, most likely some of the army officers stationed at Camp Douglas, a military post in Salt Lake City. Perhaps the story got better in the telling, but then again, as with "Mutton Chops by the Million" and "The Funeral Postponed" (Chapter 18), historical research has shown that the individuals mentioned in the stories really did exist. The people Cummings wrote about did indeed stalk the giant jackrabbit.

Today in the West, giant rabbits, featured for nearly a century on postcards, have been joined by jackalopes, rabbits wearing antelope horns. Could Amos Cummings's article have played any part in the origin of these tales? Or how about the six-foot rabbit seen only by Elwood P. Dowd (played by James Stewart) in the 1950 classic movie *Harvey*? Maybe not.

Cummings's third article, "The Funeral Postponed," set in Salt Lake City, also reads a bit like a tall tale, but research points to it too as being true. As noted in the article, Charles Yeomans, the badger-loving protagonist, had been involved in a horrendous locomotive boiler explosion, although the 1866 incident took place in Petaluma, California, not Sacramento. An account was published in 1880 in the book *History of Sonoma County* (pp. 294–295), which quotes from the pages of the *Petaluma Weekly Journal and Sonoma County Adviser*:

> On the morning of the 27th of August, the boiler of the locomotive that ran between this city and the steamer blew up, causing sad havoc. Of the occurrence an eye-witness writes: "Arriving at the depot we found the greatest consternation and confusion prevailing; people running hither and thither, some wringing their hands wildly, frantically; others using their utmost endeavors to relieve the killed and wounded from the wreck of the locomotive and one baggage-car, which were thrown against the side of the

depot building. Stepping upon the platform, the first object that greeted our sight was a human body, unrecognizable to us, literally torn from limb to limb, which proved to be Joshua H. Lewis, the owner of the depot building. Upon the top of a baggage car lay the mangled remains of Arthur Thompson, son of J. D. Thompson of this city. From these sickening sights we turned into the depot building to behold S. B. Dodge, keeper of the warehouse, stretched upon the floor a corpse, and the engineer lying on the track a few rods in advance of where the locomotive had stood, mangled and inanimate. These were all beyond the reach of suffering, and needed not to be ministered to by mortal hands. There were others, however, the sight of whom would have moved the most unfeeling heart, most prominent among them was Charles Yeomans, so well known to all who have traveled on the steamer *Petaluma*. His face was mangled in a frightful manner, rendering his recovery extremely doubtful. Kind hands did everything in human power to alleviate his suffering, and he was soon removed to his residence, where the skill of surgery was called to his aid. . . . Had the boiler exploded a few minutes sooner than it did, it is fearful to contemplate what would have been the terrible destruction of life. As it was, the word had been given, 'All aboard,' and the consequence was that sixty or seventy passengers, who a few minutes before were massed where the missiles of death swept, had taken their seats in the passenger cars, which hardly suffered a scratch. The boiler was literally blown to fragments, one piece weighing several hundred pounds falling at the foot of Main street, and another in the canal near the warehouse of McNear & Bro. The locomotive was completely demolished, not a wheel being left whole." The verdict of the coroner's jury was, "We find that the explosion occurred from the incompetency of the man in charge of the locomotive at the time."

The steamer *Petaluma* made a daily run from the Haystack, several miles south of Petaluma, across the bay to San Francisco and back.

Behind the story of Yeomans's resurrected badger is another story, that of Charles Yeomans's saloon/reading room and its cadre of intellectuals and writers, patrons like Major J. B. Wheeler, Ovando Hollister, and Standish Rood. Yeomans, as the bar was known, most likely was a hangout for Salt Lake City intelligentsia, especially those individuals who were not members of the Mormon Church. Newspaper ads in Salt Lake City newspapers and an article from the late 1870s in the *Deseret News* recounting the aftermath of a fire in town, along with the listing in Sloan's *Gazeteer* [*sic*], tell us that Yeomans saloon was in a two-story adobe building owned by a Mr. Barnes and located at 111 East Temple between Second and Third streets South.

The fourth article in this section, "Duel with Six-Shooters," reads a bit like a script for a scene in a made-for-television Western movie, although the first thing one notices is that Cummings places Truckee in Nevada, not eastern California. I suspect he was simply confused. As I noted in the introduction to this book, Amos and spouse possibly backtracked to Carson City and Lake Tahoe from Truckee and then most likely returned to that town traveling overland. That may have caused the confusion.

"Mutton Chops by the Million" was published in the *New York Sun* on July 2, 1873. "The King of Jack Rabbits" was in the *Sun* the same year on September 5; "The Funeral Postponed" appeared three days earlier, on September 2; and "Duel with Six-Shooters" was in that paper on September 16.

NOTE

1. Charpiot's Hotel and Restaurant, advertised as "The Delmonico of the West," was at 386 Larimer Street. After Denver changed its street numbering system in 1887, the hotel's address became 1540–1550. In some post-1887 directories the address is listed simply as 1540 (on Larimer Street between Fifteenth and Sixteenth streets).

MUTTON CHOPS BY THE MILLION.

*The Largest Drove of Sheep in the World—A Scene in
Denver, Col.—Three Months Going 400 Miles—A Talk with
Mr. J. J. Armijo—How to Clear a Fortune*

Correspondence of The Sun.

PUEBLO, Col., June 24.—I met Mr. J. J. Armijo in the Lindell Hotel[1] this morning. He and his brother are probably the largest sheep owners in the United States. They live in Albuquerque, New Mexico. Their herds number nearly 250,000 head. The brother has just made his appearance in Denver with a flock of 30,000 sheep, and Mr. J. J. Armijo tells me that he has a drove of 7,000 wethers[2] but a few days' journey from this city. The brother was formerly the teller of a bank in New York City, but he finds sheep raising more profitable than operations in Wall street. The father of these two gentlemen has been in the sheep business over thirty years, and the sons thoroughly understand it. I found Mr. Armijo a courteous and agreeable gentleman, willing to give the readers of THE SUN all the information in his power. We talked as follows:

WHERE THE SHEEP GRAZE.

Correspondent—You must have a large tract of land to feed 300,000 head of sheep.

Mr. Armijo—Oh, they graze upon Government lands. We divide them into flocks of 3,000 each, put a couple of herders with each flock, and let them stroll over the plains. Some of these herds are grazing as far as 250 miles from home. At stated periods we receive reports from our herders, giving the number and condition of their flocks; so that at almost any time we are able to take an account of stock and ascertain to a fraction where we stand.

Correspondent—Have you any difficulty in procuring herders?

Mr. Armijo—None whatever. We find all we want at hand. They get about $10 a month and found.[3]

HOW THE SHEEP BREED.

Correspondent—What kind of sheep do you raise?

Mr. Armijo—We raise common sheep. The breed originally came from Spain and was of the finest kind; but the sheep have been bred in so much that they have deteriorated. To preserve the quality the bucks should be changed every two years. This has not been done in New Mexico, and the result is that we raise a common but a fair sheep. Imported Spanish rams, however, improve the breed wonderfully. The ewes breed back to their ancestors very quick, and the finest grade is obtained. But while land is so plentiful we are satisfied to go on in the old way. People, however, are gradually coming in and taking up ranches, and the time will soon come when we shall be compelled to curtail our flocks and raise a blooded sheep. When that time does come we shall clip as much wool from 10,000 sheep as we do now from 20,000 or 30,000.

Correspondent—How much wool do you raise?

Mr. Armijo—It will average a pound and a half to the ewes and about a pound to the wethers. We generally send it East by way of Kit Carson and Kansas City.[4] It is consigned to a Philadelphia house. But we have no difficulty in selling the clip in New Mexico. Last year we sold the clip in Albuquerque to Eastern agents at forty cents per pound, thus avoiding the fall in the market which afterward occurred.

HOW THEY DRIVE THE SHEEP.

Correspondent—What kind of land is it around Albuquerque?

Mr. Armijo—The grass is very fine on the plains. There is plenty of water, and our flocks generally do splendidly. We have light snows during the winter, and these start up the grass and make the grazing good. Last winter, however, there was but little snow, and the grass was backward. We had bad luck, and lost many of our lambs. West of Albuquerque the country is mountainous. Of course sheep can be raised in the mountains, but they require more care and become more expensive. We prefer the plains to the mountains.

Correspondent—I see that your brother has arrived in Denver with 30,000 head of sheep. How long did it take to drive them up from Albuquerque?

Mr. Armijo—Over three months. They are usually driven about four miles a day. This gives them time to graze, and they do not fall off in weight. In moving our sheep we never take the main road, but drive them across the plains where the grass is the best. The drivers are men who know the country thoroughly, and who can tell where they are at any time by looking at the mountain ranges. I have nearly 20,000 wethers ready to butcher, but there are only 7,000 on the way here. Too many would break down the market, and it is not to our interest to throw our sheep on a broken market. These 7,000 were sheared before they started. We always shear our sheep before starting them for market.

Correspondent—I see from the Denver papers that a Mr. Evans[5] has arrived with 20,000 sheep. The paper says that there are now 80,000 sheep in that city.

Mr. Armijo—Yes, I presume the market is glutted. But my brother will probably sell the most of his sheep to the stock raisers about Denver. You see that city is a central point. Sheep can be sent from there to Kansas City, St. Louis, Chicago, Omaha, Salt Lake, or wherever they command the best prices.

WHAT PAYS AND WHAT DON'T PAY.

Correspondent—Would it pay you to ship them to Kansas City?

Mr. Armijo—That is doubtful. It would pay if we had contracts with certain dealers for so many sheep at stated periods; but to throw 30,000 sheep on any Eastern market without notice would certainly break it down, and the cost of feeding the sheep, if we waited for the market to recover, would eat up all the profits.

Correspondent—Do you like it better in New Mexico than you did in New York?

Mr. Armijo—I always like best the place where I can make the most money. I can make a great deal more money in New Mexico than in Wall street. And then Albuquerque is a pleasant place in which to live. We have butchers who supply us with juicy beef and excellent mutton every day. We can get all kinds of vegetables, and get them early. We can live almost as well as you do in New York.

Here Mr. Armijo turned the tables on your correspondent. He interviewed me as to my business in the Territory. I answered his questions with the charming frankness of a newspaper man, and we separated mutually pleased.

AFFECTION OF THE SHEEP FOR THE HERDERS.

In conversation with Mayor Rice of Pueblo[6] I learned further interesting particulars concerning the breeding of New Mexican sheep. The wool is not of a very high grade, because the sheep are hardly ever washed before clipping. Sometimes they are driven through a brook once or twice, but not enough to take the surface dust from the fleece, and a thorough scouring is a rarity. Many of the Mexicans cut the wool from the back of the animal with a sharp knife, and haggle[7] it in a shocking manner. Thus they secure only a portion of the fleece, and the sheep looks ragged and scraggy. If more care was taken with the herd, the yield of wool would be greater and of a finer quality.

The affection of the sheep for the herder is remarkable. He is with them day and night, leading them to fresh pastures and preserving them from all harm. If they are stampeded, they return at the sound of his voice. In case of sudden danger they keep their eyes upon the herder and cling to him for protection. Their confidence in him is unbounded. They follow him over the plains beneath a burning sun for hundreds of miles while being led to slaughter. He shows them water, and after drinking they await his pleasure. When night drops upon the plains and the herder wraps his blanket about him and goes to rest, the drove huddle up to him as close as possible, and fall asleep, forming an immense white circle, of which he is the centre. Up with the dawn, they patiently await his movements, and when finally corralled and in the power of the butcher, they bleat piteously for the false friend who has led them to death.

NOTES

1. The Lindell Hotel, also mentioned in "The Fate of a Gold Seeker," was on Santa Fe and Fifth in Pueblo.

2. As noted in the introduction to this section, wethers are castrated rams.

3. "Found" in this context means "food and lodging."

4. Via the Kansas Pacific Railroad east from Denver, the route Cummings had traveled west.

5. The June 19, 1873, *Rocky Mountain News* carried an article that said, among other things, that Mr. John Evans of Fort Bascom, New Mexico, was arriving with his sheep. Adding Evans's sheep to those brought by Pedro Armijo and another 30,000 that Benito Baca had driven to the city (according to an ad he placed in the *News* on June 21), the newspaper came up with the 80,000 figure.

6. James Rice.

7. "Haggle" means "to hack it unskillfully."

THE KING OF JACK RABBITS.

A Wall Street Operator's Adventures in Utah—A Night at Camp Douglas—The Wonderful Gun and Its Wonderful Shots.

Correspondence of The Sun.

CAMP DOUGLAS, Utah, Aug. 24.—A few months ago Mr. J. E. Moen,[1] a Wall street broker, came out here to look at some mines in which he was interested. Moen was accompanied by the Hon. Amasa Mason,[2] a London banker from Rochester, N.Y. They found snug quarters in Camp Douglas,[3] and recognized the faces of a few old acquaintances among the officers. One of these was the face of Maj. David S. Gordon, Col. Tompkins's right bower in the celebrated cavalry charge at Fairfax Court House.[4] Another was the refulgent countenance of Major Howell,[5] a jovial son of Mars, who was planted in the Quartermaster's Department some years ago by Gen. Rafe Ingalls,[6] and who has taken deep root in the service of the republic. A third face was that of Capt. Dinwiddie,[7] a handsome Hoosier, who once spent forty-seven days in the gloomy depths of the Black Cañon[8] of the Colorado. Moen and Mason were heartily welcomed to the festive boards of these three epauletted worthies. They made a sad inroad upon the eatables, but created a perfect panic when they tackled the drinkables. If a barrel of army whiskey had been struck by lightning the commotion could not have been greater. At one of their liquid meals Moen said he had brought a five-hundred-dollar (in gold) gun with him out here in hopes of shooting something before he returned to New York.

THE PROPOSAL.

"Did you ever see a jack rabbit, Moen?" asked Gordon.

"No," Moen said. "I never did, but I've heard of them, and would give fifty dollars for a shot at one. Are there any of them about here?"

"Oh, lots of them," exclaimed Rafe Ingalls's military plant. "You mustn't go back to New York without taking one of their hides along with you."

"I'll tell you what we'll do," said Gordon, filling his glass and starting the whiskey on its seventh round. "American Fork[9] is full of jack rabbits. To-morrow morning we'll hitch up an ambulance[10] and ride over there. Moen is sure to get a shot at one. What do you say, gentlemen? Will you go?"

"Go?" repeated Mason. "Of course we'll go. What do you think we came out here for? I'd like to see a jack rabbit myself. How large are they?"

"Well," drawled Gordon, "they're about the size of a young colt. When they start on a run, they've got the queerest lope that you ever saw. They pop over the ground as though they had the spring halt[11] in every leg."

The whiskey went round once more, and a little more intellectual conversation followed. The party then separated, but were

THE AMERICAN FORK, WHICH RAN THROUGH A PICTURESQUE CANYON, WAS
THE SITE OF THE GIANT JACKRABBIT HUNT. (WILLIAMS, *PACIFIC TOURIST*, 144;
ILLUSTRATION BY THOMAS MORAN)

brought together again by the power of attraction; all declaring
that a nightcap was necessary before going to bed. After the
nightcaps had been secured each man crept beneath his blankets, and the cool air was quickly filled with music. They snored
so loud that the corporal of the guard turned out his men, under
the impression that the horses in the camp stables were suffering from the distemper.

ON THE WAY TO AMERICAN FORK.

Day dawned clear and beautiful. The five men were in an ambulance by sunrise. They were happy. Five morning cocktails had
warmed their souls. The scenery was magnificent. The great
valley of the Salt Lake, checkered with squares of yellow grain
and green grass, and hemmed in by turreted mountains, was
spread out before them. The lake itself glistened at the base of
the far-off mountains like an immense mirror. Entranced at the

scene, the men halted, and gazed at it through the bottom of a black bottle. "Glorious, grand affair!" rapturously exclaimed the Wall street operator, waving his hand over a sea of sage brush. Dinwiddie lashed the mules, and the ambulance ran down hill with the speed of a Texas steer. Moen's gun attracted great attention. All handled it, and squinted along its barrels. The lock was clicked a hundred times. If the gun had been a second bottle of whiskey it could not have been handled more lovingly, or its good points more expatiated upon. Moen was delighted, and Mason regarded the experienced army officers and their bottles with an affection bordering on veneration.

THE KING OF JACK RABBITS.

It was well along in the afternoon when the ambulance began to roll up the American Fork Cañon. A bright watch was kept for jack rabbits. They were scarce. Hours passed, and none were seen. Moen became dispirited. At last, about 5 o'clock, Gordon saw two ears sticking up above a clump of bushes on the side of a hill.

"Hold on," he shouted. "There's one now. He's a big one, too. Get out, Moen, and give it to him. Easy, now, easy!"

The Wall street gentleman shinned out of the wagon and shoved two patent cartridges in the barrels of his gun.

"Now, then, let him have it. Give it to him," repeated Gordon.

The army officers began to laugh as Moen rested the fowling piece upon the wheel of the ambulance and squatted to take sight. They saw that the supposed jack rabbit was a jack without the rabbit. It was a *burro*, or Spanish donkey, about two-thirds grown. Moen had never seen one. The animal stood with its quaint face surrounded by green leaves, a perfect picture of contentment. The banker took good aim and fired. The *burro* threw up its ears but never budged an inch.

"You shot too high," said Howell. "Shoot lower and you'll fetch him. I never saw a bigger one. He's the king of all jack rabbits. Now, then, give it to him, quick!"

The banker squatted again and sighted his game over the wheel. There was a puff of smoke and a report. The *burro's* ears flew up a second time, but he didn't stir.

"Too low, too low, old man," cried Gordon. "Load up again and give him another shot."

"Heavens!" exclaimed Moen, "ain't he a big fellow?" He nervously shoved the cartridges into his fowling piece. "Keep quiet, boys," he whispered. "Don't scare him."

THE LAST SHOT.

"Now, then, give it to him sure," Gordon said in a low tone of voice, as the broker squatted for a third shot. As his finger touched the trigger the *burro* threw one of his ears over his eyes and began to bray. "Y-a-a-w e-e-e-h! y-a-a-w e-e-e-h!" shouted the jack. The officers burst into a roar of laughter.

The Wall street man straightened up in an instant. "Great Caesar," said he, "it's a cursed jackass! I came near killing it."

He jumped in the ambulance and put up his gun. The best of the joke is that the jack belonged to an old Mormon named Davis,[12] who collected $25 from Moen, alleging that he had shot the beast near the root of the tail, seriously damaging him. After the banker returned to New York, Davis acknowledged that the animal was untouched.

"The bullets didn't go within a mile of the jack," said he, "but what is a New Yorker good for in this country if it isn't to pluck. I plucked him."

NOTES

1. I could not further identify Mr. Moen using the 1870 New York City census and New York City newspapers.

2. In 1861, Amasa Mason had been nominated by Abraham Lincoln to be U.S. consul to Manila. The nomination was withdrawn the next year.

3. Camp Douglas was established in 1862 near Salt Lake City to "keep an eye on" Mormon activities during the Civil War. Later des-

ignated an army fort, Fort Douglas was declared surplus after World War II and the land turned over to the University of Utah. The camp originally was named for Stephen A. Douglas of Illinois, who had debated Abraham Lincoln prior to the latter's election as president and who died in 1861. The fort also was used by Reserve and National Guard units during its later history.

4. On May 31, 1861, when the Union cavalry charged the Fairfax County Courthouse in Virginia, then-lieutenant Gordon of the Second Dragoons was on temporary assignment to Company B of the Second U.S. Cavalry commanded by then–first lieutenant Charles H. Tompkins.

5. William T. Howell.

6. Rufus Ingalls remains one of the most famous United States Army quartermasters.

7. Lieutenant William A. Dinwiddie (1839–1901), who was trained as a medical doctor, is mentioned in several Salt Lake City newspapers in the 1870s as well as in various army records (as a lieutenant, not a captain, of the Second Cavalry; Cummings may have given him a promotion). Late in his career he served as a professor of military science and tactics first at the University of Illinois and then at Iowa Wesleyan University. Photographs of Dinwiddie show him sporting a dashing handlebar mustache.

8. Black Canyon, downriver from the Grand Canyon, is the site of the modern Hoover Dam.

9. American Fork Canyon, through which the stream known as American Fork runs, is about thirty miles south of Salt Lake City. The small settlement of American Fork was on the Utah Southern Railroad; a small-gauge railroad ran from the local station into the canyon, which was more than ten miles long. In *The Pacific Tourist* (p. 143), Williams hails the natural beauty of the canyon, noting it had been called the "rival of the Yosemite."

10. A two-wheeled cart pulled by two or four mules.

11. Spring halt is a condition affecting horses. It is characterized by a jerky twitch, usually of one or both hind legs.

12. This may have been James Davis, a sixty-nine-year-old farmer listed in the 1870 census as a resident of Lehi City, adjacent to American Fork.

THE FUNERAL POSTPONED.

Tears from the Eyes of the Hardest Mormon.

An Interesting Scene in the Streets of Salt Lake City—The Story of Mr. Charles Yeomans and Poor Little Dick—Shot Dead while Playing with the Muzzle of a Gun.

Correspondence of The Sun.

SALT LAKE CITY, Sept. 2.—Mr. Charles Yeomans is a character well-known on the Pacific coast. He went to California in 1849, knocked around that State for twenty years or more, and has finally settled down among the Mormons. He keeps a popular restaurant and reading room. Charles is built like a fifty-year-old Adonis. His hair curls tight to his head, and is parted just off centre, *à la Jimfisque.*[1] His features are singular, but intensely bronzed. He is said to have been blown up in California seventeen times, and his cheeks and chin bear the scars of these accidents. The last time he was shattered was by the explosion of a locomotive in Sacramento. It cost Mr. Yeomans a hole in the cheek and three tobacco-stained teeth, and it cost the Central Pacific Railroad Company $10,000 in gold besides the locomotive. Charles is pigeon-toed and walks like a Piute.[2] Major Wheeler[3] of the United States Engineers declares that he has six toes and a bunion on each foot. He wears a loose shirt without suspenders, a Byron collar[4] buttoned over his collar bone, coral studs, and a great variety of flaming neck ties large enough to cover the ground for a Mormon temple. He is never seen with a coat or waistcoat, and his pantaloons are so tightly strapped behind that the tops of his boots occasionally crop out below.

Mr. Yeomans is a confirmed bachelor. He sleeps on a cold iron bedstead in the garret of his restaurant, and pities men who have fifty wives and more or less children. Charles, however, has an extraordinary development of philoprogenitiveness.[5] His love for pets is unbounded. He would disembowel a man who kicked his dog, and scalp a man who threw a chew of tobacco at his pet parrot.

THE LITTLE ORPHAN.

About a year ago some honest miner gave Charley a badger so young that its eyes were scarcely opened. Yeomans's sympathetic heart warmed to the motherless infant. For weeks he nursed it night and day. He fed it from a bottle, and dandled it upon his knee as a father would his child. "Dick," as he called the badger, thrived wonderfully. He reciprocated Charley's affection, and looked up to him as a child would to a father. He (the badger, not Charles) was about two feet broad, three feet long, and three inches high. As he stood upon the floor he looked like a stuffed coon that had been run through a hay-press.

One day Yeomans brought home a basket of eggs. As soon as his back was turned the thin little orphan clambered into the basket, sucked a dozen of the eggs, smashed the remainder, and raised Edward generally. Charles was delighted. Eggs were high. He cuffed Dick, but said that it showed that the animal had common sense, and if he only kept on, would make an excellent Grant official. After that he fed the badger on eggs. It was really affecting to see the mutual confidence existing between the tender orphan and its benefactor. Dick had a hole under the house, and morning, noon, and night he crawled out on the sidewalk, and waddled into his master's restaurant for his little egg. Yeomans always fed him out of a tumbler, and then spent ten minutes in detailing the little fellow's good points to the bystanders.

THE LITTLE ORPHAN'S NARROW ESCAPE.

The badger was frequently sporting about the door of the restaurant. He was a general favorite. Everybody knew him. Even the Mormons began to like him. All the dogs gave him a wide berth. This was probably because they knew he was intimately associated with Mr. Yeomans. As twilight spread over the valley of the Great Salt Lake and the stars twinkled upon the Wasatch peaks, Charles shut his little protégé in a dark closet under the stairs. Dick reciprocated by scratching at the door and swearing all night. Mr. Yeomans's customers were delighted with the music. When they said they were delighted, Mr. Yeomans always asked them if they wouldn't take something, and they invariably accepted the invitation.

One day Dick was skirmishing in front of the door, and fell into the crystal irrigating ditch dividing the sidewalks and main street of Salt Lake City. The current carried him beneath a long horse-block[6] bridging the stream. Charles was terribly excited. His favorite's danger gave him the strength of a Samson. With a powerful effort he raised the horse-block and rescued the lively orphan from a watery grave. Yeomans was sick for a week. He said it was not the over-exertion, but Dick's sudden danger that caused his illness. I had almost forgotten to say that he was a Pythagorean,[7] and a firm believer in metempsychosis.[8]

THE ALARM.

Seven days ago a stranger rushed into the restaurant. He was out of breath.

"Charley," he gasped, "Dick's shot."

Yeomans's blood curdled with horror. "Great mackerel," he exclaimed, "you don't tell me so! Where is he?"

"Up back of the Constitution building, near the Cooperative institution,"[9] answered the stranger. "Some feller shot 'im. I saw him a takin—"

Poor Charles waited to hear no more. His heart was in his throat. Hatless and coatless he dashed for the Constitution building. In the yard back of it stood a group of boys and girls gazing in the grass. One look. It was Dick's dead body. Tears filled the eyes of the bereaved man.

"Who killed him?" he cried. "Where is the man? Tell me, children, who killed him?"

"The man'th up to the blackthmita'th thtore," lisped one of the little girls.

THE MURDERER.

Away went Charles for the blacksmith's shop, with the dead badger under his arm, followed by the troupe of amazed children. They pointed out the murderer. He was a brawny-looking man, with whiskers all around his chin.

"Did you kill this badger?" Charles demanded.

"Why, is that what you call it?" answered the astonished Mormon. "Well, I should never uv thought that wuz a badger. I never seen one before. Ef I'd a knowed it wuz a badger, I woldn't a shot it. You see it wuz a crawlin' around in the grass an a growlin' an the fust thing I knowed I heered the wimmin a screamin' an a squallin', an I went over fur to see what the matter wuz. When I seen this here thing in the grass, I thought 't wuz suthin wild, an I ran for a Enfield rifle what I got. When I cum back, he tuk the borrel of the rifle into his teeth, an I shottem. That's the way it wuz."

"You cursed Mormon fool," Yeomans said, while the tears ran down his cheeks, "he only wanted to play with you. That was all."

"Well," responded the stranger, "ef I'd ny knowed that he only wanted to play with me, I wouldn't ny shottem. You see them there wimmin they wuz a squallin' an a screamin', an I didn't know but—"

"Oh, you didn't know," broke in Charley, still weeping. "Have you got a double-barrelled shotgun?"

"No," the Mormon replied. "I haint got nothin' but this here Enfield rifle."

"Well," said the grief-stricken man, "I'll tell you what to do. You just go and borrow a big double-barreled shotgun, and put a half a pound of shot in each barrel, and come down to my place and I'll show you a little canary bird hanging up by the door—you can shoot that. And then I'll take you around the corner and show a little pet lamb and you can shoot that. And there's a little squirrel down the street in a wheel—maybe you'd like to shoot that!"

THE DEAD BODY.

So saying, the indignant man gathered up poor Dick's remains, wrapped them in a sheet of brown paper, and started down the street with the bundle under his arm. That night Dick's dead body lay behind the door of the restaurant. Yeomans was inconsolable. Men came into the reading room all smiles, but Charles was as sad as Niobe.[10]

"Do you remember poor little Dick," he would say, "that used to be playing around the saloon here—a little pet badger?"

"Yes. I remember him."

"Well, there he is behind the door," Yeomans would continue in a broken voice. "Some gingerbread-headed Mormon shot him. You know how he used to waddle in every night and take his little egg like a human—oh, it's rough to think that he's dead! He was one of the nicest little fellows, too—such a great curiosity. You know you hardly ever see a tame badger. I never saw one before this myself (drawing a long sigh)—oh, it's mighty tough to think that he's dead!" The tears would start afresh. "Take a drink! Take a drink!" he added, while wiping his eyes.

TOUCHING AFFECTION.

All in the room sympathized with Charley by taking drinks. They waked the dead badger by accepting over fifty dollars' worth of drinks from the bereaved proprietor. One bibulist[11] took out his pocket knife and proposed to skin the animal. He suggested that Charley could get it stuffed and put it over his bar. Yeomans fired up in an instant. His devotion to his dead friend was absolutely touching. Drawing a Derringer from his pocket, he said, "I'll put a hole big enough for a kangaroo to jump through in the first man that puts the point of a knife in Dick's skin."

After this scene, a man named Holliston[12] went to a store and bought several yards of crape. The door of the reading room was draped in black, and by 9 P.M. the restaurant looked gloomy enough. There was considerable mirth among the spectators, but Charles's heart was freighted with woe. He never smiled. Slowly and sadly he drew an empty wine box from behind the counter. It was filled with straw, and the corpse laid therein. Then Yeomans announced that he would bury his dead friend in the yard back of the saloon at 9 o'clock the following morning. He invited his friends to be present. Never was a man so sincere. He seemed to think that a load would be lifted from his mind if he gave his dead companion a decent burial.

A GRAND SURPRISE.

Recognizing his grief, his friends restrained their mirth while in his presence. They went to the telegraph office, however, and sent dispatches to Ogden, Alta, and other places, informing Yeomans's acquaintances of the death of Dick, and asking them to come to the funeral. The morning trains brought down Major Wheeler and Bishops Erb[13] and Farr[14] from Ogden, and the Hon. Standish Rood,[15] the Harkness Brothers,[16] Col. Parlin,[17] and others from Alta.

By 8 o'clock some thirty persons were seated about the crape-draped reading room, sipping free drinks. The dead badger lay in the wine box as natural as life. Charles was sobbingly relating incidents of his career, when a scraping noise and a low growl were heard at the door. In a second, Dick loped over the threshold, and walked up to Charley in his old familiar style, shoving up his peaked nose for his little morning egg.

If an earthquake had occurred, Yeomans's surprise could not have been greater. He kissed the badger over a dozen times, and gladly filled the tumbler with yellow yolks. Dick was of course delighted, and pitched in like a white man.

It turned out that there had been another pet badger in the city, and that this was the animal which the much-abused Mormon had shot instead of Yeomans's. Dick had been cavorting about more than usual on the previous day. The sun was very hot, and he crawled into his hole under the house perfectly exhausted. He had slept right through, making his reappearance in time for his usual morning meal. The best of the joke is that the dead badger was of the feminine persuasion, and none of the grief-stricken mourners discovered it until Dick's return.

NOTES

1. James Fiske, known as Diamond Jim, was a shady New York financier and associate of Jay Gould and Boss Tweed. In early 1872 in New York City, Fiske was shot and killed by a man with whom he had a

dispute about money and a Broadway show girl. Images of Fiske show he parted his hair just off-center on the right side.

2. Paiute Indian.

3. This is certainly Junius Brutus Wheeler (1830–1886), chief engineer for the United States Army during the Civil War, who was involved in various construction projects in Arkansas, Kansas, and Pennsylvania during that conflict. J.B., as he chose to be called, later taught at the United States Military Academy at West Point and authored several books on the use of fortifications in warfare.

4. An oversized pointed collar named for Lord Byron, who made them popular. It is likely that everyone reading this book has at least one winter jacket with such a collar in their closet.

5. An attachment to one's young. Cummings must have traveled with a dictionary. His use of this and several other obscure words in this article may be a gentle tweaking of Mr. Yeomans and his reading-room patrons.

6. Horse blocks were steps used to mount horses and were typically made of stone or wood.

7. Named for the Greek philosopher and mathematician Pythagoras, Pythagoreans maintain a mystical religious philosophy based on the Classical Greek and other writings; some eschew sex and marriage, the latter including Mr. Yeomans.

8. A belief in reincarnation or the transmigration of souls after death into a new being, either human or animal. Metempsychosis was a part of Pythagoreanism.

9. As we saw in "The Story of Little Emma," the Cooperative Institute was on the southeast corner of East Temple and First South streets. It was located within the old Constitution Building.

10. In Greek mythology, Niobe is a symbol of eternal mourning. After her fourteen children were killed by the gods, she turned herself into stone. Her endless tears continue to flow from her image on Mount Sipylus.

11. Alcohol drinker.

12. I believe this was Ovando James Hollister (note spelling), who was thirty years old at the time of the 1870 Salt Lake City federal census and whose occupation was "U.S. Collector." If it was Hollister, Cummings missed a real opportunity for an interview. Hollister (1834–

1892) was the author of several books, including *Boldly They Rode: A History of the First Colorado Volunteers* and *Mines of Colorado*, in addition to others on Utah-related topics. For a time he had been editor of a Gilpin County, Colorado, newspaper. Hollister is frequently mentioned in the Salt Lake City newspapers, both because he was U.S. collector for the IRS and because he wrote letters criticizing the Mormons.

13. George S. Erb, who established the Rocky Mountain Electric Light Company and was the owner of the Walker House in Salt Lake City. I do not know why Cummings referred to him as "Bishop," unless he was making a joke.

14. Lorin Farr was a prominent member of the Mormon Church and an Ogden businessman. He and his family were among the town's founders and he served as Ogden's first mayor.

15. Rood, a journalist and writer, was one of Cummings's companions to the Great Salt Lake (see "The American Dead Sea").

16. I believe the Harkness brothers were Martin K. and Henry O., both of whom were involved in the mining business. In 1874 the two brothers were living at the Townsend House hotel in Salt Lake City (Sloan, *Gazeteer* [*sic*]). Martin was mentioned in various Salt Lake City newspapers (such as the *Deseret News*) during the 1870s.

17. Parlin was in business in Alta as Parlin and Thompson, California Feed and Livery Stables (Keller, *Lady in the Bucket*, 144). The business was located at the foot of Third Street West (Sloan, *Gazeteer* [*sic*], 79).

DUEL WITH SIX-SHOOTERS.

A Startling Picture of Life in the Silver State.

A Desperate Fight in Truckee City—Both Men Empty Their Pistols—One Killed and the Other Mortally Wounded.

Correspondence of The Sun.

TRUCKEE CITY, Nev., Sept. 7.—Andy Fuget,[1] a carpenter, and Jack White,[2] a miner, fought a duel night before last with six-shooters. A feud had existed between the men for some time; and a few days ago when they met on the depot grounds Fuget said: "We might as well settle our trouble here. Draw and defend yourself." White said that he was not armed, and Fuget replied that he believed him a liar. The men then separated with the understanding that they would fight the first time they met. Night before last the men again met on the corner of Main street[3] and a little alley running up into the Chinese quarter.[4] They had no sooner recognized each other than the battle began. There were several persons in the neighborhood, but no one who saw the shooting could tell who fired the first shot. Fuget is said to have been approaching Main street from the alley, and was met by White, who was passing along the sidewalk. When the firing began, Fuget placed himself behind an awning post at the corner of the street and alley, while White stood on the sidewalk.

The firing was very rapid; so rapid, indeed, that many who heard it thought that more than two men were engaged in the shooting. The majority of those who were in the neighborhood when the shooting began ran away as fast as their legs would carry them; but two or three men, who sought shelter in the iron doorways of Burkhalter's store,[5] stood their ground and witnessed the whole battle. White fell first, and, striking on the edge of the sidewalk, rolled into a gutter about eighteen inches in depth. Fuget fell about the same time, seemingly from the effect of White's last shot, rolling into the same gutter in which White was lying, and at no great distance from him. Between the two men lay a bundle of gunny sacks, owing to which they were unable to see each other. Fuget began to crawl toward White, who lay in the gutter unable to rise. He dragged himself along the gutter until he reached the gunny sacks. He climbed up on these until he could see his mortal enemy, and then fired at him his two remaining shots. White aroused himself, and by great effort raised his pistol and fired his last shot, which rolled Fuget from his position on the sacks, and ended the desperate and bloody fight.

When the firing ceased and only groans were to be heard, the citizens rapidly collected, and soon a great crowd was on the bloody battle field. The bleeding and groaning men were carried to where they could be cared for. Fuget, however, needed but little care, as he was dying when taken up, and lived less than ten minutes. The shot which proved fatal struck him in the left groin, severing a large artery. He bled frightfully. White's wounds were three in number, and of such a nature that they must necessarily prove fatal. One shot passed through his body, from side to side, just above the hips; another entered his right breast, and ranging back, lodged against his spine; the third struck him in the lower part of the abdomen, passing through the bladder.

After the shooting and while his wounds were being examined, White said that he was fired at by another man besides Fuget. This man, he said, was a large man with heavy black whiskers, who stood in the alley leading up into Chinatown, and fired three shots at him, after which he ran away up the alley. Afterward, on being more closely questioned about this man, White refused to say anything more in regard to him, or to give his name, even if he knew it. Many persons who were in the neighborhood at the time of the shooting are quite certain that more than two men were engaged in it. They say that it seems almost impossible that two men, armed with common six shooters, could have done such rapid firing, and when the men were taken up and the pistols examined there was a general expression of surprise on seeing they were not self-cockers. Several bullets struck the iron shutters of the store, and the men who screened themselves in the doorways seem to have occupied a terribly hot position. By some it is supposed that the men were hunting each other at the same time, as but a minute before the shooting began, White came to the door of a billiard saloon near by and peered in as though looking for some one. Both men were formerly residents of San Francisco.

NOTES

1. Despite my best efforts, I could not further identify Mr. Fuget. He does not appear in any city directories or in the 1870 census. The latter does list a C. S. Fuget, a sixty-nine-year-old farmer living in Sacramento, California. Could that person have been a relative of Andy

Fuget? Review of a number of Sacramento city directories (on microfiche in the New York Public Library) for the years 1861–1862, 1863–1864, 1866, 1868, 1869, 1870, 1871, 1872, 1873, 1874, and 1875 all list a second individual whose initials and names are variously given as John, John B., J. B., and J. R. Fugitt, Fugett, and Fugets. The man, a carpenter, just like Cummings's Andy Fuget, lived at the northeast corner of Seventeenth and E streets. He, too, could have been a relative of Andy Fuget.

2. I could not identify Jack White.

3. Today Main Street is Jibboom Street.

4. At the time, about one-third of Truckee's population of 1,500 were Chinese railroad workers.

5. Frederick Burckhalter (note spelling) ran a general store that also housed a bank he owned. In addition, he operated a stage line and had business interests in Truckee. Burckhalter's general store must have extended between Front Street and Main Street (they were roughly parallel), with the foremost entrance on Front.

The Return Trip Home

MOS AND HIS SPOUSE STAYED IN CALIFORNIA for a month and a half, traveling around the state and seeing the sights. Amos apparently was not writing during those six weeks; I could not find any articles from that period in his scrapbooks in the New York Public Library, nor did I locate any in the *New York Sun*.

The trip across the United States that had begun in mid-May 1873, nearly seven months earlier, came to an end in mid-November. True to form, the Cummingses' exit from San Francisco is chronicled in a local newspaper account. The piece, like others that are found in newspapers published in towns along the route of his journey to the West, was almost certainly penned by Cummings himself. A clipping of that article found in one of Amos's scrapbooks has "November 4, 1873" written on it. That is the day he and Frances actually left San Francisco; the article appeared in the *San Francisco Chronicle* the next day.

> Amos J. Cummings, managing editor of the New York *Sun*, accompanied by his wife, sailed on the steamer *Constitution* yesterday for home. Mr. Cummings is an accomplished angler as well as a brilliant and vivacious writer. During his sojourn on the Pacific Coast he has very thoroughly explored the salmon-trout streams of California. Aside from his piscatorial investigations, he has also visited the various resorts of Eastern tourists, including Yosemite Falls, the Geysers, the Big Trees, Santa Cruz and Pescadero. He also took elaborate notes on Chinatown and on the Barbary Coast. Mr. Cummings has selected the Isthmus route for this homeward journey because a revolution is in progress in Panama, which he conscientiously feels bound to quell and write up for the paper that shines for all.

Amos had not lost his sense of humor. "Shines for all" was, as noted previously in this book, a slogan of the *New York Sun* that Cummings sometimes included in his articles, an inside joke for his colleagues at the paper.

From San Francisco, the steamship *Constitution*, whose departure from San Francisco is listed in the "Marine Intelligence" section of the *San Francisco Chronicle*, took Amos and Frances down the Pacific coast of North and Central America to Panama City, a trip of ten and a half days. There, as many travelers had done since the 1849 California gold rush, they debarked, boarded the Panama Railroad, and crossed the Isthmus of Panama (counterintuitively, the railway ran to the northwest; the Panama Canal, not in use until the early twentieth century, runs the same direction because the isthmus has an

S-shaped curve at that point). Forty-nine miles later the train with the Cummingses aboard arrived at the Caribbean town of Aspinwall, named for the developer of the railroad. The town of Aspinwall is now called Colón, Panama.

At Aspinwall, Amos and Frances boarded another steamship, the *Grenada*, a newly launched ship, which took them back to New York City. They disembarked in that port city on December 1, 1873. Both Amos J. Cummings and Mrs. Amos J. Cummings appear on the passenger list prepared for U.S. customs in New York. On that form Amos is said to be an "editor of newspaper." The ages listed for them are incorrect.

Once back in New York, the Cummingses did not linger. On December 20 they boarded a train taking them south to Florida and warmer weather. Along the way they stopped in South Carolina and Georgia. An article authored by Ziska, one of Amos's pen names, was published in the *Sun* on December 26, 1873. It is datelined Columbia, South Carolina, December 21. In it, Amos says he arrived by train from Wilmington (Delaware) that very morning. Three days later, on December 24, Cummings was in Jacksonville, Florida, where he wrote another article for the *Sun*. By early April he again was in his familiar haunts in east-central Florida, where having already slipped into his Ziska persona, he began writing more articles about Florida for publication in the *Sun*. I have not yet figured out where he was during the intervening three months.

His seven-month adventure by rail across the Great Plains to San Francisco was over. Left behind were these nineteen superb articles, each a vignette of the West a century and a quarter ago.

Bibliography

NEWSPAPERS AND MAGAZINES

Brooklyn Daily Eagle; *Charlotte Observer* (North Carolina); *Chicago Daily Tribune*; *Colorado Daily Chieftain*; *Colorado Springs Gazette*; *Denver Daily Times*; *Deseret News* (Salt Lake City); *Field and Stream: A Journal of Outdoor Life*; *Harper's Weekly*; *Inter-Ocean* (Chicago); *Life*; *Los Angeles Times*; *National Police Gazette*; *Nevada Tribune*; *New York Daily Graphic*; *New York Semi-Weekly Sun*; *New York Sun*; *New York Times*; *New York Weekly Sun*; *Philadelphia Enquirer*; *Rocky Mountain Times*; *Salt Lake Daily Herald*; *Salt Lake Tribune*; *San Francisco Chronicle*; *20th Century Cookery*; *Typological Journal*; *Washington Post*; *Winfield Courier* (Kansas).

BOOKS AND ARTICLES

Alexander, Edwin P. 1971. *On the Main Line: The Pennsylvania Railroad in the 19th Century.* New York: Clarkson N. Potter, Inc.

Anonymous. 1873. The True History of a Great Mining Enterprise. *The Nation* 442:402–404.

Anonymous. 1880. *History of Sonoma County, Including Its Geology, Topography, Mountains, Valleys and Streams.* San Francisco: Alley, Bowen and Co.

Beyer, Walther F., and Oscar F. Keydel. 1903. *Deeds of Valor; How America's Heroes Won the Medal of Honor: Personal Reminiscences and Records of Officers and Enlisted Men Who Were Awarded the Congressional Medal of Honor for Most Conspicuous Acts of Bravery in Battle,* vol. 1. Detroit: Perrien-Keydel.

Blackmar, Frank W., ed. 1912. *Kansas: A Cyclopedia of State History, Embracing Events, Institutions, Industries, Counties, Cities, Towns, Prominent Persons, etc.,* vol. 2. Chicago: Standard Publishing.

Blodgett, Richard. 2005. *The Story of Charlton Street.* New York: n.p. http://www.gvba.org/blocks.html/Charlton/charlton_street.pdf.

Bowles, Samuel. 1869. *The Switzerland of America: A Summer Vacation in the Parks and Mountains of Colorado.* New York: American News.

Carr, Albert H.Z. 1963. *The World and William Walker.* New York: Harper and Row.

Chanute, Octave, and George Morison. 1870. *The Kansas City Bridge, with an Account of the Regimen of the Missouri River, and a Description of Methods Used for Founding in That River.* New York: D. Van Nostrand.

Falk, Alfred. 1877. *Trans-Pacific Sketches: A Tour through the United States and Canada.* Melbourne: George Robertson.

Fossett, Frank. 1879. *Colorado: Its Gold and Silver Mines, Farms and Stock Ranges, and Health and Pleasure Resorts. Tourist's Guide to the Rocky Mountains.* New York: C. G. Crawford.

Harper, Robert S. 1951. *Lincoln and the Press.* New York: McGraw-Hill.

Hart, Alfred A. 1870. *The Traveler's Own Book.* Chicago: Norton and Leonard, Printers.

Haynes, John Edward. 1882. *Pseudonyms of Authors, Including Anonyms and Initialisms.* New York: n.p.

Bibliography

Hicks, John. 1950. *Adventures of a Tramp Printer, 1880–1890.* Kansas City, MO: Midamericana Press.

International Typographical Union. 1935. *A Pictorial Presentation of the Union Printers Home, 1892–1935.* Indianapolis: International Typographical Union.

———. 1964. *A Study of the History of the International Typographical Union, 1852–1963,* vol. 2. Colorado Springs: Executive Council, International Typographical Union.

Jackson, W. Turrentine. 1955. The Infamous Emma Mine: A British Interest in the Little Cottonwood District, Utah Territory. *Utah Historical Quarterly* 23:339–362.

Keller, Charles L. 2001. *Lady in the Ore Bucket: A History of Settlement and Industry in the Tri-Canyon Area of the Wasatch Mountains.* Salt Lake City: University of Utah Press.

Kendall, John Smith. 1922. *History of New Orleans,* 3 vols. Chicago: Lewis Publishing Company.

Mather, Fred. 1901. *My Angling Friends: Being a Second Series of Sketches of Men I Have Fished With.* New York: Forest and Stream Publishing Co.

McClure, Alexander K., and Byron Andrews, eds. 1902. *Famous American Statesmen & Orators, Past and Present,* vol. 6. New York: F. F. Lovell Pub. Co.

Meade, Rebecca Paulding. 1910. *The Life of Hiram Paulding, Rear Admiral, U.S.N.* New York: Baker and Taylor Co.

Milanich, Jerald T. 2002. The Historian's Craft. *Florida Historical Quarterly* 80:375–378.

———. 2005. *Frolicking Bears, Wet Vultures, & Other Oddities: A New York City Journalist in Nineteenth-Century Florida.* Gainesville: University Press of Florida.

O'Brien, Frank M. 1928. *The Story of the Sun, New York: 1833–1928.* New York: D. Appleton and Co.

Omer, George E., Jr. 1957. An Army Hospital: From Dragoons to Rough Riders—Fort Riley, 1853–1903. *Kansas Historical Quarterly* 23:337–367.

Ormes, Manly D. 1933. *The Book of Colorado Springs.* Colorado Springs: Dentan Printing.

Pennsylvania Railroad Company. 1946. *1846: One Hundred Years of Transportation Progress: 1946; A Brief History of the Pennsylvania Railroad.* Philadelphia: Pennsylvania Railroad Co.

Pond, J. B. 1900. *Eccentricities of Genius: Memories of Famous Men and Women of the Platform and Stage.* New York: G. W. Willingham.

Rambler [pseudonym]. 1885. *Guide to Florida.* New York: American News Company.

Shaw, William H. 1884. *History of Essex and Hudson Counties.* Philadelphia: Everts and Peck.

Shearer, Frederick E., ed. 1970. *The Pacific Tourist: Adams & Bishop's Illustrated Trans-Continental Guide of Travel from the Atlantic to the Pacific Ocean.* New York: Bounty Books. First published 1884 by Adams and Bishop, New York.

Siegel, Alan A. 1974. *Out of Our Past: A History of Irvington, New Jersey.* Irvington, NJ: Irvington Centennial Committee.

———. 1984. *For the Glory of the Union: Myth, Reality, and the Media in the Civil War New Jersey.* Rutherford, NJ: Fairleigh Dickinson University Press.

———. 2001. *Beneath the Starry Flag: New Jersey's Civil War Experience.* New Brunswick, NJ: Rutgers University Press.

Sloan, Edward L., comp. and ed. 1874. *Gazeteer [sic] of Utah and Salt Lake City Directory, 1874.* Salt Lake City: Salt Lake Herald Publishing Co.

Stanton, Elizabeth Cady, Susan B. Anthony, and Matilda Joslyn Gage, eds. 1886. *History of Woman Suffrage,* vol. 3: *1876–1885.* Rochester, NY: privately published.

Stevens, George A. 1912. *New York Typographical Union No. 6: Study of a Modern Trade Union and Its Predecessors.* Albany, NY: State Department of Labor.

Walker, William. 1860. *The War in Nicaragua.* Mobile, NY: S. H. Goetzel and Co.

Wallace, Irving. 1961. *The Twenty-Seventh Wife.* New York: Simon and Schuster.

Williams, Henry T., ed. 1877. *The Pacific Tourist: Williams' Illustrated Trans-Continental Guide of Travel from the Atlantic to the Pacific Ocean.* New York: Henry T. Williams.

Bibliography

Young, Ann Eliza. 1875. *Wife Number 19 or the Story of a Life in Bondage, Being a Complete Exposé of Mormonism, and Revealing the Sorrows, Sacrifices and Sufferings of Women in Polygamy.* Hartford, CT: Dustin, Gilman and Co.

Index

Page numbers in italics indicate illustrations.